LIFE
WAS WORTH LIVING

the reminiscences of

W. Graham Robertson

WITH A FOREWORD BY

SIR JOHNSTON FORBES-ROBERTSON

HARPER AND BROTHERS: PUBLISHERS
NEW YORK AND LONDON

PRINTED IN U. S. A.

L-F

Printing Statement:

Due to the very old age and scarcity of this book, many of the pages may be hard to read due to the blurring of the original text, possible missing pages, missing text and other issues beyond our control.

Because this is such an important and rare work, we believe it is best to reproduce this book regardless of its original condition.

Thank you for your understanding.

W. GRAHAM ROBERTSON
From a portrait by JOHN S. SARGENT, R.A., 1893

CONTENTS

LIST OF ILLUSTRATIONS

vii

FOREWORD

HERE is a delightful book which surely will appeal to many, for it treats of those most interesting periods, the late Victorian and the Edwardian. Mr. Graham Robertson has dealt with most of the great painters and actors of his time with a keen observation of their characteristics and personalities, and with, here and there, many quaint twists of humour all his own. I can speak for his accuracy in the matter as I knew nearly all of those he mentions personally, and many of them intimately. ' Life was Worth Living ' indeed reaches back, for in his youth Graham Robertson met and made lasting friendships with many distinguished people who used to foregather at his mother's house. In these pages the reader, too, will make friends with Albert Moore, whose pupil Graham Robertson was, with Walter Crane, Rossetti, Burne-Jones, Sarah Bernhardt, Oscar Wilde, Ellen Terry, Irving, Whistler and many others. All these have passed away, but now, under Graham Robertson's graceful pen, they live again for us.

JOHNSTON FORBES-ROBERTSON

London, May 1931.

AUTHOR'S PREFACE

WHEN I was yet a mere child of twenty-nine or thirty I once waited upon a Publisher with a picture book which I hoped he might bring out. He told me, with perfect truth, that there was no demand for that sort of thing, that it was not in his line, that—to put it plainly —my pictures and my books were not wanted, and if I would take them home and bury them quietly he would feel obliged. " But," he added, " if you would write your Reminiscences for me——"

" My Reminiscences ? " I gasped, feeling, like David Copperfield, ' very young,' " I haven't got any."

" O yes, I think so," said the Publisher.

" But I'm not a Distinguished Person."

" No," said he, " but you have known a great many Distinguished People."

Had I ? " But I can't take them and stick them into a beastly book just because I know them," I stammered. " They wouldn't like it—and I shouldn't like it—and——"

" Very well," said the Publisher. " We need not discuss it. Good morning. Take your drawings with you."

I gathered up my rejected wares and retired with what I hoped was dignity. Reminiscences, indeed ! Stories about Other People ! Naturally, in the due course of events, when I had accomplished great things and my name was a household word, I should write an Autobiography. That would be legitimate, nay, the world would demand it, and I should set about making notes for it at once ; but the time was not yet ripe for the appearance of this work and, in the meanwhile, I did not feel equal to hanging out my more notable acquaintances on a line, like washing, for the inspection of the public.

And the years passed on.

Now I am old and still quite Undistinguished and there is less occasion than ever for that Autobiography ; most of the Notable Acquaintances are in Heaven or in bath-chairs at Bournemouth, and the days when we lived and flourished seem very hazy and remote.

But now the idea of writing down my memories rather smiles upon me. It is pleasant to wander down the lanes of Yesterday into the Land of Long Ago and to bring back tales of

'Queens long dead who lived there young,'

tales now grown as discreet and impersonal as any details of the family life of King Canute or Jack the Giant-killer. And then—there is no need to publish the result. I hope I shall not do so, but perhaps it may prove a temptation, and temptations are so rare in later life.

LIFE WAS WORTH LIVING

SHADES OF MY ANCESTORS

I N a collection of Memories the author always makes a start by gracefully recalling his Ancestors, and I, anxious that all shall be set forth properly and in order, must bow to convention, but I could wish that my Ancestors had been more thoughtful in leaving interesting traces of their existence. In the Family Archives—as represented by one or two rusty boxes—I find little but indifferent miniatures of people unknown, and odd letters about nothing in particular from no one in particular to persons of no importance.

I find a row of boys in water-colour, each wearing a blue jacket and large white collar, each decidedly plain and each very like myself. These must be my little Uncles.

My father came from Banff and had numerous brothers whose names and dates are recorded in a fat Scotch Family Bible ; James, John, William, George, they march triumphantly down the page, leaving little room for Graham Moore, my father, who was evidently an afterthought and can barely squeeze in above the ' Acts for the Uniformity of Common Prayer.' These brothers went to sea and were drowned with a regularity which finally palled upon their parents ; for when Graham's turn came and he was preparing to take the same course they sent him to India, where he remained for more than twenty years.

My grandfather was, I believe, an almost professional diner out, being very much in request in that capacity. I feel sure that he knew Sir Walter Scott intimately, because I have never heard of any Scotsman between certain dates who did not, but the family hero was Sir John Moore. His brother, Graham, was my father's godfather and, in my early days, Sir John was brought a good deal to my notice ; but, as I could never picture him as otherwise employed than in being buried swiftly at dead of night with his martial cloak around him, he did not especially appeal to me as food for thought—particularly towards bedtime.

I must really try to put some more interest into my mother's side of the family. I know next to nothing about it, but with a little ingenuity much may be accomplished. ·

I take up a musty old book on Geomancy and Ceremonial Magic—fascinating subjects—and therein I come across a long-ago John Greatraikes, possessor of the Healing Touch, miracle-worker by the laying on of hands, altogether an ancestor to my mind ; and as the name Greatorex was my mother's and is uncommon, and as John seems to be unclaimed, I do not see why he should *not* be my ancestor ; in fact, I have installed him permanently as such and have developed quite an affection for my forbear, dear old John Greatraikes.

In the same reliable volume I find mention of one Sibly, author of ' Illustration of the Occult Sciences.' Does anybody want Mr. Sibly for a great-great-uncle or something of that sort ? If not, I may as well have him, for my great-grandmother's name was Sibly.

I could easily find out more about my family by this process, but as these two worthy folks turned up just when I was enquiring for ancestors I shall let them have their chance and consider myself ' suited.'

Two ancestors are quite enough, so, respectfully suspending them from the boughs of the Family Tree, I can leave the realms of pure fiction and come to my great-grandmother.

I think I have always belonged more to the past than to the present and to the future not at all, and I believe that much of this feeling arose from beginning life with a great-grandmother instead of a grandmother.

My paternal grand- and great-grandparents I never

knew, and if they were anything like their equivalents no my mother's side, it was perhaps as well : a duplicate set would have been very difficult to cope with. My mother's grandmother—always 'Granny' to me—was more than sufficient to keep any number of grandchildren in their proper places ; and to this day when I think of her I feel a crushed worm.

My mother's mother had died long ago in the time of spencers and coal-scuttle bonnets, but my great-grandmother still reigned in her stead and diffused the atmosphere of a yet remoter day. She wore little high-waisted gowns of soft grey silk and was, I firmly believed, fastened securely to a large chintz-covered porter's chair in her bedroom. Certainly I never saw her out of that chair, and naturally I drew my own conclusions.

Nothing in particular had happened to her during her last forty or fifty years, so that her thoughts dwelt much in the more active and eventful times of early life, which she recalled with such vividness that her hearers perforce journeyed back with her down the days and walked awhile in the Land of Forgotten Things.

Unfortunately I cannot speak from experience, for she disliked me extremely and never addressed me if she could possibly help it.

Had she known how deeply I admired her she would have held a better opinion of me : I thought her quite lovely and was happy to sit in a corner and stare at her. She was brilliantly pink and white, like a child or a very young girl, and her pretty little face in its surrounding aureole of lace and muslin gave an impression of extreme smallness rather than of age.

She was like a tiny grey fairy, mischievous and malign but exquisite.

She said 'yaller' and 'laloc' and 'balcōny' and 'charrut,' and when mentioning me to my mother would observe that I should live to be her 'cuss.'

Why Granny, who had been the family 'cuss' for years—of course in a perfectly decorous and becoming

3

manner—should have selected me for her successor I never discovered.

She knew little of the world of the day, as for a long time—in fact, since she was merely in her early seventies, she had ceased to leave the house and had led behind tightly closed windows a life without air or exercise which would have horrified all medical authorities and which kept her in excellent health.

She heartily despised modern theories and improvements and would quote, as thoroughly up-to-date opinions, the sentiments of Mrs. David Garrick, whom she had known as a little old woman living quietly at Brighton and who had observed, on hearing that a friend was building a bathroom, " Well, I thank God I'm none so dirty ! "

My great-grandfather had died early in life, as was only to be expected. Being what she was at ninety-six, what must great-grandmother have been at fifteen, the age at which she married ? When an old woman, she was regarded by her cringing family as a dangerous explosive, only to be approached with the greatest caution ; when a young woman—well, my great-grandfather must have been a daring man.

Young Mrs. Walford, as a decorative object, was unquestionably delightful, but as a helpmate perhaps a trifle too stimulating.

Be this as it may, my great-grandfather sought, and, I trust, found peace rather hurriedly ; leaving his pretty wife and still prettier daughter to face Life alone.

Now, when Granny faced a thing, one felt sorry for it, but realised that it stood no chance whatever : Life proved no exception to the rule. Life capitulated at once and gave Granny everything she wanted : her pretty daughter married well and early, her home became her mother's, and great-grandmother lived very happily ever after.

The pretty daughter, even after her marriage, must always have been overshadowed by her masterful mother. She was gentle, she was very pretty, she had twelve children and she died.

4

Poor little grandmamma. As a mother she can have done little but watch with vague wonder her interminable offspring tripping over each others' heels into the world.

My grandfather was a grave man, much addicted to the Old Testament, more especially to the passages wherein our enemies are disposed of in a satisfactory way, and he saw himself as a Patriarch ; indeed, when I knew him, he looked the part admirably.

It was only right, therefore, that his children should have been as the sands of the sea, but, as a student of the Scriptures, it should not have escaped him that a Patriarch's good lady received much kindly assistance in the discharge of her duties.

Poor grandmamma, single-handed, did her best, but after the birth of her twelfth child and when my mother, her eldest, was but fourteen, she faded gently out of life and great-grandmother, as Queen Regent, ascended the throne.

Pretty grandmamma. She had lived her short day in an enclosed garden where but little of the world could be seen over the high hedges ; she had known but few men or women with any degree of real intimacy, yet, like the enchanted lady of the crystal box, she had secured at least two admirers well worthy of record.

Once upon a time—in 1819, to be exact—before little grandmamma had taken any steps towards becoming grandmamma, she and her mother went to Highgate for the summer months.

Grandmamma was being instructed by her formidable parent in domestic duties devolving upon a Young Gentlewoman, and inaugurated her career as housekeeper by taking the keys out on the Common and losing them.

Wildly she searched hither and thither ; she was in despair and in terror of the Judgment : she would have to go home without the keys, and then——.

The prospect was too much for pretty grandmamma : she sat hopelessly down on the grass and began to cry.

"Why are you weeping, my dear?" suddenly said an elderly gentleman, for all the world like a Fairy Godmother. Why, by the by, is there no record of a Fairy Godfather? The God-paternal instinct would appear to be lacking in fairy circles.

"I've lost the keys," sobbed grandmamma. "What will mother say?"

The old gentleman possibly knew Mrs. Walford and was able to make a very fair guess at what she would say, for he seemed to realise that the case was desperate and joined gallantly in the search. Together they paced the Heath, at first hopeful, then more and more despondent as daylight began to fail them.

"I must tell her to-night," wailed grandmamma.

"Not to-night," said the old gentleman—to postpone the unpleasant was characteristic of him. "To-morrow will come quite soon enough. And who knows——?"

But grandmamma was past comfort and ran miserably home through the twilight.

Early next morning she received a small packet 'With Mr. S. T. Coleridge's compliments.' Those keys! The thrice-blessed old gentleman had been up half the night searching the Common with a lantern, and had at last achieved success.

Mr. Coleridge was not as a rule energetic—grandmamma must have been very pretty.

After a few more meetings he undertook to 'direct her reading,' but this post must have been more or less of a sinecure, for I fancy that pretty grandmamma did not read much. I possess a volume of *Sybilline Leaves*, containing an early and afterwards revised version of 'The Ancient Mariner,' in which the author "with best Wishes, cheerful Hopes, and most friendly recollections" begs Miss Walford to "be so good as to correct this work from the *Errata*, at page 10 (the leaf before 'The Ancient Mariner') before reading any of the poems, and to *insert* the passages added or substituted." Not a single word has Miss Walford corrected, added or substituted, so, as I

MRS. GREATOREX (the Author's Grandmother)
From a portrait by ANDREW GEDDES

am sure she was a sweetly obedient creature, we may conclude that she never read the book.

My only grudge against grandmamma is that on one occasion Coleridge at great length told her of a new idea for the end of ' Christabel '—and she straightway forgot all about it. I do not want an end to ' Christabel '; I am sure that Coleridge himself could not have ended it without spoiling it ; but I do wish that grandmamma had remembered.

Why did he not confide it to great-grandmother instead ? She would probably have told him that it was stuff and nonsense, but she would not have forgotten. And she must have been every bit as pretty as grandmamma.

Grandmamma's prettiness still lingers on many can-vases by Andrew Geddes, a Scotch painter of great talent and some note whose day has not yet arrived, but who may become a dealers' hero at any minute when the Raeburn vein is entirely worked out.

My grandfather gave a commission for his own and his wife's portraits and the result was all that could be desired —grandfather dark and impressive with his hand in his shirt frill, grandmamma trying to look sedate and elderly in an appalling and much be-ribboned cap.

But after the death of Andrew Geddes and at the dis-persal of his studio effects there was a positive eruption of portraits, finished and unfinished, of grandmamma ; an unregenerate and childish grandmamma, the girl whom Coleridge found crying on Highgate Heath. Grand-mamma in white with little blue bows ; grandmamma in a low frock and a big black hat ; sweetest of all, grand-mamma (yet unfinished) in a hazel-brown poke bonnet lined with pink sitting in an autumn wood.

When did she find time and opportunity to sit for these surreptitious and surprising portraits ? Grandmamma must have been cleverer than her family fancied.

When her gentle rule was over, the Reign of Terror, as administered by great-grandmother, duly succeeded. Mrs. Walford reigned supreme to the end of her days.

A very charming little kingdom was hers. 'Spring-field,' Upper Clapton, where my grandfather then lived, was a rambling old house with no suggestion of the town about it, and the large garden, beyond which a paddock and meadows sloped down to the Wye, was really beautiful, a marvellous land of romantic adventure for the band of children.

With my own eyes have I seen that garden of dreams, for, when I was a child, my mother and I made pilgrimage thither and trespassed all over it. I remember it perfectly.

Now the hideous and ever-advancing Town has swallowed Upper Clapton and the lovely Wye Valley, the lanes and fields have vanished, the old house of Springfield is pulled down, but the garden touched even the arid hearts of Borough Councillors and has been converted into a Public Park. I do not suppose it is the better for its conversion—this seldom happens—but it still exists.

I am glad to have walked with my mother in her dream garden, to have seen the various Sacred Places— the wall whereon she loved to sit, watching the windings of the river and eating windfalls, the hollow tree wherein she kept the 'Morte d'Arthur' and such literature as she considered unsuitable to her elders, the corner where she jumped off a laden wain on the prongs of a hay-fork, all the spots where 'things' had happened so much more important than anything that ever happens later on. We were able to mix our respective childhoods. *Arcades ambo* : I too have lived in Upper Clapton.

My mother has told me that at fourteen she felt forty. For this she received compensation in that at forty she felt fourteen, but in her early days the cares of a family weighed heavily upon her : she was the deputy-mother of a large and unruly troop.

Of course there was Granny, but then Granny was— Granny, and here a mother was wanted. She, as the eldest, must be that mother, the wise director of the children, the kindly arbiter of their fates.

8

The blind fury of her brothers and sisters when they realised this attitude may be imagined. ' Polly ' was instantly voted a Prig, a Sneak, a Spoil-sport : boys were openly rebellious, girls cold and contemptuous and, after a game struggle, my mother resigned the post.

Her first experience of maternity was unfortunate, an illusion was dispelled, she no longer wished to be any-body's mother, and I consider it very handsome of her to have reconsidered the point in after-years ; but the effort had left its mark : she had lost her childhood and never managed to recover it—until we found it again together.

Springfield serving the purpose of both town and country house (my grandfather rode up to business every day), the family seldom left home. One expedition, made with her father and a sister, always dwelt in my mother's memory ; I suppose through its appeal to her keen sense of humour.

My grandfather came of farmer folk (when they are one's relations one calls them Yeomen, probably adding ' sturdy '), and, as a mere boy, had gone away to London to seek his fortune like Dick Whittington. As soon as he began to find it he sent some of it home, and had continued this practice regularly though he returned but seldom and, later in life, when old ties were broken and memories grown dim, his visits ceased altogether.

Suddenly he resolved to seek again the Halls of his Ancestors which were situated in Derbyshire near the valley of the Dove. He would take with him two of his daughters : Marion was romantic—she should face facts, Annie was prideful—she should realise her lowly origin. Incidentally—though I am sure the thought was uncon-scious—they should both see ·him properly appreciated and should know him for the wise, kindly, generous, benevolent, becomingly humble-minded Christian Gentle-man that he was. The desire was most natural ; the fact that he did indeed possess all these admirable quali-ties seemed no reason why he should not occasionally get the credit for them, and I fancy he looked forward to a series of edifying scenes such as occur in the Moral Tales of Miss Maria Edgeworth. Toil-stained hands should grasp his, ancient dames should bless him from doorsteps, he would pat little children's heads. He could see it all.

" ' It is our Benefactor ! ' cried the worthy Family, as with tearful eyes raised to Heaven they, etc. etc. See illustration." But either gratitude was becoming rare or worthy families possessed less dramatic talent than of old ; the progress through the scenes of boyhood was on the whole rather dull. Toil-stained hands went on toiling, ancient dames made pleasant remarks from arm-chairs but never attempted to bless, little children did not want their heads patted, or the heads looked distinctly unpattable.

The reception by the comfortable and well-to-do owners of the Old Mill, which promised charming displays of Sensibility, fell very flat, and my mother's well-meant remark that the monotonous murmur of the mill-wheel was wonderfully soothing failed to please, as the mill-wheel had stopped for the afternoon and the monotonous murmur proceeded from the good gentleman of the house enjoying a nap in the next room.

One scene after another missed fire until at last my grandfather, hiring a couple of donkeys for his daughters, was reduced to doing the sights of Dovedale like an ordinary tourist. Accompanied by the donkey-woman, he set gloomily forth musing upon the mutability of human affairs while the Lady of Donkeys, no doubt to cheer him, entered at great length upon the Story of her Life. She had not attained her present position unaided—her path had been smoothed by the bounty of an unknown relative residing in London.

At last—the Situation ! My grandfather assumed the proper attitude and revealed himself benevolently. The donkey-woman got through her bit wonderfully considering the short notice, and falling upon her knees, thanked Heaven that she had lived to see, etc. etc.

My grandfather, smiling and at peace again, very properly replied, etc. etc. ; my prideful aunt writhed upon

her donkey, and my mother struggled hard against unworthy and inappropriate laughter.

All passed off most pleasantly, but, as I never met my
relative, the donkey-woman, at my grandfather's house in
after-years, I can only fear that she did not care to pursue
the acquaintance.

OF WAISTCOATS, WITCHES, AND
ELIZA'S MOTHER

LIFE went on very quietly in the garden of Springfield. The domestic circle reduced itself to more reasonable proportions, settling down finally into a neat pattern of four brothers and four sisters as if out of consideration for the family dancing-class.

The girls by imperceptible degrees became the Young Ladies and were launched upon the world of Upper Clapton. I fancy that it was not a very exciting world, for my mother had little to tell of it.

Once—tremendous moment—she was asked to a neighbour's house to meet Charles Dickens, but—it really distresses me to record it—did not like him. That is to say, she did not like his waistcoat which was of spun glass and shone like all the rainbows of the heavens reflected in all the diamonds of Golconda. It dazzled her; she could not ' beyond it find the Man '; there seemed to be nothing but flaming, scintillating waistcoat. A veil of spun glass was between her and the great and beloved creator of half our best friends, and she could not break through it.

To atone for this insult to his blessed memory I must set down an unrecorded remark of Dickens, overheard by a friend. A lady was showing him some new and many-coloured chair-covers and begging his opinion thereon. Said Dickens, after grave consideration, " They look as if they had been sat upon by a damp Harlequin."

Dickens was lost to my mother through her sense of beauty, but, on the other hand, it enabled her to appreciate and delight in the extraordinary loveliness of two girls and their mother who lived close at hand.

They were the wife and daughters of a Mr. Spartali, then Consul-General for Greece in London, and the beauty of the two girls had afterwards quite a strong influence on the Art of the day. They were ' discovered ' when, on the occasion of a garden-party, one four-wheeler miraculously wafted from London the painters Rossetti, Whistler,

Thomas Armstrong, Legros, Ridley, du Maurier, and Edward Poynter, depositing them at the feet of the Misses Spartali.

Whistler seized upon Christina, the younger, for his ' Princesse du Pays de la Porcelaine,' Rossetti secured the elder, Marie, as a model for innumerable studies and for such pictures as ' Dante's Dream,' and ' A Vision of Fiammetta.'

Armstrong himself tells of how he hurried Algernon Swinburne down to inspect the new-found treasures and of how, when Marie Spartali came towards them across the lawn in a white dress trimmed with little bunches of coloured ribbon (afterwards reproduced by Rossetti in his ' Borgia ' water colour), the young poet could only murmur feebly, " She is so beautiful that I want to sit down and cry."

Theirs was a lofty beauty, gracious and noble ; the beauty worshipped in Greece of old, yet with a wistful tenderness of poise, a mystery of shadowed eyes that gave life to what might have been a marble goddess ; a beauty which would seem to possess much of that marble's eternity.

When I myself in due time came to know the elder sister, then Mrs. Stillman, I could not conceive that she had ever been more beautiful.

Nature was loath to spoil her wonderful work, and the years crowned it with an added perfection.

In the fullness of time my grandfather moved from Springfield to London, installing himself, his family and his mother-in-law in a large corner house in Cleveland Square, Bayswater, which three of his daughters soon left for homes of their own, my mother going no farther than next door.

When I joined the family circle I was made free of my grandfather's house, and soon found that it possessed decidedly attractive features.

There was the dark cloakroom, a cave of mystery, where

the youthful explorer, straying blindly amidst vague, pendant forms, uncomfortably suggestive of Bluebeard's wives,
might chance to wake a deep, shuddering note from the
great dinner-gong like mutter of thunder in distant hills.
There was a store-room, full of possibilities ; you could
smell currants and brown sugar and yellow soap quite distinctly through the keyhole if you dared approach ; but
near it was the dread portal of great-grandmamma guarded
by her two janitors, Harriet and Jane, almost as ancient as
herself and awful in black robes that crackled. There was
a whole empty floor only tenanted by a tall clock : when
the clock was about to strike you fled—the great voice crying in the wilderness was too thrilling. There was an
enchanting lumber-room where the flotsam and jetsam of
years lay becalmed, and a box-room giving access to the
roof, so that any enterprising child could take long walks
across the tiles and bring brightness into the neighbours'
lives by dropping ' bang ups ' (small, detonating packets
purchasable in the Mews) down their kitchen chimneys.

My grandfather himself was now a very different man
from the stern parent of Springfield. He had brought up
his own children so strictly and had done his duty by them
so constantly and unflinchingly that there had been little
time for companionship or confidence. In his old age, feeling a pleasant sense of duty done, he apparently resolved
to do it no more and resigned himself comfortably to his
natural affections, with the result that never was a father
better loved.

His daughters, even after their marriages, nearly always
spent some portion of each day with him ; and indeed he was
a father to be proud of, with his strong, handsome face, his
thick, dark hair that nothing would induce to turn white,
and his grave courteous dignity.

He still showed a slight tendency to treat his family as
children, and my mother and aunts would suddenly be
called upon to ' say their pieces ' as though they had just
been brought down newly washed from the nursery. My
mother, who liked ' saying pieces ' and said them beauti-

fully, did not mind this ; others obliged with less spontaneity.

Here *I* scored, for I could always commit to memory strings of—to me—disconnected lines, and, at the word of command, I would reel off verses, mostly of a religious character, without the faintest understanding of their meaning, but with a certain feeling for phrasing which gave them a monotonous, half-chanted cadence. Grandpapa seemed to like this treatment of verse, for he usually conducted me like an orchestra with a long white forefinger and, at favourite passages, would throw in a soft but deeply booming *obbligato*.

He was certainly a very attractive old gentleman, and his charm seemed even more appreciated in the next world than in this, for grandpapa had a curious fascination for Ghosts. If there was a Ghost anywhere about, grandpapa saw it ; they came to him with their little troubles, they could not keep away from him, but—never could they induce him to believe in them.

Here was an instance of life's strange irony : many a poor member of the Psychical Society would have been thankful for the Ghosts which only annoyed and perplexed grandpapa. He disapproved and disbelieved, yet they fawned upon him, and I well remember his last Ghost which drove him from a very pleasant summer retreat near Chertsea.

He had taken the house for the summer months of two successive years, and his first tenancy passed off smoothly enough, though they *did* say below stairs that all was not as it should have been. Invisible but audible Presences walked up and down stairs behind housemaids, luminous shapes were seen in a subterranean passage connecting the kitchen and the dairy.

But during the second year the Ghost's attentions became more marked—the servants felt embarrassed by the fixed gaze of Fiery Eyes from shadowy corners, the doorbell would ring violently in the night without visible agency ; and even *I* suffered, for on two evenings my governess rushed in upon me and shook me in my bed, enquiring what I meant by coming capering in my night-gown into the next room where she was having supper. I had not stirred. Whatever had capered was not I.

At last came the climax.

One evening, early in September, when my family and I had returned to London, as was our strange and stuffy wont, ' late, late in the gloaming ' entered to us grandpapa looking—well—odd.

Even in my infant brain was born the daring thought— if it were possible for grandpapa to look ashamed of himself he was now doing so.

" Father ! " cried my mother, jumping up. " Are you not well ? "

" Quite well, my dear, I thank you," said grandpapa.

" Were you called up on business ? " asked my father.

" No," said grandpapa with elaborate carelessness. " I have no urgent business in town at present, but I find that I must beg you for a night's lodging."

Grandpapa was evidently feeling very awkward. He would invent no easy little way out for himself, no tale of doctors, dentists or lawyers to explain his sudden arrival ; that would have been against his strict code of honour ; yet he was evidently determined to keep his reasons to himself. He was asked no more questions and stayed for two days with us, by which time his own house next door was ready for him.

Soon after, by listening to my elders' conversation with a judicious semblance of inattention, I became master of the facts.

The Ghost, encouraged by its small successes, had broken out. It had materialised and had, as usual, taken a special fancy to my unfortunate grandfather. It would not let him alone, but, like a nurse with a wakeful child, would ' bring its work and sit with him ' through the watches of the night.

Grandpapa would retire to his room, lock his door, barricade it with a table and several heavy chairs, and go to bed hoping nightly that there would be ' no more of the nonsense.'

Very soon, in would trip the affectionate Ghost, a little old man, bent and grey, dressed in a long grey dressing-gown. He would pass the bed, taking no notice of its occupant's incisive remarks, and, seating himself in an arm-chair by the fireplace, would take some papers or letters from the dressing-gown pocket and set about reading them quietly.

He was really no trouble—he did not fidget about or make a noise, but he was annoying, and to my grandfather doubly annoying, because to have a thing whose existence you firmly deny plainly before your eyes *is* annoying, and had grandpapa been a modern, he would have expressed his feelings exactly by stating that he was fair fed up with Ghosts by this time.

After a week of these nocturnal *tête-à-tête* he fled ingloriously.

Deeply ashamed of the acquaintance, he had mentioned the Ghost to no one but my Aunt Emily who lived with him, and she, on her side, had made no enquiries lest she should start a panic in the kitchen. But on her last morning, before following her father to London, she called upon an old woman at the lodge to extract some information about the late owner of the house.

" He wasn't much," said the old lady.

" Not much to look at ? " enquired my aunt.

" Not much any ways," said the old lady. " Never spent a penny. Saved and saved, he did. Little grey, old, bent thing he was."

" Was he ? " said my aunt, feeling rather uncomfortable.

" Wouldn't even spare himself a suit o' clothes," went on the old woman. " Walked about in an old grey dressing-gown."

" Thank you," said my aunt, and took the next train to town.

The subject was seldom referred to, especially in my presence, but I used often to think with concern of the

Affectionate Ghost trotting in to sit with grandpapa as usual and finding the room unoccupied and his friend gone.

The gift of the Seeing Eye was not bequeathed by my grandfather to any of his descendants, and personally I have never regretted my loss of this legacy. As companions, Ghosts have always struck me as undesirable. They have no respect for privacy, no tact, no sense of humour, their conversation, as reported, is singularly stupid and often vulgar, and the hours they keep are most upsetting.

By their admirers all these little *gaucheries* are put down to the medium through whom they elect to communicate ; but why, then, have Ghosts such a predilection for low company ?

Perhaps if they could get into a better set they might improve. In after-life I came across several Seers, Witches and Warlocks, but none had his little flock in better order than the poet, W. B. Yeats. He seemed to have a way with Ghosts and Spirits, and under his kindly sway they dropped many of their ill-bred tricks and showed (occasionally) quite ordinary intelligence.

He was telling me once the true history of one of the often recurrent Catholic wonders, a picture belonging to a village priest which shed miraculous blood-drops.

" But how did you find out ? " I asked. " Did you go to——" (a distant place in France).

" No. I sent a Spirit to look into the whole thing," said Yeats, as simply as though he had said, ' I sent a boy messenger.' And certainly, under Yeats's control, the Spirit brought back as direct and fair a report as could be wished.

" The man is perfectly genuine," said the Spirit, " but there has been no Miracle. It is merely a case of self-deception." Then it described the means whereby the effect had been produced. " The next development," went on the Spirit, " will be the appearance of the Stigmata upon the person of the enthusiast," and the Spirit was quite right.

Now here was sound information given in straightfor-

ward terms. It really seemed as though the Spirit, gratified at being selected as confidant by a charming and distinguished man, had pulled itself together and minded its
manners.

When I was a boy I used to be taken by my Aunt Emily,
who from time to time dabbled daintily in Mysticism, to the
shrine of the great and wonder-working Madame Blavatsky, who was staying for an indefinite period with a friend
of our family.

I should never have gathered that she was the guest, for
the house appeared to be Madame's and all that therein
was, and the gentle hostess had faded into the background,
where she was quietly occupied in paying expenses.

Madame Blavatsky did not often oblige with signs and
wonders at these gatherings in Notting Hill, but she would
sometimes consent to ' sound the Astral Bell,' the slight
tinkle produced differing only from ordinary tinkles in that
nobody answered it.

By her many devotees the lady was held to be a holy and
saint-like being, and if this was so, Nature had certainly
treated her most unfairly in bestowing upon her an appearance and personality suggestive of concentrated evil.

I have never since come across anyone who seemed so
to radiate malific influence. No doubt I was mistaken and
Madame was all that she should have been, but it must be
admitted that she started as a saint or an angel very
heavily handicapped.

The Mystic Lady received in a small, dark and very
stuffy room and beside her hung a picture, framed in dull
gold and reported to be the true likeness of her celebrated
Control in far Tibet, though it looked very like the ordinary Russian icon of commerce.

In the dimness I saw an enormous woman who filled
and overflowed an enormous chair, a large flat face, thick-
featured and coarse-skinned, and—horrible eyes.

They were the shallow protruding eyes of the mesmerist, glittering in surface but dull and heavy in glance—
large, pale eyes, not to me impressive or alarming, but

almost unbearably ugly. The disagreeable impression was heightened by a gruff, masculine voice which poured out torrents of talk couched for the most part in vulgar slang.

Such, to my eyes, seemed the Priestess of the Theosophists. Her followers, I believe, were supposed to regard the things of this world but little, so perhaps they had not regarded Madame Blavatsky very carefully. To me, she appeared to belong completely to this world, and if she had any connection with the next she suggested dealings with its less popular hemisphere.

Once, in my early days, when staying with an uncle in a huge old tumbledown house of his, on wild and very lonely uplands overlooking the Welsh hills, I came near to meeting a Priestess of the Occult all of the olden time. I refer to Eliza's mother.

The scene where we ought to have met was all that could be wished : the spot was remote and romantic, the house neglected and almost ruinous. In its vast and mouldy library, in company with *The Mysteries of Udolpho* and *The Romance of the Forest*, I found my first Book of Magic and eagerly scanned its contents.

" How to remove warts."—I had no warts to remove.

" On the sowing of rape seed. Rape seed when sown with curses and maledictions, prospers exceedingly."—This was satisfactory, but I was uninterested in rape seed.

" How to raise a Fairy."—Come, this was better.

" Take the blood of a white hen."—How could I take the blood of any hen, let alone that the hen would be my uncle's, and I felt sure he would not care for its blood to be taken ? Would the Fairy object to the hen's being cooked, as, if not, I could save some gravy from dinner ?

I gave up my study of Conjuration, which in most cases seemed to require a little private abattoir of one's own, for want of proper professional guidance : had I known how near I was to a great expert I should have been still more ashamed of my amateurish researches.

Why did I not meet Eliza's mother ? To think that I lived for weeks so near her, within the actual radius of her

mysterious influence and yet never met her, distresses me
to this day.

For—low be it spoken—Eliza's mother was a Witch—a
real, genuine, black witch ; nothing of the modern palm-
stroking, crystal-gazing, thought-reading nonsense about
her, but the Real Thing.

The devil was known for a fact to be on an intimate
footing with Eliza's mother and to drop in frequently to see
her, and she held the rustic population for miles round in a
grip of terror.

Her name I never knew—I think there was a very
general reluctance to pronounce it—but Eliza was kitchen-
maid at my uncle's house.

No other maid could sleep in the same room with Eliza.
Things happened in the night. The furniture walked about,
and jugs and basins danced blithely in the moonlight.

Thus and thus, said the household, the Witch talked
with her daughter, and while the chairs bucked and
bounded and the washstand staggered stiffly about with its
jingling freight, the miserable room-mate cowered beneath
the sheets terrified lest, above the *charivari* of the excited
furniture, she should hear and understand some dread
message from the Abyss.

Now, in the light of modern discoveries, who can say
that the household may not have been right in its conjec-
tures and Eliza at dead of night, in awful commune with
the towel-horse or the soap-dish, may have ticked off no
more sulphurous communication than, ' Try to get next
Sunday out. Shrimps for tea.'

ACTRESSES, AUNTS, AND THE STEAM HAMMER

I T is distressing to recall the fact that I did not like my first Notable Acquaintance.

She was an actress of the Old School, and had a confirmed habit of reading Shakespeare aloud which I personally found trying. I was nearing the age of six and had been to at least two Pantomimes as well as to a circus and—well, I frankly preferred the Modern School.

I think I took Miss Glyn to have been some sort of relation of Shakespeare's—possibly his daughter—with such authority and intimacy did she speak of him. She was supposed to descend, artistically, direct from the Kembles and to hold the traditions of John Philip and the great Sarah : whether existing members of the Kemble family supposed so too I do not know.

Shakespeare, as interpreted by Miss Glyn, struck me as very dismal and monotonous. He became ' lessons,' and lessons of a prolonged and aggravated kind.

I could see little difference between the various characters as sustained by Miss Glyn. They were all haughty, with deep, solemn voices, they all flashed their eyes a good deal, they all seemed unaccountably annoyed with each other, and all their utterances were so fraught with meaning that, after awhile, they conveyed no meaning whatever.

In the course of one of these recitations, a lawyer uncle of mine read, under correction from the actress, the speeches of the Ghost in Hamlet. He had a splendid voice and must, I think, have read well, for I, holding on to my chair and thrilling exquisitely, wished, with an eye on bed-time, that Uncle George would leave off.

Then came the correction. I still held on to my chair because the lady made such a noise, but I thrilled no more. The Ghost was laid for me and had become ' lessons.' I gathered from the conversation of Grown

Ups the surprising fact that Miss Glyn was—or rather had been—*the* Cleopatra.

Odd. I had heard of Cleopatra and had pictured her to myself as strangely unlike Miss Glyn. Still I bowed to correction as was befitting, and after careful re-observation of the lady from the Cleopatra point of view, the Serpent of Old Nile became for me throughout my earlier years a stout and portentous dame in deep black, with a noble brow and a large brooch.

Once I witnessed what must have been a flash of the old fire when Cleopatra, owing to a regrettable misunderstanding, boxed my ears with great energy in the middle of the King's Road, Brighton.

I was dragging a small dog by its collar out of the way of a passing carriage, and Miss Glyn, seeing me from her window and thinking that the little creature was being ill-treated, swooped down upon me like an eagle.

For this all honour to her. Would that stalwart elderly ladies of terrifying aspect were always at hand to smack little boys who worry animals.

From that moment I reverenced Cleopatra for the love she bore to dogs and for her readiness to do battle in their cause.

Why do I remember Miss Glyn so well, and Adelaide Ristori, whom in my young days I also met, so little ? I suppose because Miss Glyn boxed my ears and Ristori did not.

My memories of the Marchesa del Grillo are of a stately figure with slow, grand movements, a quiet face, still nobly beautiful, of a gentle voice, seldom raised but with a curious resonance in it suggesting hidden reserves of power.

My mother often spoke of the never-forgotten moment in her life when she first heard the voice of Ristori in a line spoken ' off ' before her entrance in Medea—" Coraggio, figlii, coraggio ; non è lungo il passo " ; and once, in questioning me about my lessons which I cared for no

more than reason, and urging me to learn languages—
" et surtout le Latin. Ah, le Latin ! "—the actress raised
the wonderful voice and chanted a line. The words I
could not understand, but the tone and the cadence I can
hear to this day.

And from that hour I minded my book and became
a proficient in the classics ? Of course that is the proper
end to the story, but unfortunately, when later on my
pastors and masters read Latin with me, it bore no resemblance whatever to the Latin of Ristori, and perhaps that
is why it interested me so little.

And now I can get little beyond an occasional tomb-
stone or prescription.

I never saw either Madame Ristori or Miss Glyn on
the stage, but I should imagine that the former had little
of the Old School about her. To me, ignorant of Italian,
she spoke French, but I well remember her quiet, natural
tones in contrast with the declamation of Miss Glyn, whose
speech, even in private life, was measured and artificial.
No doubt she spoke most correctly, but it seemed to be
at considerable personal inconvenience.

She was great upon Elocution, which she held to be a
lost Art, and was fond of instancing the words Mayor and
Mare as sounds which when spoken correctly bore no
resemblance to each other. Certainly, when she spoke
them, May-yor-r-r did not sound in the least like Mare,
but neither did it sound like anything intelligible.

The suggesting of silent letters, such as the ' u ' in mourn
or the ' w ' in sword, the allowing them, like good children,
to be seen and not heard, is the aim of the true elocu-
tionist, but the effect is not attained simply by pronouncing the word as it is spelt, which seemed to be Miss Glyn's
method. I did not perhaps indulge in such reflections at
the age of six, but I did wonder why the lady talked like
that.

In these early days I was fortunate in the possession
of several deputy aunts—ladies outside the family circle
who had either achieved aunthood by sheer hard work

and moral worth or who had been born aunts—as to whose vocation there could be no possible mistake.

Amongst the most valued of these were ' Aunt ' Charlotte Nasmyth and ' Aunt ' Jennie Terry. ' Aunt ' Charlotte was the youngest but one of a large group of brothers and sisters, all of whom were clever and two of whom were great. Patrick Nasmyth, the painter, was the eldest and James Nasmyth, the inventor of the Steam Hammer, the youngest.

All the sisters had painted diligently and inevitably. They were all talented, but it would have made no difference had they not been so. They were Nasmyths and therefore they painted : what is more, they painted all day long. Day in, day out, the four sisters sat solemnly down together and painted, turning out large, romantic landscapes, very brown and yellow and, to speak the truth, not a little dull, yet with good feeling for composition and a certain distinction which removed them from what a friend of mine used to call ' the Spare Bedroom School.'

' Aunt ' Charlotte was the last remaining of the sisters, and now, her brush laid aside, lived with her niece Jennie Terry, a grey parrot and a cat in a little house at Putney with a delightful garden wherein I spent blissful afternoons.

She was a spirited, even brilliant old lady, full of quaint tales of bygone days and memories of her parents and brethren ; but over ' Aunt ' Jennie's birth and parentage brooded an awful silence. Being ' Aunt ' Charlotte's niece, it was to be presumed that her mother had been a Miss Nasmyth—even I managed to work that out—but for all the notice taken of his more than probable existence she might never have had a father. One day the veil was lifted for me and I learned the terrible fact that ' Aunt ' Jennie's father had been—I hardly like to record it—an actor ; and therefore by the virtuous and reputable family of Nasmyth his name could never be mentioned.

This was strange, as the family of Nasmyth was remarkable for intelligence and the name of Daniel Terry is still

25

green as that of an admirable actor, a cultivated and true
gentleman and a good friend, the testimony of Sir Walter
Scott dealing especially with his excellence in the last
capacity.

'Aunt' Jennie had accepted the situation, and never
once did I hear her speak of her father, but I think the
stage glamour lurked in her blood ; and when, on coming
out from a theatre, ' Miss Terry's carriage ' was called and
people pressed forward hoping for a glimpse of the idol
of the hour, the lovely Ellen, ' Aunt ' Jennie would hastily
veil herself and skip jauntily through the whispering crowd
to her modest hired brougham with a delightful sense of
being a Wicked Play-actress and no better than she
should be.

Of Uncle James Nasmyth she stood in considerable
awe, and before I met him I had visions of a stern and
unbending Presence who disliked little boys and who lived
amongst whirring wheels and awful machines which
banged and bumped.

I always hated machinery and had a vague notion that
James Nasmyth was mainly responsible for its existence.
He had been described to me as a Great Engineer, and I
had looked out for him uneasily at Waterloo and Victoria,
hoping that his train would not come in until ours had
started, thus averting an introduction ; so when I was at
last bidden to Hammerfield, his country home at Pens-
hurst, I went all reluctant as to the cave of a wicked
magician.

Directly the Magician appeared all was changed : I
knew that I had never met anything like this before. He
was my first Great Man, and I give myself a good mark
for having recognised him at once.

His splendid face, rugged as if hewn out of rock, the
kindly humour of his bright eyes, even the breadth and
depth of his Scotch accent, fascinated me, and he became
my first Hero.

As to his not liking little boys, that need not have
troubled me, for to my inexpressible content he did not

Believe me I am
yours very truly
James Nasmyth

JAMES NASMYTH
Drawn by THE AUTHOR from an old photograph

appear to regard me as such, but treated me with the deference and consideration due to a contemporary. When he called me ' Sir ' I nearly burst.

For enchanted hours I wandered with him, and even when he began to throw off the mask and reveal himself in his true colours as arch-magician—when he showed me stars in the daytime, an obvious impossibility save to one of more than mortal power ; when he held before me bewildering landscapes painted by him in the moon, telling me that he could find his way about that satellite blindfold—I felt no misgivings beyond the sensation that I was now in for it and completely ' under spells.'

From time to time Mrs. Nasmyth, a comely, smiling dame with pretty white hair, would collect us and look us over to see that we were all right.

" I always feel anxious if James is away for long," said she, after one of these raids. " Once I missed him for hours and then saw his feet sticking out from the end of the big telescope."

" I was cleaning it and I just slipped in and could not get back," explained James comfortably.

" How dreadful," I gasped, looking up at the great tube reared high against the sky.

" Eh, sir, it was," agreed James Nasmyth. " Man, it was the Lord's mair-r-cy I didna break the lens ! "

He, like his sister Charlotte, was full of talk of the long-ago, but his stories had in them a many-coloured magic, a blending of the droll with the romantic which held my fancy. I particularly loved a lively tale of how once in early days when it behoved him to appear at some function and he had not the wherewithal to buy a wedding garment, he had painted upon his bare legs beautiful black silk stockings with gold clocks which had excited admiration in all beholders for their miraculous fit.

Another anecdote, the more thrilling because I understood not one word of it, was of how he had stood by the side of the Wizard of the North when the Heart of Mid-lothian fell broken at his feet.

This story, which to me seemed to promise all the best elements of Aladdin and Jack the Giant-killer, was, when brought down to the adult comprehension, briefly as follows.

His father, Alexander Nasmyth, and a friend had taken little James to watch the demolition of the Tolbooth in the High Street of Edinburgh, once a royal palace but for centuries used as a gaol. Here they had been joined by Sir Walter Scott ; and while the ancient walls crumbled under the pick he had stood silently beside them until, out of an apparently solid block of masonry fell a huge mass of iron, crashing to the feet of him who had raised about it a more lasting structure ; for the iron mass was the Heart of Midlothian—the condemned cell of the old Tolbooth. Sir Walter was at that time still unacknow-ledged as the author of the *Waverley Novels*, but his claim to them was a very open secret, and the crowd exchanged glances as he stooped over the shattered ' Heart.' The wrenched-off iron door and great key were secured by him for his own house, and the young man who had come with James and his father to see the sight picked from the recesses of the cell a mummied rat, probably the last prisoner there immured, and preserved the grisly relic for long years. He was the painter, James Linnell, who soon afterwards was to give to William Blake a commission for the famous ' Inventions to the Book of Job.'

Sir Walter Scott had long been a friend and admirer of Alexander Nasmyth, sometimes called the Father of Scotch Landscape, and little James too came in for praise from him for his sketches and more particularly for his careful drawings of old coins, of which he had amassed a small collection. The kindly ' Wizard ' won the child's heart for ever by producing a beautiful little silver coin of Mary, Queen of Scots, and presenting it to his ' young brother antiquarian.'

What a bridge across the years that little coin seemed to throw when that same ' young brother,' now grown old, showed it proudly to me.

Round and round his garden he would take me, a veritable wonderland to a child. The acres were not many, but were planted thickly with spreading trees among which little paths wound bewilderingly in and out, so that the explorer lost himself afresh at each turn. Through these mazes we would go, he sometimes telling a tale of Faerie, for of the Faerie he could speak delightfully ; aye, and could limn them too. It seemed strange that the same brain and hand that had conceived and directed the mighty Hammer could have produced ' The Fairies are out,' a black and white drawing full of microscopic detail and dainty, gossamer charm.

I think that it was the poet in Nasmyth that led him, despite his passion for mechanics, to spend his leisure moments in regions where rivets and nuts and cog-wheels are unknown, where he would wander lonely with the moon over the blue fields of Heaven.

A gigantic telescope, made by himself, stood in a clearing at the end of a long brick path edged with flowers. Nearer the house was the Magician's Tower, workshop beneath, observatory above ; and, on the rapturous occasions when I was caught up into this thick mystery, my cup was full.

It was a wonderful companionship and a wonderful experience for an imaginative child ; and when we were alone in the dim observatory, when he would set the sidereal clock, ordering the huge telescope to ' mind ' a particular star like a sheep dog until he should want it again, and I knew from the measured throb that the giant tube and the very roof itself were, at his command, swinging slowly westward to the music of the spheres, I felt that he and I stood together on the pivot of the universe and that he could, if so he willed, ' bind the sweet influence of Pleiades and loose the bands of Orion.'

How that moment of enchantment came back to me when, in long after-years, I stood again in the Hammerfield Observatory with a very different man at my side.

A querulous pedant to whom all Nasmyth's beloved tools and instruments, bought for a song, were 'out of date' or 'altogether useless'—as indeed they were to him who neither knew their uses nor could have used them if he had. He could not refrain from sneering at and trying to belittle the Mighty Dead whom he had never known and in whose shoes he was standing.

"That Nasmyth"—he always alluded to him thus—"knew nothing. He was no man of science. His Steam Hammer is now absolutely superseded."

"So is James Watt's Steam Engine," I observed.

"Just so," cried the learned gentleman. "Now here again, you see. His telescope is useless. It merely commands a small portion of the sky through that hole. In all *modern* observatories the telescope and the roof move by machinery to allow the astronomer to sweep the Heavens."

I glanced at the clockwork at his elbow, but said nothing. Should I who had sailed with the Master Mariner over the Seas of Night put out again with this novice? I held my tongue with some small difficulty and was truly glad when the new owner, speedily tiring of a toy with which he could not play, resold Hammerfield to Lord Ronald Gower, who, being an artist, was able to hold in due reverence the name of its late master.

Dear James Nasmyth. He honoured me with his friendship to the day of his death, extending to the awkward schoolboy and callow youth the same kindly tolerance which he had shown to the child. Here is his first letter to me written not long after the Hammerfield visit.

> PENSHURST,
> KENT.
> *Nov.* 1, 1875.

MY DEAR GRAHAM,

We were so much pleased with your illustrated note. I send you by this post a rare book by John Parry! being graphic illustrations of

Musical Terms, and hope it will be as amusing as it is instructive to you. He is a first-rate Musician as well as artist.

With our united kindest regards to your dear Mama and Papa,

Believe me, I am,

Yours very truly,

JAMES NASMYTH.

Have you been to see the Death and Burial of Cock Robin ?

What a comfort he was to me later on when my parents were conscientiously and vainly trying to educate me.

" My dear-r-r mad'm," he would say to my mother, though he had known her as ' Polly ' in short skirts, " the sole reason why I have succeeded in life is that I never had any education. If you cram a boy's head full of other folk's ideas, where's the room for his own when he begins to pick them up ? "

When I went to school he sighed ; when I entered Eton he fairly howled, and the letter of congratulation which he sent me when I left I still possess, though its social blasphemies must not be recorded ; the last and mildest being, " I truly rejoice that you have escaped from that hot-bed of young snobs."

He need not have distressed himself. I never learned anything worth speaking of at either of my schools, and Eton in my case failed signally to fulfil her historic boast, for I left as unmistakable an outsider as I entered. But I fear that it is easier to empty a head of all ideas than to refill it according to the Nasmyth standard.

Since his death I have sometimes heard James Nasmyth and his wife spoken of as having been rather ' near ' and unduly careful of their worldly goods, but my own experience is in direct opposition to this theory. My mother went to see Mrs. Nasmyth after her loss and expressed surprise at her intention of leaving Hammerfield. " I could not live here without James," said Mrs. Nasmyth quietly. " But it's a dear old place. I wish you would have it, Marion. Let me give it to you just as it is, furniture and everything. James was always fond of you. Do take it."

We could not accept from our old friend this gift of a beautiful and valuable property, but as an example of the Nasmyth ' nearness ' it was very characteristic.

EXCEPT for my mother's great love for poetry and her real appreciation thereof, we as a family were not artistic.

My father could draw, but never did so, and he had sufficient knowledge of a good picture to dislike a bad one ; but these two negatives did not succeed in producing an affirmative, and our house was pictureless save for the inevitable Landseer engravings, without the aid of which a respectable Bayswater family could hardly have been expected to eat its dinner.

Yet, though he had not collected round him many *objets d'art*, he had done wisely and well in his omissions. Though he had been for over twenty years in the East our house contained no carved wood screens, no Koran stands, no Benares brass work, no dusty, grassy objects with discs of red and green talc stuck about them, no coloured photographs of the Taj by moonlight.

The few things he had cared to buy were all Chinese, which says much : lovely little tables of black lacquer, lacquer jars faintly patterned and of the tint of faded roses, thin shell-like cups of porcelain.

Our house was no uglier than most ; in fact, my father's instinctive rejection of rubbish and my mother's ' way ' with furniture which coaxed the most hopeless room into looking twice as well as it had any business to look, made here and there for something that was almost beauty.

" Pooh ! " will remark one of my few remaining contemporaries. " What about the large green table with beadwork roses round it in the middle of the drawing-room ? What of the sham flowers in the grate ? And didn't you have an imitation marble paper on the stairs —and grained doors—and a handsome hat-stand ? "

Ye-e-es, I admit the hat-stand and the marble, but not the grained doors—and the table wasn't in the middle of the drawing-room and the roses were woolwork, not bead, and anyhow it might have been ever so much worse.

But just about when I was passing from the nursery to the schoolroom a strange influence was astir in the town. The stagnant waters of Victorian indifference had been troubled and something was slowly rising to the surface. Would it prove the very Venus reborn from the foam—was Beauty on her way to Bayswater at last?

Elderly ladies painted feverishly upon drain-pipes and door panels.

London watched, waiting for a sign.

Then came my Nursery Governess and with her Culture. I had always tried to draw, and my attempts kept me ' good and quiet ' and had therefore been encouraged : now I learned that, all unawares, I had been perpetrating Art with a large A. If I persevered—well, there was no telling to what heights I might attain. It was conceivable that I might in time colour texts, yea, even the advanced ones with birds'-nests and angels in the capital letters, I might draw groups of flowers upon little mats with marking ink, I might even, if my talent had an original bent (I felt ever so original), one day design antimacassars.

I gazed at the jack towel upon which my instructress was then embroidering Love-in-a-mist in faded grey and green wools (Love-in-a-mist is really bright blue, but in Art it was grey) and felt that this could never be. The height was too giddy, such eminence could not be mine. But my ambition and enthusiasm were alight and I owe many thanks to the lady who set torch to them.

She was, as James Nasmyth would have put it, ' quite unspoilt by education.' She loved the Arts and could deal bravely with the lower branches such as fretwork, embroidery in wools and the making of shell pincushions ; higher she could not go, but she looked eagerly upward through the mists of a charming, childish ignorance and saw—considerably more than might have been expected.

Friends had she, co-labourers in Art's vineyard, and

34

into their mysteries I was initiated. I remember a certain old Mrs.—Mrs.—the name escapes me—whose prowess in the field of crewel work was at once a wonder and an example. Every now and then we would receive a note trumpeting the news that Mrs.—what *was* the name now? —had yet another pattern for an antimacassar, and the arbitress of my education and I would exchange a silent look of awe and thankfulness, wonderingly glad that to us was vouchsafed the knowledge of this rare woman, this Mighty Mother of Antimacassars, this

> " Endless fountain of immortal drink
> Pouring unto us from the heavens' brink."

Hastily we would set off and find the Wonderworker seated in a vast chair and surrounded by the implements of her craft, while about her, over the backs of chairs, round the edges of tables, pendant from the mantelpiece, prone on the piano, was on view her gallery of many and marvellous works.

At her touch the furniture grew speechful and exchanged sly badinage.

" Where are you going to, my pretty maid? " jocularly enquired the arm-chair, while the sofa coyly replied, " I'm going a-milking, sir, she said " ; and the milkmaid on the sofa shot soft glances from her crooked woolly eyes at the bowing green-coated gentleman on the chair.

These figures, I was told, were ' copied from Walter Crane.' I mentally uncovered. I knew my Walter Crane : he, or rather his picture books, had seen me through measles and whooping cough, and I looked doubtfully at the miserable caricatures which in no wise recalled the dainty originals. Still—the master-hand that had thus thrown them higgledy-piggledy upon the jack towelling could hardly have erred—they *must* be all right. I marvelled and came to heel, but at the back of my mind remained a doubt. What would Walter Crane himself—if so lofty a being could have any actual existence —have thought of the woolly milkmaid? Ought she to

35

have been so *very* unlike his drawing ? Were all these things perhaps not quite—I choked down the daring blasphemy and that very afternoon designed my first antimacassar, a spray of grey convolvulus wriggling up a stick. I can see it now and earnestly wish that I could not.

In truth, my feet were set in dangerous ways. These industrious old ladies, happily sewing away at their crooked milkmaids and lumpy flowers in the back parlours of Bayswater and Brompton, were in all innocence the pioneers of the great, so-called ' Æsthetic ' Craze which later on swelled to a flood of absurdity and vulgarity, quenching and sweeping away the only genuine Art Movement that I have seen originate in England.

Tangled in this web of woolwork, a helping hand was extended to me by my Aunt Emily. She was my mother's only unmarried sister, and after my great-grandmother's death had taken command and gone her own way.

She was much at the house of a very old family friend, Barbara Leigh Smith (Madame Bodichon), and there, it was darkly whispered, she ' met people.' I myself had heard her remark that she knew George Eliot, and thought that she must have known him very well to refer to him thus familiarly. Madame Bodichon's circle was fond of celebrities, and I rather gather that it had just then exhausted a very popular brand of Italian Patriot and had for the moment fallen back upon painters. Be this as it may, my surprising aunt one day electrified me by saying, " Come with me to see Walter Crane." Had she said, " Come with me to Heaven," I should have been no more surprised and far less pleased.

To enter the unknown land where pictures were born ! To see a real painter in a real studio ! A glimpse of the New Jerusalem would have been but a poor exchange.

Glowing with bliss, I was wafted with my aunt in a hansom to Shepherd's Bush, a likely and suggestive address ; and indeed in those days though the shepherds had departed several bushes remained, and the lanes were sufficiently suburban to appear rural in my town-bred eyes. We stopped before a little low house standing in a garden which seemed to me limitless. Here were spaces of daisied grass, old apple-trees bright with blossom, dogs, guinea-pigs, all that the heart of child could desire, yet I passed these delights as though I saw them not. What were guinea-pigs to me at this solemn moment?

The house when we entered seemed strangely dark, and we groped our way down a long room, shying nervously at the chairs as they emerged from the gloom. I ran into a curtain worked in crewels and thought of Mrs.—I never can remember her name—then straightway forgot her, for we were in the presence of the Master.

Even in the semi-darkness I noticed several things. The Master looked very young, almost a boy. The Master did not seem very masterful; had it been possible I should have said that the Master was shy.

I had quickly to readjust my ideas: I had expected a tremendous personality like that of James Nasmyth, and behold a slim, gentle youth with a deprecating manner.

Entered Mrs. Crane, then a beautiful woman with great grey eyes, black-lashed, and a quantity of golden brown hair with a lovely ripple in it. Then followed an anxious period of delay. Tea was brought—who wanted tea? Stout and placid babies were exhibited who eyed me with a friendly interest that begot uneasiness, and I hoped and trusted that the object of my visit had been made quite clear to these infants. Good Heavens, suppose there were a Nursery Tea upstairs and I banished to it while my elders battened on pictures!

I should have trusted my adroit aunt, who soon manœuvred herself and me along with the Master down a twisting garden path toward the studio. Even before we reached it I knew that just this and nothing else was what I wanted.

Now we are led to believe in Moral Tales (or rather

we were in my day when morals still existed) that a gratified wish usually brings with it disappointment, but the Tales are wrong on this point, as on some others.

If you do as you like and get what you want you will be perfectly happy, but—the catch lies here—you must be absolutely certain of what you *do* want, and this is where many people slip up. To long for a thing, to get it and then to tire of it only proves that you never really wanted it. The moral does not seem to come in at all.

I must apologise for keeping myself waiting at the studio door to let off this little address, but that door was my first big milestone : beyond lay the clear knowledge of what I wanted to do with my life, and with its coming something of childhood fell from me.

My first studio. I can remember the impression perfectly. It seemed very large and rather dark, a dim cathedral fit for the celebration of strange rites. It was very dirty : that was good, for I liked dirt and had never been allowed to indulge my taste to any satisfactory extent.

Then through the dusty gloom pictures began to appear. In one the Three Sirens, lightly linked together, paced rhythmically on yellow sands the while a fated vessel with languid oars and drooping sails drifted nearer and nearer over seas of misty opal.

In another Venus, wringing the water from her hair, stepped from blue sunlit ripples to a shore where little white temples nestled among blossoming almond-trees. I thought these pictures beautiful. In support of my infant judgment I may add that I still think them beautiful, but—they are the only two good pictures that Walter Crane ever painted.

He was young, he was ambitious ; these pictures were his first bid for recognition as a painter ; he had taken immense pains and had done his best.

The painting was thin and tentative but delicate, the colour clear and pitched in a very high key and the dull surface, producing the effect of fresco, was pleasant and decorative.

The Venus, the larger canvas of the two, was the supreme effort, and prayers had been put up to the Olympian Frederick Leighton that he should descend to Shepherd's Bush and pronounce upon it ; which he had duly done according to his good-natured custom. I did not then hear his criticism, but learned later on (and elsewhere) that he had delivered himself thus. " But my dear fellow, that is not Aphrodite—that's Alessandro ! " —Alessandro being a well-known male model who had in fact materially assisted in the genesis of the Anadyomene.

For alas, the fiat of domestic authority had gone forth against female models as being neither necessary nor desirable additions to a young artist's equipment, and thus Walter Crane's goddess showed a blending of the sexes which was mystically correct but anatomically surprising.

Still she was a fine, upstanding slip of a boy, and in the clear sunlit atmosphere and the charming colour scheme of ivory, blue and almond she passed for Venus pleasantly enough, and later on, finding grace in the eyes of G. F. Watts, the painter, she hung for many years on the stairway of Little Holland House.

The second picture in the course of years came into my hands, for my grandfather in his will leaving me a sum to be spent upon a token of remembrance, I proudly bought ' The Sirens ' and have got much pleasure from it.

It is strange that these two pictures should have been Crane's Ave and Vale as an oil painter : he never approached their accomplishment again.

His extraordinary facilities for graceful design beguiled him into over-production and hasty, scamped painting. He never tried to master his material when working in oil or to correct the rapidly growing mannerisms which finally wove a veil between him and the whole face of Nature. His pictures with their boneless, sexless figures are well forgotten, but his name lives in his illustrated

39

books for children, exquisite in design, charming in fancy ; a delicate, playful art of which he was at once the pioneer and the supreme master. These books, well within the reach of all, yet works of art of the highest value, probably did more to improve the public taste just at this time than anything else. Notwithstanding their beauty and merit their vogue was tremendous ; they found their way into every house and their influence soon made itself felt in the decoration and dress of the day. It was the hour of Walter Crane, an hour that lasted for many years.

Many sketches for these books and designs taken from them and further developed were scattered about the studio, which we explored for a palpitating forty minutes or so and from which I emerged dusty and happy beyond description and now quite ready for converse with the fat babies and the less rarefied atmosphere of guinea-pigs and white rabbits.

The babies were affable, the rabbits bland and restful, and the exciting afternoon ended pastorally in their society under the pink and white apple-trees. When we left I was invited to return, and many afternoons, equally bliss-ful, I spent at Shepherd's Bush.

Walter Crane and his wife were always most kind to me throughout my boyhood. He was, I think, at his best with children ; his sympathy with them, so plainly seen in his picture books, was a very real thing.

When some years later I was at a tutor's at Tunbridge Wells and the Cranes were living in a little house on the common, the kindness and hospitality they showed to a rather lonely little boy lived long in that boy's memory.

Mrs. Crane had made up her mind that I was under-fed—she was not altogether wrong—and at whatever hour I might appear she insisted upon regaling me with a mutton chop. I did not require much pressing, but was deeply grateful and glad to make any little return I could—the Venus tradition still surviving—by posing to Crane as Diana the Huntress, holding in leash a large lean hound which had bitten the butcher during the foregoing week and always seemed to me to be looking round for more of him.

A thing that caused great detriment to the later work of Walter Crane was the sudden overflow into it of his political opinions. A mild attack of dilettante Socialism, contracted early in life, developed all the usual symptoms in after years and taught his Art, if not to ' fold her hands and pray,' at least to wag her finger and preach, producing symbolical compositions in which god-like though rickety British workmen, appropriately dressed in tight *suède* knee-breeches and Liberty silk shirts, lounged about —presumably during the lunch hour—with female Allegories, winged indeed, but otherwise attired with a far stricter regard to economy. The workman may have been pleased with these designs but his wife must have regarded the promised Utopia with uneasiness.

The ritual of costume which plays so large a part in fancy Socialism has always puzzled me.

Knee-breeches proclaim Nature's Nobleman, yet they are never worn by that worthy, but rather by the slaves of tradition in attendance on an effete Court : dress clothes in the evening are the sign of infancy, yet they may be worn blamelessly in the morning by a white-souled waiter : a dinner-jacket is dissolute, while a velvet coat clothes the wearer with virtue as with a garment, yet a velvet coat costs more than a dinner-jacket and wears less well.

I never obtained a key to these mysteries from Crane, for in those later times when Social Reform occupied his thoughts so much we saw little of each other ; we had drifted apart I hardly knew how, but I suppose that his work appealed to me less and that my personal shortcomings struck him more than of old. Also he had come to live much nearer to me, which in London is a great bar to intimacy. We can always run round and see our neighbour—to-morrow will do just as well as to-day. And to-morrow so seldom comes.

I rejoice to think that on my last meeting with him

and his wife we walked together for some time in Kensington Gardens and I then returned home with them, staying long into the twilight and finding all the old relations quite unbroken.

Kindly, gentle Walter Crane ; I fear that life was rather a disappointment to him. He was hardly strong enough to bear the burden of his own great gifts which were, in a way, a misfit and made for a bigger man. His art did not advance, its movement rather was retrograde. He was shy and without self-confidence, making few friends and seeming to find communication with his fellow-men increasingly difficult. He looked weary : a friend of mine, meeting him for the first time towards the end of his life, exclaimed passionately to me, " No man has the *right* to be so dull " ; and with the end came dark clouds and the shadow of tragedy.

Yet at the outset the world had seemed full of possibilities for so gifted a youth. He somehow missed his way, but left a deeper mark upon the art of his day than many an artist of far more certain accomplishment.

A VERY different type of man was another painter, Thomas Armstrong, who was also a most kind friend to me in my boyhood.

He had graduated in Paris, along with Whistler, du Maurier, Poynter, and Lamont, and had all the knowledge and training that Walter Crane lacked. If Crane painted too much, Armstrong painted too little : he worked slowly and carefully, and in middle life was obliged almost entirely to give up painting ; his duties, as he understood them, as Head of the South Kensington Science and Art Department leaving him no time for other work.

Those pictures that he might have painted were a real loss. His art had much of the calm beauty of Albert Moore's decorations, much of the tone magic of Whistler, yet it was in no wise imitative, but keenly personal. I have seen no such restful schemes of blue and grey with a hint of veiled purple as in many of his works in which shadowy mountains brooded dreamily over grey olive woods in a silver twilight.

But against the loss of the pictures must be set the gain of a born teacher, a man who, while holding all the traditions of the schools, would so modify and adapt them in individual cases as to bring out any lurking originality in those who worked under him ; abating no whit of their drudgery, but encouraging and helping them along the particular road that they wished to follow.

Though I was never under him at South Kensington —I served my little time there before his appointment— yet I can speak from experience, for he took a most kind and helpful interest in my work from very early days. He was against desultory scribbling and picture-making as tending towards inaccuracy and the development of mannerisms, and would have me work from Nature only ; but one day, to my dismay, he picked up some effort of mine which I had by no means intended to fall into his hands.

43

"What did you copy this from?" he enquired.

"I didn't copy it, I did it 'out of my head,'" I confessed, meekly bowing before the expected storm. But no storm burst.

"H-m-m," said Armstrong. "Well, look here. Mind you always do a bit of drawing of this kind every day. Of course you'll never turn out anything decent until you have *learnt* to draw, but this is a trick that you lose if you don't practise it. Lots of good draughtsmen can't draw a thing out of their heads to save their lives."

This advice, in those days, was most revolutionary and dead against all the teaching of Paris. Few who knew the grave, quiet Thomas Armstrong of later life could picture him in these earlier days, for the shadow of a great sorrow fell upon him and neither he nor his beautiful young wife ever recovered from the loss of their fine little boy, Ambrose, who died at the age of eleven. They would hardly recognise the jolly, rollicking man whom I used to find in the old Charlotte Street studio where, originally smuggled in by my indomitable aunt, I gradually gained right of entry.

I loved the picnic teas in the dusk when he could paint no more, the kettle that would never boil or else boiled over, the cake that was ordered but never sent, or else sent somewhere else, and the genial, laughing host, quite unperturbed and apparently regarding it as somebody else's tea-party which perhaps was not going off very well but which was no concern of his.

Often would come in Randolph Caldecott, a charming and lovable man who had achieved a success almost equal to that of Walter Crane in the making of picture books, though the art of the two in no way clashed. Crane's designs were gravely beautiful decorations, Caldecott's brilliant sketches full of nature and high spirits, of the life and laughter under the sun.

Of Caldecott I saw only too little, though his delightful personality makes his figure stand out brightly, but, alas, it is shadowed by the memory of a day in 1886

44

which I spent with Armstrong at the little house in Holland Street, going through and arranging innumerable drawings and sketches after the news of the artist's early death had come from Florida.

About the time of the Charlotte Street teas—in 1877, I think—came a stirring among the studios as of a rushing mighty wind. Something was going to happen.

There were rumours of a wonderful new picture gallery wherein pictures would be treated as pictures and not as postage stamps ; that is to say, they would be hung more or less as if in a private house, thus giving them a chance to decorate instead of disfiguring the rooms.

Here would be seen the works of painters who, finding the crowded walls of the Academy do little justice to their pictures, had left off exhibiting for many years. Strange names were whispered—Rossetti—Madox Brown —Burne-Jones.

Burne-Jones : where had I heard——? Ah, I remembered.

One day in Walter Crane's studio I had noticed a canvas quite unlike any of the others. It spoke with authority while the rest bashfully murmured ; its note was deep and solemn. It was unfinished, a mere *ébauche* in monochrome. A procession of heavily draped figures bearing strange instruments of music passed slowly across from right to left against a line of desolate hills.

" Please, what's that ? " I piped.

" That ? " said Walter Crane. " O, that's an unfinished thing of Burne-Jones's."

There was a tone in his voice which told me that undue interest in the ' thing ' would not be advisable just then, and being a tactful child—which is to say a delicate and habitual liar—I masked my excitement and asked no more direct questions. I thrilled, but rejoice to remember that I kept my thrills to myself.

Gradually I learnt that Crane and Burne-Jones were painting together a decorative frieze for the house of Mr.

George Howard (afterwards Lord Carlisle) on Palace Green ; or rather, that Burne-Jones had designed it and, not having time to carry it through, had handed it over to Crane to finish. I also gathered that Crane had disagreed with Burne-Jones about something or other in connection with the work. This feat did not strike me as remarkable at the time, but I did not then know how difficult it was to disagree with Burne-Jones.

And now I was to see more pictures by him and many other wonderful things. The opening of the Grosvenor Gallery was to be an epoch-marking event, said rumour, and for once rumour spoke the truth.

This enterprise, undertaken not with the hope of gain, but with the certainty of loss, was a genuine offering at the shrine of Beauty, a gallant blow struck in the cause of Art.

It was conceived, financed and carried out entirely by Sir Coutts Lindsay with the help of Lady Lindsay and C. E. Hallé, the son of the great pianist.

Sir Coutts I never met, but when in course of time I began myself to perpetrate pictures I saw a good deal of Hallé and found in him a delightful companion and a kind friend.

Charles Hallé was certainly an artist ; he loved art truly and well and served her faithfully, yet he never found his proper mode of self-expression. What he ought to have done I do not know ; what he should not have done was apparent to all—he should never have attempted to paint. His pictures do not bear thinking of, so I will not think of them, but only of the witty, interesting man who I feel sure could have done something or other most beautifully if only he had happened to find out what it was. His appearance was romantic, contrasting oddly with his impish sense of humour, and his most fascinating accomplishment to me was the narrating of screamingly comic and slightly Rabelaisian stories with a look of brooding melancholy in his great dark eyes that would have done credit to Manfred or the Corsair.

Between them, he and Sir Coutts Lindsay made the opening of the Grosvenor a memorable triumph.

The general effect of the great rooms was most beautiful and quite unlike the ordinary picture gallery. It suggested the interior of some old Venetian palace, and the pictures, hung well apart from each other against dim rich brocades and amongst fine pieces of antique furniture, showed to unusual advantage. I can well remember the wonder and delight of my first visit. One wall was iridescent with the plumage of Burne-Jones's angels, one mysteriously blue with Whistler's nocturnes, one deeply glowing with the great figures of Watts, one softly radiant with the faint, flower-tinted harmonies of Albert Moore. Here too was the sombre work of Legros, the jewelled fantasies of Gustave Moreau, and (or was it in the following year?) the wonderful ' Hay Harvest ' of Bastien Lepage and his portrait of Sarah Bernhardt.

The impression left upon me—and upon most other people—was unforgettable. To this day old fogies speak of the first two or three exhibitions at the Grosvenor Gallery with undiminished enthusiasm : there has been no such delightful surprise in the world of pictures since.

The only people who did not appear to be pleased were the critics ; they howled, but this I suppose they consider their unpleasant duty.

If a painter is asked his opinion of an exhibition he will mention the pictures that pleased him ; the critic, on the other hand, will only have noticed the pictures that did not please him, and of these he will speak at length. The weariness of the lives spent by these gentlemen in the contemplation of pictures which they do not like forms a pathetic apology for their existence.

Much must be forgiven them, for they have loved little. Here was an opportunity for them ; here at last were the pictures of Burne-Jones and Whistler put forth for all to see.

In the centre of the south wall hung the ' Seven Days of Creation,' flanked by the Mirror of Venus and Vivien and Merlin. All were impressive, but the Beguiling of Merlin wrought the most potent spell.

It was mercilessly ridiculed. The lovely and intricate patternings of the blossoming may-trees, the sinuous poise of the malign sorceress passed unnoticed, while the critics proclaimed that the head of Vivien was too small for her body.

The head obviously *was* too small, but did these clever folk really think that the painter did not know it?

The Vivien of his picture is a Lamia, a Melusine, and as she puts forth her powers she is all serpent and in act to strike. The dull greenish garment, tightly clinging like a wrinkled skin, the curve of the lithe body, the narrow eyes *and* the small flat head all reveal the triumphant snake swaying slowly before the eyes of its helpless and mesmerised victim. It is a great picture, and perhaps the most individual that the artist ever painted. When I saw it again, twenty years after, it impressed me in precisely the same way, though I was better able to appreciate the loving labour that had gone to its making.

The Whistler nocturnes did not as yet say much to me beyond—blue—blue—the intense but tender blue of twilight seen through the windows of a lamp-lit room.

I was still a little boy, and a Burne-Jones is far easier to appreciate than a Whistler.

With Burne-Jones's pictures one can get a ' book of the words.' The inspiration is derived from a book, the treatment has been thought out *in words* and contains ideas from other books. The vision is that of a man to whom inspiration has come not from without, but from within, not from observing Nature with the eye of a painter, but from gazing at a dream world with the eyes of the spirit.

And for this the work is no less beautiful, but it is easier to understand in that, not being direct observation, it must be, to a certain degree, reminiscent, nor an entirely original point of view.

In Whistler's pictures of the river at dusk the inspiration comes direct from Nature, the treatment is the result of a mood—the effect of the actual scene and hour upon the artist's mind, the vision is that of one who has seen something that man has looked at for centuries and never seen before.

Burne-Jones's art is the exquisite accompaniment to another's voice ; Whistler's is the song itself.

Thrilled by Burne-Jones, bewildered by Whistler, I arrived at the Albert Moores and, so to speak, sat down to rest among them.

How lovely they were, what clear colour, what perfection of workmanship ! The paint was solid, yet light and crumbly as pastel, there seemed to be a delicate bloom on the surface as though they were viewed through a veil of gossamer or pearly mist. They were like flowers ; one expected them to smell sweet.

" Good heavens, what must it be to paint like that ? " I thought. " And, for all its delicacy, the work is so sure, so absolutely certain. The man who made these pictures must know all there is to know about painting ! Would he——" I wondered——" that is, could I——? "

And at about this point I was taken home and sent to school.

I had been in Wonderland, but the Gate of Ivory slammed to in my face and the high-class, wrought-iron entry of Dr. Hawtrey's excellent preparatory school for young gentlemen yawned in its stead. It seemed hard. I didn't want to be a young gentleman ; I wanted to be a painter. Why couldn't I be prepared by Albert Moore instead of by Dr. Hawtrey ? But of course I asked no such questions, accepting my fate with the hopeless apathy of childhood, and was soon plodding down the colourless ways of school life, yet trailing a little private cloud of glory picked up at the Grosvenor Gallery. The usual attempt had been made to raise my spirits by the assurance that my schooldays would prove the happiest of my existence.

I have a great regard for truth, so much so that I

only produce it upon special occasions, and I do trust that I shall never catch myself passing on to any child this blatant falsehood which would put Ananias to the blush.

How could the schooldays of any reasonable being be the happiest of his life ? The only conceivable case would be that of a very wealthy man with nothing to do and with no wish to do anything. At school he would have been provided with employment, would have been faintly interested and mildly amused, and might in after years of dreary inertia look back upon the period with longing. For my part, had I believed the statement, suicide would have been my only sensible course, but luckily its fallacy was obvious.

I had been far happier before I went to school—this alone threw it out of court—and I fully intended to be far happier when I left. I had never been bored before I went to school and I have never been bored since I left. It remains with me as the only time in my life when I was helplessly, hopelessly bored.

One blessed memory I still hold, one fragrant breath from that waste of savourless days still perfumes for me the dawn of every Thursday.

In the dull grey void hung tremulous like a star Thursday morning—sausage morning.

In the dreary school hours or still drearier hours of play a vague joy would fill me and I would ask why and whence this balm that soothed, this force that sustained, and an inner voice would reply, " The day after to-morrow will be Thursday."

Why this Thursday sausage so transported me I cannot tell. Never before or since has a sausage woven about me precisely the same spell. I was not a greedy child and we were always well fed, yet that Thursday sausage seemed to fill a blank in my existence, it whispered of hope, of the world without the walls, of the life that had ceased when I entered school and would begin again when I left.

With the coming of the great dishes a peace would fall upon the throng, boys' shrill voices were stilled, and the sausages could be distinctly heard fizzling as they passed up the hall. Even to the pale faces of the Masters would come a smile almost human as they watched their flock choking and gasping through a first sausage with hopeful eyes upon a second. Our places at table were arranged according to our precedence in class, and I noticed that those at the head of the table got a second helping more often than those lower down. I took three prizes during my first term in consequence.

Beyond these sausages I remember little of interest in those early schooldays.

The only friend I made who overflowed into my real life was Ambrose Poynter, the son of E. J. Poynter, afterwards President of the Royal Academy, and in the holidays I was duly presented to his father and to his lovely, witty mother, who fascinated me as she did everybody.

Poynter himself I always found difficult of access, though he was kind to me in his remote way ; putting up occasionally with us boys in his studio and suffering us in his house, though I think not gladly. Many of his old friends have assured me that his heart was in the right place, but I feel certain that the same could not be said for his liver, and chronic dyspepsia is not very improving to the temper.

Models, I know, used to find him a little trying, though when they became accustomed to his ways they usually grew loud in his praises and contended for the honour of sitting to him. Yet at first these ways must have been discouraging.

A young and timid aspirant who had obtained an introduction to him once rang his studio bell on one of his bad days. The door opened by unseen agency (worked by a latch from the room above) and a rather unpromising voice roared, " Well ? "

" Please," faltered the girl, " Miss (let us say) Bosanquet Jones sent me to you. She thought I might suit.

She——" Her words died away : it was eerie standing in the dark passage talking to nobody. An awful silence fell, then came again the voice from above, speaking very clearly and with passionate emphasis, " It makes me *sick* to think that Miss Bosanquet Jones is still alive." And the invisible agency slammed the door with an echoing bang.

I should mention that the lion-hearted girl, returning again to the charge in a more auspicious hour, met with a kindly reception and sat to the artist many times to her great pride and satisfaction.

OF THE LADY OF BELMONT AND ALBERT MOORE

I HAD reached the ripe age of thirteen and had for years been an earnest student of fairy-tales, ballads and romances. In the course of my studies I was continually coming across dazzlingly beautiful ladies, princesses lovely as the day, radiant fairies, exquisite though distressed heroines. There was never any doubt as to the beauty of these ladies ; it took you flat aback at first sight and you knew at once that you were in the presence of a Fairy or a Princess or at least of an ill-used stepdaughter—which came to the same thing in the end. And there seemed to be any amount of these amazing creatures about ; in fact nothing very interesting ever happened to any lady who was not beautiful as the day.

I looked round me in the solid, comfortable, mid-Victorian world. There were pretty girls and girls who were not pretty ; there really seemed very little difference between them. They roused no particular interest, and as to taking one flat aback—well, it was not in their line. I concluded, after some research, that the race of Fairy Princesses was extinct, and I didn't much mind. I had never been able to fit one of these ladies very comfortably into my schemes for the future, and the removal of her figure from my Air Castle—where she had naturally occupied a very handsome suite of apartments—left me a nice lot of room.

But one day in 1879 I was taken by my mother to see 'The Merchant of Venice' at the Lyceum Theatre. I was delighted to find Venice all that I had pictured it, and soon old friends began to take shape : Antonio, Bassanio—rather stouter than I had fancied—and above all, the terrible, fateful Shylock with his pale face and glittering eyes. Then came Belmont and Nerissa and— O, my goodness ! Flat aback was I taken in quite the correct and conventional style.

There she was at last, from head to foot all gold—the Impossible She—the Fairy Lady, beautiful as the day ! As I had imagined, there was no mistake about it. The Princess suite in my Air Castle was opened at once and thoroughly aired—it might be wanted at any minute. In fact, before I could turn round, there was the Lady installed.

' Portia, Miss Ellen Terry,' read the programme.

Well, she solved many difficulties.

If Miss Ellen Terry were possible anything might be possible, including dragons and roc's eggs. The Gates of Elf Land had been closing ; Miss Ellen Terry flung them wide again : the Lady Beauty had revealed herself just as I was about to say, " I don't believe there's no sich a person."

And what was she like ? How is it possible to describe to a generation that knows her not the beauty of Ellen Terry ? Her portraits will remain showing an appealing, arresting personality, a haunting glance, a grace of softly falling raiment, but no portrait can reflect a shadow of her beauty.

Pale eyes, rather small and narrow, a broad nose slightly tilted at the tip, a wide mouth, a firm, large chin, pale hair, not decidedly golden, yet not brown—by no means a dazzling inventory of charms, yet out of these was evolved Ellen Terry, the most beautiful woman of her time.

I knew that her radiance was not the mere glamour of the stage, for I was, at that age, a hardened theatregoer. I was familiar with the machine-made beautiful fairies and Princesses of Pantomime and had accepted them placidly, as a child accepts bad illustrations to an interesting book. But here was no painted show from the land of Make Believe—here was the real thing.

Her charm held everyone, but I think pre-eminently those who loved pictures. She was *par excellence* the Painter's Actress and appealed to the eye before the ear ; her gesture and pose were eloquence itself.

ELLEN TERRY

From a portrait by THE AUTHOR, 1891

She was a child of the studio, having always been much with artists, and during her brief married life she must have sat almost continuously to her husband, G. F. Watts, who afterwards destroyed many of his studies made from her, but the few that escaped are among his very best works. The wraith-like Ophelia, the eager, wistful youth in 'Watchman, what of the night?' the running girl in blue with clasped hands, which he presented to her after time had swept away all bitterness between them, and best of all, the picture called 'Choosing' in which she stands against dark camellia leaves, a girl of sixteen in a dress of golden brown with beribboned sleeves—her wedding dress, designed by Holman Hunt —are records of a period which left a great mark upon her art.

She had learnt to create Beauty, not the stage beauty of whitewash and lip salve, but the painter's beauty of line, harmony and rhythm.

Meanwhile I was sitting absorbed in 'The Merchant of Venice.' What stands out most clearly in that wonderful evening? In spite of the gracious charm of the Fairy Lady, what rises first and last in my mind is the face of Henry Irving.

The memory of the Lady's Portia (oddly enough, I never saw it again) is like a dream of beautiful pictures in a scheme of gold melting one into another ; the golden gown, the golden hair, the golden words all form a golden vision of romance and loveliness ; but of Irving's Shylock I seem to remember every movement, every tone.

Later on, when I came to compare it with his other parts (Irving could never be compared with anyone but himself), it was not among my favourites. His readings of characters were nearly always most sympathetic to me, but I feel that, for once, he was wrong about Shylock.

His dignified, heroic, intensely aristocratic Martyr was magnificent and unforgettable, but it upset the balance of the play and it ruined Portia's Trial Scene.

How small and mean sounded her quibbling tricky

speeches when addressed to a being who united the soul
of Savonarola and the bearing of Charles the First, with
just a touch of Lord Beaconsfield that made for mystery.

After her best effect we momentarily expected the
doge to rise exclaiming, " My dear sir, pray accept the
apology of the Court for any annoyance that this young
person has caused you. By all means take as much of
Antonio as you think proper, and if we may throw in
a prime cut off Bassanio and the whole of Gratiano we
shall regard your acceptance of the same as a favour."

Still, right or wrong, his Shylock was a living thing,
a haunting, memorable figure, and I left the theatre
with the profoundest sympathy for the noble, ill used
Jew and with the name Ellen Terry graven indelibly on
my heart.

Both these sublime beings were as yet unknown to
me personally and seemed denizens of a region fascinating but remote, all inaccessible to the mere mortal :
how could I dream that the golden Portia was in the
future to be one of my dearest and closest friends ?

Henceforth the Lyceum became for me a temple, and
I worshipped there whenever I got the chance.

My schooldays still dragged their weary length along,
but O, the holidays ! So much to do and see, and so
little time to do it. Far from sleeping between term and
term like ' lawyers in the vacation,' the holidays were
my periods of activity. I worked at free-hand drawing
by Armstrong's advice and scraped through the little
examination into the South Kensington schools, where I
managed to put in some time drawing from the antique.
Poynter then reigned there—the rule of Armstrong had
not yet begun.

The Grosvenor Gallery was still the cave of Aladdin,
hung with jewels. Burne-Jones had made good each
year with the splendid ' Laus Veneris ' in '78 and the
palely beautiful ' Annunciation ' in '79 ; Whistler had
shown the masterpiece ' Miss Alexander,' round which
scoffers were already remaining to pray, and groups and

single figures exquisite in colour and execution still flowed from the brush of Albert Moore.

The technical perfection of his pictures fascinated me ; the rather uninteresting Græco-West Kensington young woman who invariably appeared in them did not appeal very strongly ; they were a little monotonous in their calculated loveliness, but—if one could only paint like that !

I forget how an introduction was effected, but one day my mother took some drawings of mine to him and asked if he would take me as a pupil. Albert Moore looked vaguely at the drawings, vaguely at my mother, then, quickly taking a fancy to her, dropped into intimacy at once with the remark, " Well, I could draw a great deal better than that at his age." And goodness knows he could. I have seen a little drawing by him of his father done at the age of about eleven or twelve which could not be described as wonderful work for a child because it was not a child's work. It was the work of a master, fully developed and equipped.

Before she left him my mother extracted a rather unwilling promise from the kindly painter to take me ' on approval ' as a studio pupil, and before long, by the blessing of Providence and the timely intervention of chicken-pox and other small complaints, there came a lull in my schooling and I had a year ' off,' which I spent with Albert Moore.

His was a strange and interesting figure in the world of art. Few people knew him well, for he seldom took the trouble to make friends, yet he was the most gentle and affectionate of men. His splendid Christ-like head with its broad brows and great visionary brown eyes was set upon an odd awkward little body that seemed to have no connection with it.

His favourite attitude of repose was squatting on his heels like a Japanese, and when settling himself for a talk, would suddenly subside thus upon the floor, to the amazement of casual beholders.

His usual indoor costume was a very long and very

large ulster, far too big for him and once, in remote ages, the property of an elder and taller brother. With this he wore a large broad-brimmed straw hat without a crown.

He lived then in a curious building at the corner of Holland Lane, its accommodation consisting of two huge studios, a sitting-room with nothing to sit upon in it, a bedroom and, I suppose, a kitchen. His constant companion was Fritz, a dachshund of depressed appearance reported by models to live entirely upon sardines and oranges. Fritz's sole accomplishment was ' doing George Eliot,' in which impersonation he sat up with folded paws and looked down his long nose while his ears flapped forward like cap lappets.

He *was* very like portraits of the distinguished authoress, but he did not realise it, and the performance bored him. The great embitterment of his life was cats. Cats pervaded the whole house ; vaguely, unofficially, holding no recognised position, they swarmed in the studios and passages, were born abruptly in coal-scuttles, expired unpleasantly behind canvases, making the place no home for an honest dog and taking, as it were, the very sardines out of his mouth.

Albert Moore regarded them mournfully but placidly as inevitable. There *were* the cats. There also were the spiders and their cobwebs, the dust, the leaks in the pipes, and other like phenomena.

They were perhaps not pleasant, but they were endurable, and certainly could not be got rid of without admitting tiresome people to the house who would hammer and move things about—which would be unendurable.

I sided with Fritz about the cats, which infested the studio in which I worked, and I made one determined effort to suppress them. I turned out all I could find, rummaging out coy or morose specimens from behind dusty pictures until I felt sure that the room was clear ; then I banged the door and started work again in a catless void with a charming sense of quiet and privacy. I would be careful to keep the door shut in future ; I would not open the low window on to the leads where perhaps—— Bump ! A heavy object fell from the ceiling, smearing a long streak down my canvas and landing at my feet. " Pr-r-r-ow," said the object, regarding me malevolently out of evil yellow eyes. It was a new cat —fallen through the skylight.

I gave up. If the Heavens themselves were against me and rained cats like manna from above, I might save myself further trouble. Henceforth I was cat-ridden like Fritz. Yet Albert Moore could never have liked cats : his was emphatically the dog nature, loyal and affectionate. He had the eyes of a dog ; beautiful, tender eyes which could light up with a brilliant smile that never reached the lips.

Nothing in the way of papering, painting or white-washing was ever done in the house, and even of ordinary dusting I saw no sign, nor was anything ever mended.

Many years afterwards, when I was fully fledged and had a studio of my own, I remember calling upon Albert Moore with Whistler, who had a very real admiration for his work and a great respect and liking for the man him-self.

We found him in his huge, desolate workroom solemnly painting, surrounded by a circle of spoutless, handle-less jugs each holding a large cornucopia of brown paper.

Whistler was instantly fascinated by the jugs and could think of nothing else, but he remembered Moore's dislike of being questioned. He edged nearer to me.

" What are the jugs for ? " he asked in a whisper.

" I don't know."

" Ask him."

" *You* ask him : you've known him longer."

" You're his pupil. You *might* ask him."

I summoned my courage. " What are the jugs for ? " I enquired.

" The drips," said Albert Moore laconically.

" The drips ? " whispered Whistler. " *What* drips ? *Ask* him."

Luckily at this moment a fat water-drop oozed from the ceiling and fell with a plop into one of the receivers.

The roof leaked. It had probably leaked for months, perhaps years, but Albert Moore sat dreaming among his jugs and never thought of repairs.

Whistler was always at his best and gentlest with Albert Moore ; he understood the rather slow working of his brain and knew that his thoughts were worth waiting for. Moore on his side adored Whistler, whose quick wit stimulated him. He was a sad man, and loved to laugh.

Whistler once told me that he had tried hard to bring about a friendship between him and Rossetti, knowing how Moore would have delighted in the poet's unexpected turns of humour ; but Rossetti was impatient and would not respond. " He's a dull dog," he pronounced. " A dull dog."

" He thinks slowly, but he's not in the least dull," persisted Whistler—but it was no good.

However, Rossetti had already won Albert Moore's heart entirely on the occasion of their first meeting.

As they sat down to dinner the poet was served with soup. " I say, what a stunning plate ! " cried Rossetti —and instantly turned it upside-down to look at the mark. The ensuing flood seemed to come upon him as a complete surprise, and Albert Moore laughed whenever he remembered the incident for the rest of his life.

That life was in many ways a very lonely one. He lived apart, absorbed in his work, knowing and caring little about the outside world, whose ways sometimes puzzled him very much. At such moments he would hastily seek advice, and his choice of mentors was distinctly original. When in difficulties with a picture he gradually formed a habit of consulting my mother, whose suggestions he often adopted, to her unbounded surprise, but for an opinion on any social or economical point he always went to the cab rank near the gates of Holland House and the men gave him much good counsel, although sometimes the language in which it was couched provided him with an additional puzzle.

One morning I found him at his door, fingering a collection of dirty slips of paper.

" The charwoman has gone," he sadly announced.

I thought that her absence would make little if any difference and ventured to say so.

" Yes, but she's sent me these," said Moore, gloomily exhibiting the bits of paper. " Look, they're all numbered. The cabmen say they're pawn-tickets. They say I had better see whether I have lost anything."

We saw—and he *had* lost several things, including his blankets.

" What's to be done next ? " I enquired.

" I suppose," said Moore slowly, " that I ought to go and *see* her—oughtn't I ? "

I privately thought that the less he saw of her the better, but I did not feel competent to advise.

" Ask the cabmen," I suggested ; and he went like a lamb.

" The cabmen think *not*," he said on his return. " They say that before I get there she will have slung her hook. That means—they think that she will have changed her address. But one of them will come with me to the pawnshop."

Certainly Albert Moore could always find good friends when he wanted them.

He was an untiring worker ; seldom have I known him to take a holiday or even a ' day off.'

He built up his compositions very slowly and laboriously, making elaborate charcoal cartoons of the whole group, then of each single figure, first nude, then draped. Then came chalk studies of the draperies, colour studies of the draperies, rough photographs of the draperies, so that before the great work was actually begun he had already produced many pictures. The colour studies of draped figures, done straight off while the model stood and never retouched, were his most perfect works. The touch was so light, the paint so fresh and exquisite in texture, the drawing and colour so true and sensitive, that they were miracles of artistry.

After they had served their purpose as studies he would often complete them by adding heads and backgrounds, and thus it came about that many of his pictures were so much alike : two or three only slightly varying studies for the same figure, each in turn developing into a finished painting.

When the studies had all been made, the first step towards the actual picture was the putting in of the whole composition in grey monochrome. Over this, when it was dry, came a thin, fluid painting very delicate in colour through which the grey design clearly showed. Next came heavy impasto, strong and rather hot in colour, over which, when dry, was passed a veil of semi-opaque grey, and on this was wrought the third and final painting, thin and delicate like the first.

In later years he modified this process slightly, merging the first and second paintings into one richly toned impasto painting which, while still wet, he stabbed into the canvas with a great brush until the grey drawing beneath became again visible through it.

He would always make his pupils work exactly in his method while they were under him.

" You will not want to paint as I do when you are doing work of your own," he would say. " You cannot know as yet *how* you want to paint, but what I am teaching you will help you to find out."

ALL too soon my period of work with Albert Moore came to an end and I returned to the enforced idleness of school. This time I went to Eton, and I shall of course forfeit the respect of all properly constituted people if I confess that I liked it very little better than my preparatory school.

I suppose the fact was that I could never be happy where I could never be alone. I had been much by myself in my childhood and a certain amount of privacy had become a necessity to me : at school I used to keep awake at night in order to indulge in the luxury of solitude.

I found the cool cloisters and dark, oak-beamed corridors of College most attractive, and used to fag myself there with bogus notes from no one to nobody so as to sit for awhile in the grey quiet atmosphere.

I loved the time spent in the dim Chapel, reading a little copy of the *Vicar of Wakefield* which fitted exactly into a hymn-book cover, or studying the card on which the Anthems for the day, together with the names of their composers, were set forth with a lack of punctuation which led thoughts into strange channels.

" Sing unto the Lord a new song George Macfarren," suggested that George had been detected in an attempt to palm off old ones upon a benignant but unmusical Providence ; while the abrupt request, " Wash me thoroughly Joseph Barnby," was hardly delicate.

I had an *écorché* figure and one or two other casts in my room and tried to do some work from them, but the world was too much with me, and I found it a world singularly incapable of amusing itself which seemed to throw it upon my society. That I might secure some time to myself I therefore deliberately thought out ' amusements for the masses ' and scored one or two marked successes. A pastime entitled ' Gyration ' first made my name as an entertainer. Unfortunately it could only be enjoyed in my room which contained the necessary plant, but as it emptied many other rooms I was able to find refuge.

The Gyrator suspended himself by a rope of knotted comforters to a hook in the ceiling (*my* ceiling) and, resting lightly, Mercury-wise, on one toe upon a wooden knob in the floor, he was wound up with a long rope and spun like a top; the spinners running away with the rope down the passage. A really successful spin made the human top sick and giddy for the rest of the day, and the recreation had an immense vogue. It made much noise, and the Powers that Were who objected to us small fry encroaching on their own noise-making prerogatives were constantly putting a stop to it—then falling victims to its fascinations.

The following scene would usually take place :

Enter to me a Power in wrath.

He : Robertson, what's that confounded noise in the passage ?

I : I think it must have been some fellow gyrating.

He : Doing *what* ?

(*Here followed explanations.*)

He : Well—it's to stop.

I : Yes.

He : You understand ? It's not to go on.

I : No.

He : Just remember that. Er—how d'you do it ?

I : You stand on one toe on that little knob.

He : So ?

I : No—so. Then you catch hold of those comforters and you are wound up with this rope.

He : Like this ?

I : No, like this. Right up under your arms.

He : I see. And then——

I : Then you're spun.

He : Could *you* spin me ?

I : No. You're too heavy. It would want two or three.

He : Go and get 'em.

I : But I thought you said——

He : Go and GET 'em.

Gyration was succeeded by the Comb and Bath Band (led by an excellent fiddle and reinforced by a flute) which played on stated evenings on the upper landing to an audience of appropriately costumed promenaders. This relaxation was hardly more popular than the last with the Powers, but I could name several Olympians who came to kick and remained to promenade.

Aviation by mice in parachutes was also all the rage during a summer term. It was really helpful to us who were overrun by mice and constantly confronted with heart-breaking washhand-basin executions, and pleasant for the mice, who always landed safely in neighbours' gardens and ran rejoicing away.

But on one unfortunate and breezy day the tutor next door gave a tea-party, and when the revelry was at its height, a mouse seated in a parachute drifted in through the open window and disembarked among the ladies. It depressed me to find that this really charming incident was regarded next door as a deliberate insult. As if one could not have thought of a better insult than a mouse in a parachute.

One kindred spirit I met at Eton in the person of Hedworth Williamson (now Sir Hedworth), and we saw much of each other during his too-brief sojourn there, but he had wonderful luck, departing in a cloud of glory to the sanatorium with something scarlet and catching in the middle of his first term, and leaving altogether at the end of his second with well-developed ophthalmia. We usually met early in the week at the top of our class, whither we had always been wafted for answering some question that had nothing whatever to do with the lesson. From this eminence we were invariably cast down for talking, and spent the rest of the week comfortably at the bottom together.

He was a literary gent, and his compositions and my illustrations to the same got us through the monotonous school hours quite briskly. He had a genuine imaginative gift which should have carried him far had he cared to cultivate it : I well remember a dream of his which, as says Scheherazade, I will forthwith proceed to relate, for it still seems to me an unusual dream for a schoolboy.

In his dream he was at a country fair, and as he walked among the booths he noticed a black-browed gipsy standing apart who held in his hands a large cage. Someone whispered, "That is the man who has caught the Fairies"; and the gipsy looked up, holding out the cage towards the dreamer.

Within couched several tiny figures with drawn, white faces and thin lips tightly closed. Miserable atomies they looked, huddled sullenly together like moulting sparrows, while with a stick the man stirred up his withered but immortal prisoners as he chanted :

> "Dance, my Moppets, dance, my Minions.
> Time hath no feather in his pinions
>   To wing an arrow with
>   Against your shadowy kith.
> Dance in your death-debarred dominions."

Here the dreamer woke, but the fragment of weird verse stayed with him and has always remained in my mind.

Of my tutor I was very fond. He hated boys, and as I, up to a certain point, hated boys too I was able to regard him with feelings of commiseration which helped me to overlook many of his little faults.

He was a nervous man, full of sensitive refinement, and used to grow absolutely livid with rage at the crudities and imbecilities of his classes. Often he would come into the pupil room, take one look at us assembled urchins, mutter to himself, " Pigs ! Beasts ! ! " and retreat hastily, slamming the door, unable to trust his knuckles near our heads.

Sometimes his sorrow would burst from him when I had brought him some work bad beyond the ordinary. Its quality was no business of mine, as work in our house was got through on the co-operative system and the gentleman who usually did my Latin verses was unfortunately in the Modern Division and his classics were not his strong point : on the other hand, his mathematics were so good that I was put to the trouble of going over his calculations and inserting mistakes so as to give a little local colour.

" What is the use of my trying to stuff things into your odious skulls ? " my tutor would wail, gazing at me with mingled despair and disgust. " *I* gain nothing by it. If ever I begin to notice in any one of you the slightest inclination to rise above the level of the beasts that perish, that boy is instantly removed—off he goes to College—and I am left with a set of absolutely beastly new ones instead. *Yours* is a type that I especially dislike," he would go on pleasantly. " You do nothing in particular, but you are one of the greatest nuisances in the house ; you'll do neither me nor yourself any credit, and yet I suppose you are not altogether a fool."

This was a point upon which I have never been able to make up my own mind, so I could not help him.

I looked forward to these little chats with my tutor : he was very human.

Meanwhile in London, where the magic hours of the holidays were spent, Art was upon the town.

The very serious and genuine Movement that had produced the group of painters whose works the Grosvenor Gallery had revealed had rushed onwards in a flood over the arid sands of Philistia, sweeping all before it, and the startled natives, taken off their feet and struggling in deep waters, did strange things. Determined at all hazards to be ' artistic,' women arrayed themselves in amazing garments embroidered with sunflowers ; their dishevelled hair streamed down their backs, by a projection of their extraordinary imitative gift their faces grew thin and cadaverous.

Oscar Wilde, who was largely responsible for the absurdities of these worthy folks, had written a sonnet to Ellen Terry in which he described her in a pathetic part as

" Like some wan lily overdrenched with rain."

All the women at once saw themselves as wan lilies and—well, it is not a style becoming to everybody.

The men, after abortive efforts to look like Greek gods, tried mediæval saints instead and cultivated pale, ascetic faces with dreary eyes and unkempt locks ; the more daring soaring to Liberty silk ties and brown velvet coats.

It was very deplorable ; for the Æsthetes by their antics killed the thing they proposed to love as dead as a door-nail, and the great Art Revival of the 'seventies from which so much had been hoped passed away in the 'eighties amidst peals of mocking laughter.

Still I must admit that the Æsthetic Burlesque was very good fun while it lasted, and I for one thoroughly enjoyed it ; it was like living in a Harlequinade.

Suddenly, as if in reproof of the artificial and unhealthy type then masquerading as beauty, there glided across the social firmament a vision of that divine loveliness dreamed of by painters and sculptors since Art began.

One day I was crossing the road at Hyde Park Corner and idly noted a figure making its way past Apsley House towards the Park.

At the first glance it seemed a very young and slender girl, dowdily dressed in black and wearing a small, close-fitting black bonnet : she might have been a milliner's assistant waiting upon a customer for all her gown said to the contrary, or a poorly paid governess hurrying to her pupils. As I drew near the pavement the girl looked up—and I all but sat flat down in the road.

For the first and only time in my life I beheld perfect beauty.

The face was that of the lost Venus of Praxiteles, and of all the copies handed down to us must have been incomparably the best, yet Nature had not been satisfied and had thrown in two or three subtle improvements.

The small head was not reared straight on the white column of the throat as a capital crowns a pillar, but drooped slightly forward like a violet or a snowdrop, the perfect nose was made less perfect and a thousand times more beautiful by a slight tilt at the tip. The wonderful face was pale with the glow of absolute health behind the pallor, the eyes grey beneath dark lashes, the hair brown with glints of gold in it, the figure in its poise and motion conveyed an impression of something wild, eternally young, nymph-like——

Dear me. Were there not uncomfortable stories of mortals who had looked upon nymphs and——

Here the Barnes bus drifted gently into me.

" Where are yer gittin' to ? " enquired the driver, but when I looked about me the Venus of Cnidus had vanished. Clearly she had been an hallucination, she had no real existence. No human woman *could* be like that, and if she appeared to me again I should certainly consult the family doctor about her.

In the spring of the next year I was wandering in the Row one Sunday morning when I became aware of a commotion among the solemn promenaders ; a crowd collected, women scrambled on to chairs to get a better view, from all directions people converged towards some hidden centre of interest. As the hustle surged past me I suppose I must have stood open-mouthed and obviously interrogative, for a total stranger gripped my arm in passing and panted : " Mrs. Langtry—run ! "

I had heard of Mrs. Langtry and I ran. Being very slender and compressible, I wriggled easily through the struggling throng and peeped into the clear space of enchanted ground at its midst.

There, conversing with a tall and distinguished man (I feel sure that he was tall and distinguished, though naturally I did not look at him), stood a young lady in pale cream colour. Her back was towards me, but, as she talked, her head in its little close bonnet drooped slightly forward like a violet or a snowdrop—— Good heavens ! No wonder that I had all but sat down under the Barnes bus ! My dowdy divinity of Hyde Park Corner, my pathetic nursery governess, had been the world-famous Jersey Lily, the Venus Annodomini, the modern Helen.

Never since the days of the Gunnings had such universal worship been paid to beauty. The Langtry bonnet, the Langtry shoe, even the Langtry dress-improver, were widely stocked and as widely bought ; photographs of Mrs. Langtry papered London. Yet the Jersey Lily of the 'eighties remained very simple in her dress and manner, her grey eyes looked gravely out at a city in undignified prostration at her feet ; she made no parade of her beauty ; indeed, none was required.

" The Lily is so tiresome," once sighed Oscar Wilde to me. " She *won't* do what I tell her."

" How wrong ? " said I with mental reservations.

" Yes," murmured Wilde, " I assure her that she owes it to herself and to us to drive daily through the Park dressed entirely in black in a black victoria drawn by black horses and with ' Venus Annodomini ' emblazoned on her black bonnet in dull sapphires. But she won't."

I agreed that it was a pity : I should have liked to see the pageant and I knew how the Lily looked in black.

That year portraits of the marvel filled the galleries ; by Poynter a bad one, fussy and unlike, by Millais a so-so one, the commonplace likeness of a dull photograph, by Watts a fine one, giving much of the radiant youth and vitality of the sitter, and innumerable weak but lovely studies and drawings by Frank Miles. But this was a beauty beyond reach of the brush : Praxiteles, who had first conceived it, should have returned to earth to carve it afresh. It was the only human beauty that ever wrought the effect often produced upon me by a magic line of poetry, a lovely sky or a haunting piece of music, that of moving me to tears by its perfection. Curiously enough, a picture has never affected me thus but sculpture many

70

times. I well remember one winter afternoon at the British Museum standing in the Egyptian Gallery when the lights had just been kindled and looking through an arch into an unlitten hall where the Demeter and Persephone of Phidias gleamed mysteriously through a blue twilight.

I gazed and gazed until I could see no more, and putting up my hand in alarm at the sudden loss of sight, I was amazed to find tears pouring down my cheeks.

It was strange to me that the beauty of Mrs. Langtry attracted the public so much : those who thronged to stare at her could have obtained precisely the same thrill from the Metope of the Parthenon, yet the Elgin Room at the British Museum was never inconveniently crowded.

The admiration, I suppose, must have been merely a passing fashion, for when later on the Beauty went upon the stage where all who would might see her, she never commanded a large following. Certainly she was not a good actress, yet neither was she a bad one, and that is saying much.

Her voice and speech were beautiful, and when she had beautiful words to say she said them simply, not chopping them up with ' business ' or strangling them with ' suppressed emotion.' Her Rosalind is one of my pleasant memories. She gave no ' performance,' no new readings ; she was not coquettish or hoydenish, she did *not* sing the ' Cuckoo ' song, she did so few stupid things that the part began to play itself and at times the true Rosalind stood before us. In short, she gave Shakespeare a chance, and the poor man really came through very well. One bit of original business I remember which I have never noticed in another Rosalind. She carefully avoided all vulgar clowning in passages referring to her male attire, but when she spoke the line—' Here, on the skirts of the forest, like fringe on a petticoat,' she put out her hand with a perfectly natural gesture to pick up her own petticoat, and finding none, paused awkwardly for half a second.

She also provided the only Audrey that I have ever

seen on the stage. In appearance exactly right, an apple-cheeked maid with a touch of rustic dignity, shy in manner, her awe of Touchstone only overcome by her deep curiosity. The line—' Is it honest in deed and word—is it a *true* thing ? '—usually drawled with a leer between two bites at a property turnip, came earnestly, falteringly, with the intent gaze of a puzzled child and with a child's reluctance to put a grave thought into words. It brought no foolish laugh, but made the little figure of Audrey live.

I never saw much of Mrs. Langtry, though she came to my studio on several occasions and we met from time to time. It was good to know her, for the bending of her head and throat as she bowed in recognition was a thing never to be forgotten ; it was good to hear her speak and to find her voice an added charm, but I could never feel that she had actual existence—the fantastic unreality of a dream was about her ; she was a ' Museum Piece,' and subconsciously I missed the glass case and the plain-clothes policeman.

Once in a moment of madness I asked her to sit to me and she graciously gave assent, but no sooner was my request granted than I regretted it. Who was I that I should add another name to the list of those who had ingloriously failed to ' paint the lily ' ? I promptly dropped the subject, the lady as quickly forgot all about it, and I shall always regard that unpainted portrait of Mrs. Langtry as my artistic masterpiece.

U NTIL about this time I had never known Edward Burne-Jones personally, though I had fallen under his spell since my first sight of his pictures at the Grosvenor Gallery. For some years I had met and played rather solemnly with his little daughter, a shy and very grave child, at the house of her aunt, Mrs. Poynter, and knew slightly his equally shy but restless and voluble son who was a few years my senior, but as yet I had not been admitted to the inner shrine ' occult, withheld, untrod,' where dwelt the Master, and should never have ventured to make pilgrimage thither had not Mrs. Poynter, a lady of charmingly quick perceptions, fathomed my secret aspiration and sent me off one day with her son, Ambrose, to the longed-for goal with a message to her sister, Mrs. Burne-Jones.

The goal was certainly some way off. The direction once given to an address in the wilds of Fulham—" Go down the Cromwell Road till your cab-horse drops dead and then ask someone "—would apply almost equally well to the Grange, West Kensington ; but once reached it was well worth the journey.

The Grange, an old, dark red house, once the home of Samuel Richardson of ' Pamela,' stood back from the road behind a wall and an iron gate. Within the gate, and even more within the large low hall, furnished like a living-room, into which the front door opened, the impression conveyed was that of unusual quiet, a hush almost suggesting the Sleeping Palace of Faerie lore save that there was no drowsiness in the spell ; the house seemed to hold its breath lest a sound should disturb the worker.

The hall was dark and the little dining-room opening out of it even more shadowy with its deep-green leaf-patterned walls ; and it is strange to remember that the Brotherhood of Artists who so loved Beauty did not love light, but lived in a tinted gloom through which clear spots of colour shone jewel-like. At the end of the dining-

room stood a dark green cabinet, painted with designs
partly raised in gesso and enriched with gold and brilliant
hues, wrought by Burne-Jones in the early days when he,
with Morris and Rossetti, was devising wondrous furniture
and house decoration. Above it hung a small painting, a
little figure in magical red. Burne-Jones long afterwards
told me how he had prized it for the lovely colour of the
red robe, but had been much puzzled by the rest of the
picture, for the figure was then seated upon a crudely
daubed bank, holding in her hand an odd and unexplained
object which stuck up out of the ground : he felt that the
painter of the robe could not have painted the bank, and
one day began to clean. To his delight the bank began
to come away—something was beneath, something that
glowed softly, blue and golden. Gradually the ugly daub
disappeared, and behold a milk-white bull bearing Europa
across a sea of deepest blue, beyond which gleamed a
little golden city ; Europa still grasping what was now
seen to be the bull's golden horns.

It was certainly a Giorgione. It is true that we know
—at least it has been clearly proved by the learned—
that Giorgione painted none of the pictures formerly
attributed to him ; yet he was a painter and must presumably have painted something, so why not this exquisite
little Europa ?

Beyond the hall was the drawing-room, which struck a
different note. Here all was simple to austerity, and there
was light in plenty from two large windows opening on
to the garden. The furniture was plain, almost the only
ornaments were pale casts ; the Night and Morning of
Michelangelo brooded over the hearth, Theseus and a
pleasant-faced owl looked down from a cabinet ; there
were many books and book-cases, Mantegna's ' Triumph
of Julius Cæsar ' passed along the right wall : it was less
a lady's bower than a student's study.

Out through the window I was led, across a lawn to
where under a big mulberry-tree sat a tiny lady : as she
turned to receive me I met her eyes and became aware

of a great personality. The quiet in those wonderful eyes of clearest grey was, I knew, the centre of the strange stillness that lay upon the place, yet beneath and beyond could be sensed an Energy, dominant, flame-like. Eyes like those of Georgiana Burne-Jones I have never seen before or since, and, through all our long friendship, their direct gaze would always cost me little subconscious heart-searchings, not from fear of criticism or censure, but lest those eyes in their grave wisdom, their crystal purity, should rest upon anything unworthy.

After a moment—we often gain more knowledge of people from a first glance than they allow us to gather in many after-years—the impression of awe passed, the grey eyes became merely beautiful and kindly, and the tiny lady was making an awkward boy feel quite comfortable and happy.

We were joined by the grave little girl, whom I could hail as an old acquaintance, but with diffidence : she had put up her hair and let down her frock in rather an alarming manner and had become distinctly less grave and almost unnecessarily pretty. Her brother, Phil, came in, hospitable and excitable, but as yet there was no sign of the Master.

At last he walked out of the house and came down the garden towards us, and I was at once relieved to see that he was not going to turn out a disappointment. His face with its great width across the eyes and brows, tapering oddly towards the chin, was strangely like his own pictorial type ; its intense pallor gave it a luminous appearance added to by his large grey-blue eyes and silvered hair ; his long coat and high waistcoat produced an impression indefinitely clerical ; he wore a dark blue shirt and a blue tie drawn through a ring in which was set a pale blue jewel.

He might have been a priest newly stepped down from the altar, the thunder of great litanies still in his ears, a mystic with spirit but half recalled from the threshold of another and a fairer world ; but as one gazed in reverence

75

the hieratic calm of the face would be broken by a smile so mischievous, so quaintly malign, as to unfrock the priest at once and transform the mage into the conjurer at a children's party. The change was almost startling ; it was like meeting the impish eyes of Puck beneath the cowl of a monk. Yet neither of these entities was a disguise ; the monk was quite genuine, so was the elf, and in the uncertainty as to which of the two might turn up lay a strange fascination.

And—as is not always the case with a dual personality— each was equally to be relied upon. You might be making your confession to the monk and suddenly find yourself being absolved—or the reverse—by Puck, but it didn't matter. Puck was gently wise too and full of infinite understanding.

He greeted me very kindly, as was his wont, and put me at my ease by taking no particular notice of me but giving me permission to prowl round the great studio at the end of the garden, to which I quickly made off.

It was a huge barrack of a place, like a schoolroom or a gymnasium, containing none of the usual properties and elegancies of a ' show ' studio, but round the walls were ranged the studies for the Perseus and Andromeda series, paintings in *gouache* of the full size of the proposed oil pictures and far surpassing any of them that ever reached completion. They followed the adventures of Perseus from his call to the Quest by Athene to his marriage with Andromeda, and, as far as I can remember, only three or four were ever carried to a finish in oil.

The finest of all, the Gorgon Sisters, wakened by the death-cry of Medusa, circling wildly in the air in search of the slayer, was never even begun, but the water colour is all sufficient and could not have been improved upon.

Down the whole length of the bare whitewashed wall ran the scenes of the pictured story : the mysterious goddess flashing her will into the hero's brain, the Gratiæ in steel-grey robes groping blindly for their single eye, the weary figure of Atlas bowed beneath the weight of the

76

EDWARD BURNE-JONES
From a pencil drawing by THE AUTHOR, 1895

heavens, the daughters of the Evening Star, a beautiful group, black-robed Medusa looking out with eyes of boding while behind her the winged Fate drew swiftly near, the victim on the Rock of Doom and her rescue, and the quiet closing scene in which Perseus and Andromeda with linked hands bent over still waters wherein was mirrored the image of the Fatal Face.

Many other pictures, more or less incomplete, hung on the walls or stood dustily in corners, for the artist seldom worked continuously on the same canvas, but laid one after another aside, sometimes for years, while he developed other designs. Here were the beginnings of ' Love the Pilgrim,' ' The Prioress's Tale ' (the last picture completed by Burne-Jones), ' The Masque of Cupid,' various designs for the Romaunt of the Rose and the first panel of the Briar Rose series, the Prince making his way through the wood towards the enchanted castle.

Familiar as that studio soon became to me, and the still more sacred one within the house itself, I always recall it as I saw it first on that spring afternoon ; yet the sombre stately paintings there had only shown me a side of the painter which I already knew and which he had given to the public. In the garden, on my return thither, I found on exhibition other specimens of his work in a style quite new to me. The drawings which he had made for his children in their very early days had been preserved and pasted into books, and upon these treasures I was permitted to gaze. The babies must have found these pictures thrilling and delightful to the last degree in broad daylight ; how they had felt about them towards bedtime I did not like to enquire.

They nearly all had a hint of the nightmare about them, treating of the adventures of helpless midgets lost in vast lands of towering mountain peaks, fathomless abysses and trackless forests. One, I remember, showed an immense valley—all was on an impossible scale of grandeur—smooth and polished like a basin into which a tiny insect-like man had slipped and was sliding miserably

77

down the side towards a dark hole which yawned at the foot. Beneath was the cheering inscription—' Inside that hole there is a Thing,' and the series was entitled, ' The Horrors of Mountainous Lands.'

Another set had been begun, probably under pressure, called ' The Pleasure of the Plains,' but after an enthusiastic start on a line of preposterously fat pigs inspiration had flickered and gone out. ' The Pleasure of the Plains ' proved all too tame and the artist returned to Horrors with renewed zest, though occasionally in a lighter vein dealing with the life and habits of an animal called ' The 'Spression.' One has met with people whose beauty is said to lie in their expression, but not only the beauty but the very excuse for existence of the 'Spression lay in his. In actual form he was undistinguished, being something between a wombat, a poodle, and a pig, but his expression, now joyous, now melting, here deeply tragic, there raffish and rollicking, lent him a charm all his own. One particular drawing, ' Stampede of Wild 'Spressions in the Pampas,' showed him in almost every mood and is a joy to remember.

I fancy that some of the Horror Sketches had proved rather strong meat for the catered-for babies, for when in later years their author was looking forward to thrilling his grandchildren with Shapes of Terror, a check was put upon his invention by their mother. " Margaret says I mustn't draw bogies or devils, or Things for Angela," he complained to me. " It seems such a pity because I'm quite sure she would like them and I'm so tired of pigs ; yet if one isn't to draw devils, what is left but pigs ? " However, it soon became apparent that his strong-minded granddaughter was more than a match for any bogy yet invented and only too delighted to exchange placid idylls of the pigsty for the latest news from Nightmare Land, whence its special reporter seemed ever to draw fresh inspiration. Even I didn't much like the look of ' The Mist Walkers ' and ' The Heath Horror.'

I suppose that my earnest efforts to give satisfaction

on that first Sunday afternoon must have proved mildly successful as, far from being cast forth, I was invited to return and soon found kind and fast friends in all the members of the family. The master of the house was understood to say that I was very much like the young Ruskin, and as he evidently regarded the remark as a compliment I tried to feel gratified, and to forget how extremely plain Mr. Ruskin has always appeared to me in his portraits.

Burne-Jones would speak of Ruskin, the man, with great affection and even reverence ; of the critic he had his doubts, though from me, whom he suspected of un-sound views, he would try to conceal all misgivings. Nevertheless, he could not withhold from me a tale of how some patron of the Arts was being taken round his studio by Ruskin and the Great Teacher wound up a glowing eulogium with the statement—" And every one of these works is in pure water colour." The painter gasped— then shut his mouth tight. The Master Critic was of course infallible and yet—and yet—every picture in the room was in oil, and he had never produced a pure water colour in his life.

The artist had always delighted me ; the man himself, fascinating from the first, charmed me more and more as years wore on, and he gradually admitted me to intimacy ; we seemed to become ' of an age,' his ever-youthful sym-pathy and insight enabling him to meet me more than half-way. He was to me a kind and much-loved friend to the end of his days, a friend upon whom I could always depend to enjoy with me a certain aspect of things— curiously enough, the comic side of life. To this day I find myself thinking, " This will amuse or interest E. B.-J. : I must remember it." I particularly loved to draw from him a laugh, of which he had three varieties : the first an ordinary, modulated, drawing-room affair that did not count for much ; the second a loud and very deep ' Ha ! ha ! ' like a big dog barking ; the third and most valued complete silence accompanied by a general doubling up and shaking of the shoulders. This I regarded as First Prize and to gain it collected matter assiduously, undeterred by the distressing experience of Mrs. Burne-Jones, who, while similarly employed, once achieved catastrophe.

She was paying a round of calls, amongst which was a duty visit to some noble patrons of the Arts whom she knew only slightly but to whom it was befitting and advisable to show attention. The prospect bored her and she left this visit to the last. At a friend's house she heard a story about a cook who, being found under the kitchen table in an advanced state of intoxication, had said— What was it?—ah yes, she remembered, but she would write it down at once for home use lest she should forget it. Making a note of the remark she waded steadily through her visits, coming at last to the long-deferred duty call. "Not at home." A direct interposition of Providence, but had she cards enough? No—yes—just enough ; but as she turned away with a pleasant sense of ' something attempted, something done ' a terrible thought struck her and she wildly searched her card-case. It was empty, and that last fatal card left upon the august patrons had borne the inscription,

Mrs. Burne-Jones.
It's not drink—it's worry.

However, her reward lay in the fact that she had made history—a history which Burne-Jones loved to relate.

Another favourite, though I always feared apocryphal, tale of his was of the new man-servant who came hastily in one morning announcing, "Please, sir, your Aunt Nelly."

" *My* Aunt Nelly ? "

" Yes, sir."

" But—I haven't got an Aunt Nelly."

" No, sir ? Gave that name, sir."

" But—what have you done with her ? Where is she ? "

" Ran straight up to the studio, sir."

The artist bounded upstairs fearing he knew not what,

flung open the door and disclosed—Antonelli, the male model.

A third pretty tale designed to show his innocence of the Italian tongue was of the hesitating entrance of a model come for his first sitting. " Buon giorno," said the lad nervously.

" Quite right," said the painter, nodding encouragement, " Burne-Jones—that's the name. Come in."

He soon became wonderfully tolerant of me, even admitting me to his studio when he was at work, an unusual concession the excuse for which no doubt was that I kept very quiet and he quickly forgot that I was there. Indeed, I remember one day after a long silence and evidently imagining himself alone he suddenly and in the deepest bass remarked, " N-n-no ! " in a tone of absolute finality. " Why not ? " I enquired.

" Why not what ? " said E. B.-J., coming to himself and realising me with a start.

" You said No."

" Did I ? I believe I often do. Now, it's a very curious thing," he went on, putting down his pencil and giving his mind to the subject, " I'm what you would call a pleasant man, am I not ?"

" Yes," I admitted, " though I'm not sure that I should use the expression in describing you."

" Still we can leave it at that, can't we ? A decidedly pleasant man."

" Yes."

" Well, when I am alone and speak unconsciously to myself I always say No very firmly and deeply, though it is a word that has been a difficulty to me all my life. Now Edward Poynter, whom some perhaps might not call a pleasant man——"

" Perhaps," I agreed.

" —when *he* talks to himself always says Yes most amiably, and that's about the only time he ever does say it. Why should this be so ? Why does not he say No and I say Yes ? "

I could throw no light upon the subject.

As our friendship developed I found that where he differed most diametrically from other painters of my acquaintance was in his attitude towards Nature, which seemed hardly ever to inspire him directly. I cannot remember once to have heard him express pleasure at a natural effect except when it reminded him of a picture or a story. His outlook was that of a man of letters.

I, who had been much with painters, noticed very soon when walking with him that wonderfully quick as he was to observe and note passing events of a sad or comic or quaint character, all such material as would be useful to the novelist or the poet, he saw nothing from the purely pictorial point of view.

Albert Moore would come in from a walk full of almost inarticulate delight at the memory of black winter trees fringing the jade-green Serpentine, or of a couple of open oysters lying on a bit of blue paper or of a flower-girl's basket of primroses seen through grey mist on a rainy morning. Burne-Jones would have woven a romance or told an amusing tale about the flower girl, but would not have noticed her primroses, the combination of the silvery oysters and the blue paper would not for a moment have struck him as beautiful ; he had not the painter's eye.

He saw colour with the eye of a jeweller ; certain spaces in his design were to be filled up with various hues so as to make up a beautiful pattern ; he coloured his drawing as a child will colour a black and white outline, and for his particular form of decorative art no method could have been better. Some of his pictures, the ' Laus Veneris,' for instance, were like clusters of many-coloured gems or stained windows through which shone the evening sun.

He indeed made studies, was always making them, and most exquisite in themselves they were, but for all the use they could have been as Nature notes they might never have been drawn. They were ' all made out of the carver's brain,' like Christabel's chamber ; Nature was merely called in as consulting physician to confirm an opinion or to suggest a change of treatment.

I have often watched him drawing from the life, and so strong was his personal vision that, as I gazed, Antonelli the model began to look very like Burne-Jones's study, although the study never began to look like Antonelli.

After the hard and fast rules of Albert Moore and his exact knowledge of the capabilities and limitations of his material, Burne-Jones's methods seemed to me very amazing.

Like the

> ' old man of Thermopole
> Who never did *anything* properly,'

whether working in oil, in water colour, in pastel or in pure line, he appeared wilfully to ignore the possibilities of his medium and to put it to uses for which it was never intended.

In water colour he would take no advantage of its transparency, but load on body colour and paint thickly in gouache ; when he turned to oil he would shun the richness of impasto, drawing thin glazes of colour over careful drawings in raw umber heightened with white ; if he used pastel, it was to imitate oil ; when he designed stained glass he did so in black and white cartoons without hint of colour and—most surprising of all—with no indication of the leading ; when he drew for the woodcuts of William Morris, decorations in strong line, thick and black, he would do so in palest softest pencil, the drawing most delicate, the line shadowy and hesitating. What chiefly puzzled me was that many of the things he left undone he was pre-eminently fitted to do. Who like him could have arranged the jewelled splendour of stained glass, fitting the bits of glowing colour into their setting of leaden tracery ? Yet, as far as I know, his first design for a window, a commission obtained for him by Rossetti from Messrs. Poel, and the panels in oil for the great

Friedeswede window in Christ Church, Oxford, are the only instances in which he attempted to do so.

It all seemed very strange to a would-be student ; all the more so in that the results of these (from my point of view) malpractices were so hauntingly beautiful.

I have often wondered what Burne-Jones would have produced had he never seen the works of the early Italian school. The world of everyday was of no use to him, but he saved himself the trouble of creating a new one by straying into the back gardens of Mantegna and Botticelli. His own dream world would have been as lovely as theirs and, I think, even more interesting—what a pity that it was never open to the public.

I have noted down these few details of his procedure and technique as memories of a great artist, and therefore of interest, but by no means as criticism.

If Burne-Jones, as was said of Rossetti, painted poems, why on earth should he not ? Having something to say, why should he not choose his own way of saying it, and who can contend that his way was not beautiful ?

I have seen it laid down by critics that Burne-Jones could not draw. He was pre-eminently a draughtsman, and one of the greatest in the whole history of Art.

What the critics meant, I imagine, was that, in some of his earlier work, his figures were not anatomically correct ; which was true to a certain extent, and he took great pains in later days to rectify this fault—with some slight loss of freshness and spontaneity.

But as a master of line he was always unequalled ; to draw was his natural mode of expression—line flowed from him almost without volition. If he were merely playing with a pencil, the result was never a scribble, but a thing of beauty however slight, a perfect design.

The possession of this faculty, even in a much slighter degree, is to be met with amongst artists far less often than might be imagined. Whistler, the magician of the paintbrush, had it not at all ; his scribbles were scribbles and not very suggestive at that. Sir Edward Poynter, perhaps the finest academic draughtsman of his day, was helpless without the model before him.

Burne-Jones, like William Blake, drew from 'vision' and, as with Blake, Nature occasionally 'put him out'; but, unlike Blake, he had developed his power of vision by many years of patient study. He did not throw Nature overboard, but hitched his star to a wagon, not allowing it to stray too far beyond our mortal perceptions.

A superior person will here remark that his curious atmosphere of dreamy sadness, the boding glances of his wistful women, were tricks which grew monotonous by repetition. But, my dear sir, all painting is a trick, and the conjurer must really be allowed to perform the trick as best pleases him. So long as the live rabbit and the half-dozen eggs duly appear out of the empty hat, the means employed are no concern of yours, and you must allow that Burne-Jones's rabbit nearly always emerged kicking lustily, and his eggs, though not always new-laid, were beautifully fresh.

O, that ' Burne-Jones trick,' how many—myself among the number—thought they had found it out and could reproduce it ; but their rabbits, if ever forthcoming, were poor specimens, and their eggs were ' shop 'uns.'

A T about the time when I began to visit the Grange occurred the death of D. G. Rossetti and the first public exhibition of his collected works, which left upon me one of the most profound impressions of my life. To certain minds the art of Rossetti is as a spark to tinder, setting light to the imagination, devastating and sweeping away preconceived ideals, dazzling the eyes with fires, false perhaps, but superlatively beautiful.

I well remember my first sight of the pictures. Before the glamour fell upon me, I had time to look round in amazement and to think—" But these things are—surely —*bad*, ill-painted, ill-drawn, hot and heavy in colour "— then my reason fled and I was led captive.

Why had the critics said with a sneer, " He should have painted his poems and written his pictures " ? He *had* done so : here were painted poems which exercised as potent a spell as any written ones. ' The Blue Closet,' ' The Christmas Carol,' ' Paola and Francesca,' ' Borgia ' were all pure lyrics in water colour, exquisite in music and rhythm, and most of the larger oils, though finer in intention than in execution, spoke with melodious utterance.

I sat down comfortably at the feet of the poet painter and have remained there ever since, though later on I became better able to analyse his weird charm.

Any intelligent art student could out-paint Rossetti, nearly any member of a life class could draw better, and yet what they would produce would be of no import, while his slightest scribble is full of suggestion.

With him all is suggestion, intention. He expresses himself with difficulty ; but how much he has to say !

A few years ago I was straying through some loan collection. Like most painters, I get through an exhibition very quickly : in the first look round I see what to avoid and this saves much time. On this occasion I shied violently across the room at a terrible work which, to my shocked and instantly averted gaze, announced itself as an unusually bad Rossetti. I saw—against my will—a lilac face with purple lips, huge lilac arms sprawling over lumpy fulvous folds, distorted drawing, tortured, ' gormy ' paint.

For very love of Rossetti I would not look again ; I would forget as soon as possible.

Some days afterwards I began to be haunted by a beautiful Presence, vague, half-remembered. A wonderful face, gentle and noble, with eyes that dreamed and lips that faintly smiled, a lovely pattern woven of clinging white fingers and clustering apple-blossom, the gracious fall of glowing draperies. Where had I seen this ? In a picture, surely, but in what picture ? I had seen no such beautiful picture very lately. Suddenly it came to me—it was the picture that Rossetti was trying to paint when he produced the lilac and purple horror.

How strong and insistent must that original purpose have been, that the mental photograph, taken during that momentary glance, should be that of the picture that might have been instead of the picture that was. Through the slimy surface and muddy colour the beauty, dreamed of but unattained, had shone out and stamped itself upon my mind despite the evidence of my eyes.

I was now full of enthusiasm for the newly realised Wonder Man and eager for all the information I could collect as to his life, sayings, and doings.

More especially did those interest me who had known him in his brilliant youth and ranged themselves with him under the Pre-Raphaelite banner.

Burne-Jones I did not like to question too closely, as I knew that actual friendship between the two had been at an end for some years. Of the poet he spoke but seldom and with something like reluctance, but always in terms of affection and admiration.

As a young man his devotion to the great genius, both artistically and personally, had known no bounds, and I think that the misunderstanding and estrangement which came between them during the later darkened years of Rossetti's life must have been a sorrow to him.

When, later on, he most kindly began to help me with my work, both by advice and by actual demonstration, the name of his first master was often upon his lips. "How are those roses stuck on to that girl's head?" I remember his enquiring à propos of a picture of mine.

"I don't exactly know," I admitted. "Do you think it matters?"

"Yes," he replied, "I think it does—but Rossetti didn't. I once asked him why he had introduced some inexplicable object into a picture, and he would only say in a deep voice, 'To puzzle fools, boy, to puzzle fools.' But I don't altogether recommend the practice."

Two other survivors of the gallant band I was able to observe from time to time at the Grange, in the persons of F. G. Stephens and William Michael Rossetti, but I never came to know them in any real sense of the word. To tell the shameful truth, they both seemed to me rather dull old gentlemen : I was surprised and shocked at myself, but—there it was.

I hope that, in the case of W. M. Rossetti, I was not influenced by a story indiscreetly told me by Burne-Jones. Once upon a time William Morris had been trying to interest D. G. Rossetti in the mythology and legends of Scandinavia, from which he was taking the theme for his 'Sigurd the Volsung.' Rossetti was unsympathetic, and the entrance of Fafnar into the tale brought his objections to a head.

"I never cared much for all that stuff," he said. "There's something unnatural—monstrous—about it. How can one take a real interest in a man who has a dragon for a brother?"

Morris weighed the advantages and disadvantages of the inclusion of dragons in a family circle for some moments in dead silence, and then remarked, gazing fixedly at Rossetti, "I'd much rather have a dragon for a brother than a bloody fool."

Rossetti's fraternal delight in the answer gave it a deplorable immortality, and this unconventional and quite undeserved sobriquet stuck to W. M. Rossetti for some time.

Against these slight disappointments I was able to set the grand personality of Ford Madox Brown, the father of the school and incomparably its greatest painter. I think he never came in my day to the Grange, but I had managed to scrape acquaintance with him through mutual friends. But I knew him too late ; he was kind and courteous, yet remote, and over the dark little house by Primrose Hill there seemed to brood a shadow of I know not what sorrow or disappointment. Yet it was tremendously individual, and the dim rooms, crowded with ugly, fascinating pictures, I can see as though I had but now quitted them.

Large water colours from ' Silas Marner ' and ' The Deformed Transformed ' dominated the drawing-room, from the brush of the wonder-boy Oliver, ' Untimely Lost ' in the dawn of his promise, and round them hung small paintings purporting to be by Elizabeth Siddall (Mrs. D. G. Rossetti) and indeed drawn and tinted by a faltering and unskilful hand but quite obviously, in all save execution, fresh from the brain of her magician husband. On the opposite wall was a portrait of the child Oliver by his father and a most beautiful though unfinished picture of the painter's wife holding a naked baby, the artist's reflection appearing behind her in a mirror. Below this hung a little figure in brilliant red, Gabriel Rossetti's second attempt at water colour and presented by him to his kind friend and helper.

The studio, two bare rooms very dimly lighted, was on the first floor, and I well remember my last sight of the great painter there among the dusty canvases. He was ill—had a headache and would not come downstairs —but had allowed me to come up, and we talked awhile as he worked upon an old picture which he had taken up again—a quite peculiarly ugly picture it seemed to me.

The plant Love-lies-bleeding was the principal feature, and its stringy ugliness, like the chenille bell-ropes to be found in seaside lodgings, was reproduced with loving labour. Two plain girls in hideous dresses also figured in the composition, and I sat there marvelling how a picture could be so ugly and yet so full of arresting interest.

Once again I was to see the dark house and the haunting pictures, but, alas, their frames bore sale numbers, and thick-booted men tramped about dismantling the solemn little rooms. The great man had passed away, but leaving a rich inheritance to the years to come, and the painter of ' The Last of England,' ' Work,' and ' Christ washing Peter's feet ' will assuredly be remembered after most of his contemporaries are forgotten.

With Holman Hunt also my acquaintance was but slight, though it extended over many years. I think I was not more than once or twice in his studio.

On one occasion he showed me the ' Triumph of the Innocents,' a large picture which he told me he had been forced to repaint owing to a defect in the first canvas, and I remember feeling sorry that so much intricate and—to me—singularly unattractive work should have been undertaken all over again. At a loss for something to say, I gazed round the studio at a few portraits which pleased me not at all, until, in a corner, I caught sight of a most beautiful design faintly sketched upon a large canvas.

" O," I cried, " the Lady of Shalott !   I'm so glad you are going to paint that." For the drawing in the Moxon Tennyson was an old love of mine, and ranked with the five Rossetti designs as prime favourites.

" Yes," said Holman Hunt, " I have always wanted to paint it, and now, at last, I am going to begin."

Yet it was more than twenty years afterwards that the finished picture of the Lady of Shalott was exhibited ; the last work of the artist and completed, it is said, by another hand, though only in a few unimportant details.

The painter told me that he had always been fond of the design, yet when it was shown to Tennyson, who seemed blind and deaf to the sister arts of painting and music, the bard's only remark was : " But I never said that her hair was flying about all over the shop like that."

Holman Hunt always appeared to me particularly gentle and unassuming, and the strangely acid and vindictive tone of his Autobiography came as a great surprise to most people. Why he seemed so anxious to belittle Rossetti and to assume his sceptre I cannot imagine. He was never born to be a leader or to found a School : his infinite capacity for taking pains (in his case an inadequate definition of genius) he could not have passed on to others, and his odd, prismatic view of Nature could not have commended itself to many. This point of view was, I think, mainly owing to defective eyesight and detracts much from the effect of almost all his pictures, with the exception, perhaps, of three beautiful and memorable works, ' Strayed Sheep,' ' The Hireling Shepherd ' and the early version of ' The Light of the World.'

Another interesting member of the group I did not meet until many years later, the great draughtsman and painter, Frederick Sandys. He had never been one of the Brotherhood, nor, I think, a friend of Burne-Jones, but was for a time very intimate with Rossetti, from whom he drew much beauty of form and colour with which to clothe his own more sombre and virile imaginings.

In appearance he was like a Duke from Stage-land, tall and thin, handsome in a way that now recalled Don Quixote, now Mephistopheles, and with the courtly manners of the (stage) *grand seigneur*.

His stately calm and incorrigible Bohemianism formed the subject of a Hundred Merry Tales in which Rossetti and Whistler used to delight, and many of which the latter related to me.

One in particular I remember. Sandys was, as usual, in pecuniary difficulties, and several of his friends had assembled at Rossetti's house to discuss the raising of a sum that would enable him to emigrate. Sandys, during the conference, lounged on a sofa, apparently taking not the faintest interest in the whole affair, but when his would-be benefactors had departed, he slowly sat up.

"Whistler," he said, in deep, meditative tones, "if I got that money to go away with—I could stay here!"

A strange, wayward man, neither able nor wishful to obtain cheap popularity, his name and works are but little known, yet, amongst a brilliant company, he was one of the most highly gifted. Towards the end of his life there was a slight falling off in his work; his fancy heads became pretty instead of beautiful and his portraits began to coincide rather too much with the sitter's own idea of him or herself, but he left record of his genius in a few magnificent subject pictures, a brilliant series of black and white drawings and two portraits of old ladies, Mrs. Anderson Rose and Mrs. Lewis, which will certainly take their place among the highest achievements of modern art.

Of all the ancient company William Morris was the most often to be found at the Grange. He came to breakfast regularly every Sunday with two other old friends, known respectively as ' Uncle ' Crom and Luke (Ionides), and I used to reflect how lofty and permeated with beauty must be the converse of the painter and the poet at this weekly symposium, until I discovered that they usually read aloud to each other from a comic paper called *Ally Sloper*.

Morris's friendship with Burne-Jones and admiration for his work remained unshaken to the end; in fact, I do not think he recognised the existence of any other painter.

No one but Burne-Jones must illustrate his books, and this, despite the fact that he, of all artists, was the least fitted to depict the lusty full-blooded folk of Morris's romances, men and women full of the joy of life and the love of woods and waters and open skies.

Burne-Jones returned this affection deeply and sincerely, though I think he always disliked the flamboyant form of Socialism adopted by Morris. He would never discuss it, but one day said to me, "All that does not really belong to him at all, you know ; it is merely an attitude of mind and may pass at any moment. In fact, from day to day I expect to see him turn completely round and rush off in the opposite direction."

In truth it must be very difficult for an artist and devotee of beauty to keep an even mind in these matters. His sympathy is naturally with the democrat and Socialist, while his instincts and interests are ranged with the opposition, for it is unfortunately certain that whatever those twin gods of Democracy, the State and the People, touch they blast with a monstrous and soul-destroying ugliness.

Still, though he would not speak of them, Burne-Jones had great respect for the opinions of his friend, and when, in later years, he accepted a baronetcy, was very nervous as to how Morris would take it.

I remember finding him in his studio, staring in dismay at a great parchment which looked business-like yet ornate, like an illuminated address.

" Look here," he said, making room for me beside him, " the Queen has sent me a picture—not at all a nice one —and underneath are a lot of questions ; am I clean and sober ?—why did I leave my last place ?—that sort of thing. And I can't answer any of them. What am I to do ? "

I inspected an undoubtedly villainous print of Britannia doing nothing in particular at the head of an imposing document, over which we pored together. It was couched in stately legal phrase, and I could make no more of it than the bewildered recipient. Suddenly I was inspired.

" Mr. Morris is downstairs," I exclaimed. " He'll understand it. Let me take it to him."

I was almost out of the room with the paper when I was violently detained by my coat-tails.

" For Heaven's sake, don't ! " shouted the embryo Baronet. " What are you thinking of ? He'll tear it up or—no, he'll write the most awful things all over it and I shall never be able to send it back ! "

Mrs. Morris required to be seen to be believed, and

even then she seemed dreamlike. In her habit as she lived did Rossetti paint her over and over again, all the pictures striking likenesses, many of them most faithful portraits, yet her face is almost invariably looked upon as a figment of the painter's brain, a strange and impossible ideal.

When I first saw her, the dusky wonder of her hair was threaded with grey, but the face seemed to change hardly at all ; it was as if cast in pale bronze, the lines of the low brow and the carven lips remaining firm and sharp.

Five faces had notable effect upon the art of Rossetti : first the face of his sister, Christina, followed by that of Elizabeth Siddall, his wife ; then began to appear the faces of two professional models, Fanny Cornforth and Alice Wilding, and finally, like Aaron's rod swallowing up all the rest, came the face of Mrs. Morris, and so potent was its influence that it is now universally accepted as the ' Rossetti type,' the absolute invention and patent of the poet-painter.

I fancy that her mystic beauty must sometimes have weighed rather heavily upon her. Her mind was not formed upon the same tragic lines as her face ; she was very simple and could have enjoyed simple pleasures with simple people, but such delights were not for her. She looked like the Delphic Sybil and had to behave as such.

She was a Ladye in a Bower, an ensorcelled Princess, a Blessed Damozel, while I feel sure she would have preferred to be a ' bright, chatty little woman ' in request for small theatre parties and afternoons up the river. Brightness might equally have been expected from Deirdre of the Sorrows, chattiness from the Sphinx. She was Venus Astarte, ' betwixt the sun and moon a Mystery,' and there she had to stay.

She required appropriate setting and was perhaps at her wonderful best in her own house, standing in one of the tall windows against the grey river or lying on a low couch with beyond her the dim splendours of a great

"PROSERPINA," by D. G. ROSSETTI

From the Author's private collection

cabinet painted by Burne-Jones with the legend of Little Saint Hugh of Lincoln. There she seemed to melt from one picture into another, all by Rossetti and all incredibly beautiful.

I can well understand that her type was too grand, too sombre to appeal to every eye.

When she travelled in France, our light-hearted and often beauty-blind neighbours found her appearance frankly amusing and would giggle audibly when she passed by, to the astonishment and rage of Morris, who was with difficulty restrained from throwing down his gage in the cause of his Ladye.

I always recommended would-be but wavering worshippers to start with Mrs. Stillman (Marie Spartali) who was, so to speak, Mrs. Morris for Beginners.

The two marvels had many points in common : the same lofty stature, the same long sweep of limb, the ' neck like a tower,' the night-dark tresses and the eyes of mystery, yet Mrs. Stillman's loveliness conformed to the standard of ancient Greece and could at once be appreciated, while study of her trained the eye to understand the more esoteric beauty of Mrs. Morris and ' trace in Venus' eyes the gaze of Proserpine.'

As he foretold in a poem, those who would look on her now must come to Rossetti, and in the portrait in blue, holding a rose, in the ' Mariana ' and the ' Proserpine ' and in the chalk drawings, ' Aurea Catena ' and ' The Prisoner's Daughter ' (to quote a few out of many) they will find her exact presentment, set down without exaggeration.

Hers is one of the few World Faces, unique, yet each representative of a great type of which it is the supreme summary : for the moment I can only recall the Sphinx, Lisa Gherardini and Napoleon, but to the list, however short, must certainly be added the name of Jane Morris.

William Morris, looking like a burly sea captain with deep voice and brusque manner, was a curiously vivid figure among the folk of the Rossetti period as I met them at the Grange, who all seemed a little remote and out of focus. I never knew them very well, but the atmosphere of the Grange was not conducive to intimacy : there was a hush in the shadowy rooms, people moved slowly and spoke softly in carefully chosen words, and the Oxford voice was much in use among the younger visitors. This Oxford voice, a gentle murmur, a species of *voix d'or*, had been, I always imagined, invented by Walter Pater as an amusing foil to his personal appearance. For though the mellifluous coo, emanating from a rather ladylike young æsthete, was distinctly irritating, from the lips of a man with the face of Mr. William Sykes and the shoulders of Samson it was interesting, even fascinating.

This great poet who never wrote verse was a kind friend to me, and when I was sometimes allowed to dine *en famille* with him and his sisters at the little house in Earl's Terrace, Kensington, I was always intrigued by the contrast between the rugged masculine features and the delicate preciosity, which never became affectation, of voice and speech. Monna Lisa, sitting among her rocks on the wall behind him, used, I fancied, to look faintly amused too.

Sometimes, at the Grange, one had an uncomfortable sensation of sitting up and balancing a biscuit on one's nose—a feeling always left behind at the studio door, within which the master of the house would drop from his pedestal with a disconcerting bump. Yet, when on the pedestal, his pose was not a conscious one ; the reserve and gentle dignity in which he wrapped himself from all but chosen friends was, I imagine, half shyness, half an instinct of self-preservation.

Journalists and reporters, if they ran him to earth, which seldom happened, found in him a most unsatisfactory subject who would never take the required attitude, whether artistic, heroic, or sympathetic. " A dreadful woman has been asking me what is my message to the people of Hackney Wick," he complained one day, hurrying me upstairs. " I was very nice and did my best. I said I hoped they were pretty well and that I was pretty

well and—that was all I could think of. But she wasn't
pleased."

Another interviewer had better luck when his quarry,
at bay in the hall, darted behind an open door which an
orderly minded servant instantly closed, revealing the
flattened form of the master. The reporter brightened ;
the elusive and mysterious artist was evidently in a holiday
humour and bidding him to a game of Peep-Bo or I Spy.
" Child of nature," he observed waggishly, but in spite
of this very promising opening the interview was not a
real success.

OF A POET, A POODLE, AND A COOK

By this time I had left Eton, not deeply to my regret
and to the unseemly delight of James Nasmyth, and
was working with a tutor in Hertfordshire with a view to
college.

In the holidays I continued to haunt all the studios to
which I could gain admittance—for the most part inflicting
myself upon Burne-Jones, Poynter and Albert Moore, and
sometimes venturing into the strongholds of Leighton and
Alma Tadema, who was then moving into his newly built
palace in St. John's Wood, where the styles of Ancient
Rome, mediæval Holland and modern Britain met and
tried to mingle, with surprising but uncomfortable results.
There, on Sundays, flocked musicians of all descriptions
and there too was usually to be seen Mary Anderson, just
then the idol of London and drawing crowds to gaze upon
her as ' Galatea,' the living statue.

She was extremely beautiful and of the pure classic
type not infrequently to be met with in America ; I
have seen several such statue-girls, especially among
Californians.

Her plastic loveliness and slow dignity of poise and
movement fitted her essentially to represent Pygmalion's
marble goddess, but her best work was done in the
' Winter's Tale ' as ' Hermione,' with which rôle she
doubled that of ' Perdita,' and here she had the support
of Johnston Forbes-Robertson's admirable ' Leontes,' a
wonderful character study. Her dancing, as ' Perdita,'
was the perfection of rustic grace, joyous and expressive,
a delightful memory. She looked and seemed much
younger off than on the stage, not the triumphant actress
but a simple girl, kindly and unaffected.

One Christmas I remember taking part in theatricals
at the White House, Chelsea, which had been built for
Whistler by E. W. Godwin but was now inhabited by Harry
Quilter, a critic, writer, and would-be painter. He was a
man of means and pursued Art as a hobby without ever

98

quite succeeding in catching it up. The theatricals—an
adaptation of Emile Augier's ' La Cigue '—remain in my
memory because the company included Florence Terry,
the first of the wonderful Terry group to be known to me
personally. Shall I confess that she was a slight disappointment ? In another family she would have held her
own but, as a Terry, she seemed a pale sketch for Ellen or
Marion which had been left incomplete. Nevertheless,
she acted prettily and gracefully and I regarded her
with due awe, for had I not seen her as Nerissa, conversing familiarly with the Golden Lady of Belmont
herself ?

In the summer of that year I was in the Engadine, and
there fell in with a new friend, Comte Robert de Montesquiou Fezensac, the poet, whose strange but winning personality attracted me from the first.

Unlike the generality of poets, he looked the part ; his
beautifully chiselled features and slender figure, lithe and
active as an Indian's, produced their effect without the aid
of unkempt locks and Guy Fawkes-like garments.

He was a man with many sides to his character : to
walk with him through the Galleries of Versailles, in the
bosquets of Trianon or in the stately gardens of St. Cloud
was to see the deserted palaces in their ancient glory and
to breathe the very atmosphere of the past. In the country
or among the mountains he became a creature of the woods
and fields, whimsical, mischievous, faun-like, an early riser
and tireless walker, a lover of silence and solitude and
responsive to all the moods of Nature. In his fantastic
rooms in Paris, he was, as absolutely, a man of the passing
hour, a typical member of that curious little world of
amateurs which hangs midway between the worlds of Art
and Society.

He could be an ideal companion, witty and sympathetic, and I have delightful memories of long days spent with
him among the mountains, beginning with an early breakfast at about six at a little *crémerie* in the woods and always
ending with a rush home through the twilight, just in time

99

for dinner in a state of indecent hunger and dirt—though now I come to reflect, I only was dirty ; he had the gift peculiar to certain Frenchmen of keeping perfectly clean and unruffled under any circumstances.

Later on I saw much of him in Paris at his father's house on the Quai d'Orsay, where he had a suite of apartments just underneath the roof.

It was curious to leave the stately, almost austere rooms of the old Comte and to climb up a dark stairway, through tunnels of tapestry to the eyrie which Comte Robert had elected to inhabit, and to come into the exotic atmosphere of his extraordinary rooms, like a vague dream of the Arabian Nights translated into Japanese : the room of all shades of red, one wall deep crimson, the next rose colour, the third paler rose, and the last the faintest almond pink ; the grey room where all was grey and for which he used to ransack Paris weekly to find grey flowers ; the bedroom, where a black dragon was apparently waddling away with the bed on his back, carrying the pillow in a coil of his tail and peering out at the foot with glassy, rolling eyes ; the bathroom, where one gazed through filmy gauzes painted with fish into a green gloom that might have been ' full fathoms five ' under waves. It was all queer, disturbing, baroque, yet individual and even beautiful, and as a trans-mutation of a set of unpromising attics into a tiny fairy palace, little short of a conjuring trick.

Robert de Montesquiou was a most kind friend to me for many years and showed me much in Paris that I should never have seen without him. Together we visited innu-merable private collections of pictures which were either shown to us, in the absence of the family, by caretakers, whom my companion always treated with almost exagger-ated courtesy and consideration as our esteemed host and hostess, or by the polite and usually Semitic owner, whom he appeared, as invariably, to regard as a caretaker—and a caretaker without a character.

More especially did we search such houses as contained works by the mystic painter for whom there was then a

ROBERT DE MONTESQUIOU AND SARAH BERNHARDT
both costumed as " Le Passant "
From a hitherto unpublished photograph

cult in Paris much like that for Burne-Jones in London. The fantastic art of Gustave Moreau appealed strongly to Montesquiou, and he passed on his enthusiasm to me. The large water colour, ' The Vision,' representing Salome stayed in her dancing by the apparition in the air of the Baptist's severed head, I had seen some years before at the Grosvenor Gallery and had not greatly cared for, but the smaller works now revealed to me were fascinating in the extreme, particularly the lovely ' Europa,' a smaller version of the ' Salome ' without the ghostly head, and the jewel-like ' Galatea.'

Moreau was then almost a hermit and lived in rigid seclusion. Montesquiou, who knew him slightly, wished to present me to him, and I still possess his letter in reply to my friend's request, bravely denying himself the proffered pleasure.

When I was eighteen occurred the death of my father, who had been an invalid for some years and upon whom my mother had been in almost constant attendance. After his loss we went abroad together and remained out of England for nearly a year, my mother taking a house for the winter at Biarritz, then a small town, hardly more than a village, in the midst of quite unspoilt country. Now, I believe, it almost joins Bayonne, the great cork woods are cut down, there are golf courses and ' every modern improvement,' and I do not wish to see it again ; but then I loved it dearly.

Soon after we arrived I made a friend who was my constant companion for the next sixteen years, a large grey poodle of the St. Jean de Luz breed.

Though only two years old, he had already had a career, beginning as a fisherman, when he used to go out with the sardine boats, then becoming a photographer's assistant. He was loath to give up his master for me, and at first would leave the house in a marked manner whenever we had the slightest difference ; but when he discovered that we were ' carriage folk,' that is to say, occasionally hired flies or went by train to Bayonne, he threw in his lot with us gladly. Carriage exercise was an unwaning joy to Mouton, especially if there were other dogs about to witness his triumph. He was terribly self-conscious and conceited, though in the years to come his affectations fell from him, and he had a genuine dramatic gift. I dislike to see dogs perform tricks and would teach him none, but he rapidly evolved a whole programme of his own which we used to find him going through in the street in the midst of an admiring circle. He was always jealous of rival artistes and particularly disliked two small green parrots, the property of the cobbler who lived opposite and who had taught the birds to break into a lively dance while they shrieked out the chorus of an old *café chantant* ditty, ' Te voilà, Nicholas ! Ah ! Ah ! Ah ! ' It was a charming performance ; the three singing cobblers sitting cross-legged on their bench under a tree, the little parrots, perched on a low wall with grey toes uplifted, ready to dash into the refrain and dance, were irresistible and drew the town, or rather the village ; but Mouton, parading on his hind-legs on the opposite pavement, would gradually draw off his audience and get in his turn despite the counter-attraction.

Biarritz did not encourage the Arts much. There was a steady demand for black-eyed, mantilla-ed ladies on fans or stout toreadors on tambourines, and sunsets, with the sun setting due south behind the Pyrenees, were occasionally enquired for, but beyond this, little or no business was done.

Nevertheless, after some exploration, I found a studio with a painter in it, one Monsieur Achille Zo. He was not a remarkably good painter but well up to the average of the school of Madrazo, and quite competent to portray the rather stout and *passée* Spanish belles who gave him his few commissions.

I was admitted to his studio ' on liking,' and I suppose he liked me, as I stayed on. There was one other pupil, a Basque peasant boy who cleaned and tidied up Monsieur Zo in return for instruction received : a very charming boy with much talent and a delicious sense of colour ; some of his flower studies were curiously beautiful.

We three painted solemnly together in the small studio, solemnly watched by Mouton who sat close beside me for hours, quite motionless—at least, we all thought he was motionless, though it afterwards appeared that he was not. One thing disturbed our serenity : no one could keep a stick of charcoal. If laid down for a moment it vanished, and brimming boxes were mysteriously emptied as soon as opened.

The Basque boy cherished dark suspicions of the English interloper, I had the worst opinion of the Basque boy, and Monsieur Zo laid the blame upon both pupils quite impartially. A cloud settled down upon our amicable trio which might never have been dispersed but for the detective qualities displayed by the Duc d'Osuna. This potentate was practically the only visitor to the studio. He loved pictures, and when he could not see good ones, preferred bad ones to no pictures at all and would often drop in and sit chatting as we worked, without disturbing us in the least. He was a curious man with a bitter cynical wit and, apparently, little liking for his fellow-creatures, yet when he talked of Art—and he did so brilliantly—he became another being—gentle, sympathetic and kindly.

I suppose he noticed the disturbed atmosphere of the studio since *l'affaire du charbon*, for he evidently kept his eyes open, and one day we discovered him to be convulsed with inward laughter.

" Do you not really know who takes the charcoal ? " he asked at last.

" Who ? " we gasped.

The duke pointed a long, accusing finger at Mouton, who sat beside me, as usual the picture of innocent unconsciousness.

" *Mouton ?* " I cried. " But Mouton doesn't care for charcoal. See ! " I offered him the small piece with which I was drawing, at which he sniffed disparagingly then turned away his head.

" That's a clever dog ! " cried the duke with enthusiasm. " A very clever dog."

" But he never moves from my side."

" Doesn't he ? " said the duke. " Watch him."

Monsieur Zo brought out a new stick of charcoal and
laid it carelessly on a chair beside him, then resumed work,
as did his pupils. I was just becoming absorbed when I
noticed something like a shadow flit noiselessly across the
floor ; I looked down ; Mouton was hastily resuming his
seat and—the charcoal was gone.

From the first the thief had been Mouton, who had
developed a craving for charcoal, first, I suppose, swallowed experimentally, and would stick at nothing to get
it.

" That's a very remarkable dog," said the duke, who
seemed to have a taste for crime. " I wish he were mine."

But I could not part with Mouton.

However, the Duc d'Osuna bore no malice and often
gave me very valuable criticism and advice, as well as
occasional presents which were even more acceptable.

" Why do you draw on that ugly white paper ? " he
once enquired when looking over some of my black and
white.

" Because it's the only paper I've got," I replied.

" I'll give you some paper," he grunted, and next day
bestowed upon me a packet of paper for which an etcher
would gladly have committed murder. Delicate as withered leaves, strong as parchment, thin sheets of pale gold,
mellowed by time like old ivory. I had the sense to know
its value and kept it carefully. Years after I gave some
sheets to Whistler, who almost fell down and worshipped
them.

Another Distinguished Personage I came across while
at Biarritz, and though I did not actually meet him, his
spell is upon me to this day.

In a little whitewashed inn of which he was the *patron*,
far away among the hills, there lived in retirement one who
had been—nay, who still was—one of the greatest artists

the world has ever seen. As a youth he had been cook to
the Emperor of the French and had carried all before him.
So meteoric a career has seldom been witnessed.

Already the crowned king of his profession at an age
when ordinary mortals are toiling up the lower slopes, he
had grown weary of his greatness ; his still youthful head
was bowed beneath the weight of his laurels. Masterfully
he had won them, masterfully he laid them by. Moved
by no threats, touched by no entreaties, he had stepped
down from his throne and in a little village among the
woods, in that strange, debatable Basque land which is
neither France nor Spain, neither highland nor lowland,
he had sought and found that peace which in glittering
courts may not be known. There he lived his quiet
cloistral life, regretting no whit the stalled oxen of the past
and all-satisfied with a dinner of herbs—nicely served in
an omelette and washed down with thin, delicious *vin
ordinaire*. Millionaires had wooed him with their gold,
crowned heads had abased themselves, our own Edward
VII had besought him almost with tears to return to
public life, but all in vain : the enchanter would work no
more wonders, deeper than ever plummet sounded had
he buried his wand.

But one day in spring-time when all the world was
young, when the windflowers woke in the coppices, when
the snow streams dashed singing down through fields of
violets, and the pale asphodels unfolded their mysterious
blossoms in the sedgy woods, a great longing fell upon
him, he was shaken by a very passion of creation.

As in a dream he strode into the kitchen, as in a dream
he took his Art to him again and—Cooked.

Mute with wonder the simple servitors stood about him
until, his task done, the Master looked upon his work and
saw that it was good : and as he looked the inspiration
faded and he passed out of the kitchen, again a simple
man amongst men.

And at this supreme moment my mother and I, Fate-
led, were lumbering up the hill in a hired *fiacre*.

A POET, A POODLE, AND A COOK

Frank trippers were we, carelessly bound no whither for no particular purpose, yet Fate, still playing up, led us straight into the little whitewashed inn, into a newly scrubbed room, and there laid before us the Luncheon of our lives.

We came slowly from that little white room, held in the hush of a great awe, grave with new knowledge, with shining faces, like Moses fresh from the Mount. Never again would we speak lightly of Food ; we knew it now for what it was or could be, a mystic rite, a sacrament.

" We will tell everyone in Biarritz about it ! " cried I in the thoughtless generosity of youth.

" We will do nothing of the sort," said my mother, " but we will mention it to a few particular friends, and we will come back ourselves—come back often."

This programme we carried out but soon noticed that our particular friends seemed to be growing less particular and to seek other society than ours. At length, one, either shorter in the temper or more deeply wounded than the rest, gave us the key to the mystery.

" How could you send me to that odious place ? " she wailed. " I never had a more disgusting lunch in my life ! "

Then the pack turned upon us and rent us ; some cold and reserved, observing that it was a pleasant drive and that no doubt the luncheon was excellent if that was the sort of thing we liked, others openly reviling us in good round terms.

Never again had the Great Man cooked—ours had been a marvellous and unique experience, and the glory of it is with me still.

We watched the passing of our friends almost with indifference : inwardly stayed by a mutual memory of perfection : we were no longer as they, for

> " We on honey dew had fed
> And drunk the milk of Paradise."

106

OF THE DIVINE SARAH

AFTER our year of wandering we returned to England
through Paris, where I again spent most of my time
with Robert de Montesquiou. His surroundings were
more amazing than ever and he had developed a habit of
sitting for his portrait which filled all available space (of
which there was not much) with his counterfeit present-
ments. Among them I only can recall one by Jaques
Blanche, destined for the grey room, an upright panel in
all shades of grey, and a dark, Ribera-like study by Antonio
de la Gandara, then a very young man, representing the
poet seated *en profil* in a long robe of Chinese embroidery,
clasping his knees with long, jewelled fingers.

One day, while exploring amongst the curious objects
strewn about the rooms, I came upon a tiny photograph
in a black frame, the photograph of a dead girl in her
coffin. There was nothing of horror in the picture, only
pathetic loveliness, and I felt that I had surprised some
tragic secret as I hastily replaced the frame and Comte
Robert looked up quickly.

" You know her, don't you ? " he asked.

" No," I whispered. Did I ever see her ? Could I
have known her when she was alive ?

" She isn't dead," he said, smiling. " That is Sarah
Bernhardt."

Sarah Bernhardt. Yes, indeed I had seen her, and not
long before : I had found her prodigious, marvellous ;
but the play in which she had appeared had been a melo-
drama by Sardou, called ' Fédora ' and the panther-
heroine seemed altogether of the stage, a creature who
could have no real existence and who made no personal
appeal. The little figure in the coffin was different,
spiritual, ethereal, but movingly human.

Soon afterwards I saw the great actress again, but this
time in ' Phédre,' and only those who have seen her
' Phédre ' at its best will understand what a revelation it
was.

From the moment that the white-clad figure of the unhappy Queen appeared I was enchained. Here was a new experience, acting such as I had never dreamed of, such as I can hardly believe has ever been equalled.

Here was the girl of the coffin, grown to a woman but pathetically lovely as ever.

Her gestures were few and slow, she seemed to move hardly at all, even when the tragedy deepened and the dream-filled eyes blazed with unholy fires, the golden voice grew harsh and strident with horror.

She was a slender white column set in an angry sea ; the waves of crime and shame beat against her but could not mar her.

My mother, who had seen Rachel as Phédre, much preferred Sarah Bernhardt, who, she said, softened by nobility and beauty a part which her great forerunner had made almost unbearably horrible. Rachel had been an incarnate devil, Sarah was the victim of Fate, the sport of the gods, a noble nature in overthrow.

When I next met Robert de Montesquiou I suppose I must have raved ceaselessly of the divinity, for, to pacify me, he gave me a letter of introduction, which I was not able to present at the time as the lady was away in America, but on her return she passed through London and I tremblingly approached the Métropole Hotel, where she was then enshrined.

What should I find there—Phædra or Fédora, the girl of the coffin or the monster of newspaper stories, the malign, mysterious sorceress ?

Somewhat to my relief for the moment, I found nobody ; Madame was out, as I afterwards found Madame was accustomed to be when inquisitive strangers called.

However, the next morning brought a message from her asking me to lunch and I bought a beautiful pair of new gloves and set forth, consoling myself with the reflection that I could not look a greater fool than I felt.

I well remember her first coming to me with outstretched hands across the great empty room, her russet

SARAH BERNHARDT
THE " COFFIN " PORTRAIT
Private photograph taken in the early 'seventies

hair loosely wisped up, her long robe of cream-coloured velvet falling over an under-dress of mauve silk gathered into a silver girdle. Several other people were there, but I have forgotten all about them, as one generally did in the presence of Sarah. Old Madame Guèrard I know was one, who always lived and travelled with her and had been much more to her than her own mother throughout her life.

My hostess placed me beside her at table where I sat tongue-tied and gaping like a fish. I remember that the conversation fell upon the rôles in life which we should each choose to play.

" I should like to be a queen," said Sarah at once.

" My dear child," protested Madame Guèrard, " what people do you think would ever stand you ? You would find yourself with your head off in a week."

Sarah reflected. " Yes," she said gravely, " I suppose I should, but "—brightening up—" I should have had lots of other people's heads off in that week."

During the next spring I was again in Paris for a few weeks when I saw much of the divine Sarah, and we laid the foundations of a long friendship which I have always valued most highly.

On my first visit I found her in dejection in her studio before a huge mass of clay out of which she had been trying to evolve Love doing something or other—Triumphing, I think. Death was also somewhere about and a few other rather unconvincing allegories.

Sarah barely nodded as I was shown in and we gazed together at the unpromising-looking lump.

" It's bad," she murmured at length. " Very bad. There's nothing good in it—is there ? "

I tried to say that I thought it a masterpiece, though of course unfinished, but I suppose my French failed to disguise my feelings.

For a moment more Sarah glared murderously at the wobbly lop-sided Love, then seizing a strong piece of wire, she sliced off a considerable portion of his anatomy.

" You help," she cried. " I'll scrape, and you take the bits in that basket and throw them out of the window."

Having ascertained that the window gave on to a small flagged court and that I was not expected to bombard passers-by in the Boulevard Pereire with dismembered fragments of Love and Death, I fell to work and we soon reduced the unfortunate group to an innocent-looking mud-pie and began to feel quite cheerful and intimate.

I was able to look round the large hall which served as studio and reception-room, at its red walls hung with trophies of arms, Mexican hats, lassos, lariats, savage masks and weapons, at its floor strewn with rugs, hides and cushions, at glass cases full of golden laurel wreaths, golden vases and other souvenirs, at the huge aviary of twittering birds which stood in a corner near the fire-place.

" Why has that cage such very strong bars ? " I asked.

" I kept a lion there once," said Sarah.

" And—and it died ? "

" No," said Sarah. " He didn't die," and her tone implied that there were things worse than death. I afterwards learned from Madame Guèrard that the lion had been one of Sarah's failures.

" I am going to keep a lion," she had announced.

" Yes, yes, of course a lion," her friends had agreed, knowing the futility of argument, " but doesn't he—won't he—— ? "

" Won't he what ? " asked Sarah.

" Won't he—perhaps—smell a little ? "

" Smell ? " cried Sarah. " Smell ? The lion, the King of Beasts ? No, of course he won't smell."

So the lion came—and he smelt.

Sarah bore it bravely and made no sign, but gradually the smell crept from the studio to the dining-room, from the dining-room to the bedrooms. Sarah became pensive but no one ventured to make a suggestion, until at last one morning she descended, took one final and comprehensive sniff and exclaimed. " He smells. Take him away." No word more was said, good or bad, the King of Beasts was hurriedly removed, and lions, as a topic of conversation, were avoided for some time after.

His Majesty was succeeded by a long train of pets, ordinary and extraordinary. It was never safe to reckon upon what manner of beast you might be called upon to fraternise with upon your next visit.

Dogs of all kinds were always to the fore—Osman, a huge wolfhound, was a magnificent creature. The tiger cub (his day was later on) I never found attractive, though lovely to look upon. " Don't hold him near your face," said Sarah as she handed the formidable baby to me to nurse. " He has a way of dabbing at your eyes," and truly a dab in the eye from that heavy paw, small though it was, would have been anything but beneficial. He was sometimes allowed to walk about the dinner-table, which excited and made him fractious, and I was always rather relieved when he had tottered snarling past my plate without paying me any marked attentions.

The most fascinating of the pets was the lynx, a really lovable beast who ranged about the house at his will and was gentle and affectionate as well as graceful : the mysterious, white-robed figure of Sarah coming down the steps into her studio with the lynx gliding noiselessly beside her was so suggestive of Circe that one looked about for the pigs.

Was Sarah Bernhardt beautiful ? Was she even passably good looking ? I have not the slightest idea. Beauty with her was a garment which she could put on or off as she pleased. When she let it fall from her she was a small woman with very delicate features, thin lips, a small beautifully modelled nose, hooded eyes of grey-green shadowed by a fleece of red-gold hair, strong slender hands, and a manner full of nervous energy. But when she would appear beautiful, none of these details were to be perceived ; her face became a lamp through which glowed pale light, her hair burned like an aureole, she grew tall and stately ; it was transfiguration.

This strange dream-beauty was impossible to transfer to canvas ; no portrait of her holds even the shadow of it.

The very clever picture by Bastien Lepage is little more than a caricature, though a very charming one and giving the intense vitality of the sitter. It was finished like a miniature, and Sarah confessed to me that she had grown utterly weary of the endless sittings and had led the painter a pretty dance in her efforts to escape them. At last he had arrived bearing his impedimenta and a camp stool upon which he had planted himself outside her bedroom door, daring her to pass in or out without posing for him, and thus, by force and violence, the picture got itself completed.

Georges Clairin's immense canvas, full of frills, flounces, fringes, dogs and cushions, like an odd lot at a jumble sale, is of no value as a likeness ; Gandara's portrait is a clever study of a pink dress, but Sarah is not inside it. She looked so paintable, yet no one could paint her.

She sat very kindly and patiently to me for many studies in her big studio, often with the wonderful cloud of hair loose about her head, from which it stood straight out like delicate crinkled wire, and her hasty toilette, if visitors were announced during one of these séances, always amused me. Three lightning quick movements, a vigorous brush down over the forehead, two wisps up at the sides and the jamming in of a single hairpin, and she rose quietly to greet the new-comer, *coiffée* as usual.

Sometimes, for a change, she would draw me and usually got a very recognisable likeness, though she did not take any pride in her drawing or painting, but rather fancied herself as a sculptor, in which capacity she had certainly achieved success more than once. She laughingly told me of the mistaken kindness of an unknown admirer who had attended one of her enforced sales and made a purchase which he had forwarded to her. With it came a note expressing his sympathy with her in her difficulties and begging her to accept the accompanying package which contained something that he felt she must value most highly and which he craved permission to restore to her.

"I *was* delighted," related Sarah. "I had been miserable all day thinking of my beloved possessions being sold, and now came this charming letter and an enormous packing-case—what could be inside? I went over all my lost treasures while it was being opened, wondering—Could it be this?—could it be that? At length the last wrapper fell away and the gift was disclosed—it was the largest and worst of my own pictures! A dreadful thing, to be rid of which had almost consoled me for the sale! This was the poor dear man's notion of what I would value most highly. I cried with rage, until I began to laugh."

She showed me a photograph of the picture in question and I was able to understand her disappointment. It was called 'La Jeune Fille et la Mort' and showed an oddly banal treatment of the well-worn subject. The 'jeune fille' in evening frock and 'picture' hat of black velvet (half mourning—a delicate touch) seemed to be alarming herself unnecessarily, for she was evidently in robust health and more than equal to repelling the advances of an insignificant little skeleton in white muslin who smiled coquettishly in the background. But when the picture was painted, Sarah Bernhardt was very young and very fragile. She imagined, and indeed had been told on good authority, that her days were numbered, and with characteristic bravery she faced the thought of death, keeping it constantly before her and surrounding herself with the emblems of mortality. Hence the coffin, the skeletons, the gristly paraphernalia of her early days, but as her magnificent constitution gradually asserted itself, she passed from this eerie Shadowland into the sunshine of life, all morbid eccentricities were laid aside and her outlook became thoroughly normal and healthy.

Once I found her in the highest spirits, evidently raised by some paragraph she had chanced upon in a newspaper.

"There goes the last of them!" she cried, with a flourish of the paper.

I gaped unintelligently. " The last of——? "

" The last of the doctors who gave me only one more year to live when I was a girl. There were any amount of them, and they all talked and wagged their heads and passed their final sentence upon me—and now they're *all* dead and here I am ! "

There she certainly was ; a more vivid, vital being could not be imagined.

Stories innumerable have been told about Sarah Bernhardt ; of her extravagance, her love for *réclame*, her tornado-like rages (these with many grains of truth in them), of her cruelty (invariably false), and of her numerous caprices and escapades ; but of her kindness, her generosity, her whole-hearted sympathy in sickness or distress, few have cared to tell except those who have known her personally, and if such tales were even briefly recorded they would form a volume of inconvenient size.

I remember, during a performance in London, one of the scene-shifters, new to the theatre, falling backwards down a concealed stairway and injuring himself severely.

Sarah sent for doctors and did all that was to be done at once, and after the curtain fell I came to bid her good night.

" He is going on all right," I said. " You can go home quite satisfied."

Sarah looked surprised. " But I'm not going home."

" You are going to stay here ? "

" Of course."

" All night ? "

" Yes."

" But the man is being well cared for : you may be sure that he has everything he wants."

" I shall be sure if I stay here," said Sarah simply. " If I go home I shall not."

So there she stayed, but the newspapers never got hold of that eccentricity of hers ; it would have been no use as a Sarah Bernhardt story, yet nothing could have been more characteristic. She would always give *personal* service, the most precious gift of all.

On one of my visits to Paris I caught a bad chill and had to stay within doors for a week. Sarah was at once to the rescue.

" You'll be miserable shut up in a stupid hotel room," she said. " If you must keep to the house, there is my studio ; you can go on with your work there and I will look after you."

So every morning I bundled myself into a *fiacre* and set in for the day at the Boulevard Pereire, Sarah driving me back on her way to the theatre in the evening. To burden herself thus for days with a gawky boy and his rudimentary French would have been an impossibility to the Sarah of legend, but was just like the real Sarah, than whom never was a kinder or truer friend.

There I painted two small portraits of her, one by the great wood fire, under the Clairin picture, one on a divan heaped with furs ; there I saw her rehearse ' La Dame aux Camélias,' and was most interested to note the absolute precision with which she built up her apparently spontaneous effects.

There was a new Armand Duval, and over and over again they practised the wonderful death-fall in the last act when the body of Marguerite used to drop from his arms with no more weight than a snowflake or a feather.

" I know I shall break my neck over that some day," observed Sarah cheerfully. " If Armand does not keep tight hold of my hand as I swing round I'm done for."

But the thought did not seem to depress her, and the new Armand held tight as requested and acquitted himself well throughout. He was Camille Dumény, who later made a fine position for himself on the Paris stage, and he and I soon became friends.

I have pleasant memories of *déjeuners* at his little flat near the Comédie Française, for he was a great lover of music and had considerable skill as a pianist and a sister with a voice, a combination which made for harmony.

Her tastes lay in the direction of the florid and dramatic, but Duményk knew my preferences and would say, after an outburst of ' Samson et Delilah,' " But now—for him—some Gluck," and we would plunge into the calm deeps of ' Orphée,' ' Armide ' and ' Iphigénie.'

To Sarah Bernhardt music was an unknown quantity and was without meaning.

" After all," she would say, " it is merely noise, and I recognise two kinds of noise—loud noises and soft noises : I don't particularly mind the soft, but I can't bear the loud. When people come here and bang the piano, I want to stop my ears and rush out of the room."

There I was able to join hands with her, for the professional pianist, let loose in a private room, is usually a torture and an outrage, and to me the piano itself is by no means an improvement upon the delicate instruments for which were written ' the gentle music of a bygone day.'

Alexandre Dumas (fils) came once or twice to the studio, though not to attend rehearsal. I do not think he ever rehearsed Sarah in Marguerite Gautier and I know that, before she took up the part, he had pronounced her to be unsuited to it, but he had evidently altered his opinion.

I used to stare at Dumas, trying to reconstruct his father out of the author of ' La Dame aux Camélias ' and ' La Femme de Claude ' and sometimes for a moment would appear a suggestion of that wild negro face, but fading back at once into an affable, pink gentleman with masses of white hair.

IT is perhaps a pity that this incomparable artist lingered upon the scenes of her triumphs so long that a new generation of playgoers learned to associate her illustrious name with a tiny, shrouded figure that tottered through an act or two, chanting dreamily like an echo of past sweetness, or uttering short, raucous cries with the shreds of an exhausted voice. For those who had known her in her great days these performances had an interest that was bitter-sweet, they brought up evergreen memories of beauty and melody, but to the new-comer they must have conveyed an entirely false impression of the greatest actress of our time.

To my mind her claim to this title is beyond dispute. Towards the end of her supreme period critics began to weary because she appeared so much in the clap-trap, stagy dramas of Sardou, though whenever she was seen in work worthy of her she resumed all her old sovereignty. They began to carp at what had charmed them for so long and to say that the much-hymned ' golden voice '—a soft chant, little above a whisper, yet of a penetrating and bewildering sweetness—was a trick commonly practised by High Church curates, that it was no natural tone but a false voice.

Who ever said that it was not ?

Sarah Bernhardt herself told me that she had hit upon this false voice as a means of saving her natural voice, which was, in her youth, easily exhausted ; that she achieved it—as does the curate—by pitching the voice up in the head and producing it through the nose, and that, by alternating it with her natural utterance, she could come safely through long tirades which otherwise would have left her speechless.

But to produce a false voice and to use it beautifully are two different things ; with the curate it is sing-song and dull monotony, from the lips of Sarah Bernhardt it was the cooing of doves, the running of streams, the falling of soft spring rain. And its carrying power !

I remember calling at the stage door of some theatre in London to leave a message and asking the doorkeeper whether the Act was finished or if Madame Sarah was still on the stage. The man merely said, " Listen." I listened, and up from the far-distant stage, along passages, up stairways, through heavy swing doors, came the murmuring chant of the *voix d'or*. No other voice was audible ; when the voice of Sarah ceased there was silence till it began again. " Rum, ain't it ? " commented the stage doorkeeper.

' Phédre ' was undoubtedly her greatest part. She brought all her powers to bear upon it and gave herself up to it in a way that was unusual with her.

I have often been amazed by her double consciousness when acting ; have found her at the close of a great scene weeping bitterly, panting, half fainting from the emotions through which she had apparently passed, yet with her mind centred upon some subject far away from the part she had been playing, as, for instance, some curious figure among the audience which had attracted her notice and to which she had been giving her almost undivided attention.

But ' Phédre ' she approached in a different spirit. She would speak little during the day before a performance and, if she could help it, not at all between the acts. She seemed actually to become the passion-tossed queen and to realise nothing outside her mimic kingdom.

Once I met her at the wings as she tottered off, hardly able to stand, after the terrible scene in which she urges Hippolyte to kill her. Her hands were covered with blood—blood was streaming down her white robes.

" What is the matter ? How have you hurt yourself ? " I cried.

She stared at me with unseeing eyes. " I have not hurt myself," she said slowly. " Nothing is the matter. What do you mean ? "

I pointed to the rapidly spreading stains and, with an effort, Sarah seemed to emerge from Phædra and looked in astonishment at her bleeding hands.

" It was the sword," she said at last. " It must have been Hippolyte's sword. I seized it and held it—it has cut deep into my hands—but I felt nothing at all—nothing."

This species of ecstasy, this careful husbanding of her strength always ceased with her last great scene of passion : the final act, though she played it as exquisitely as the rest, took nothing out of her.

" I have only to die," she told me. " The last act is nothing at all " ; and when her call came, she would cry ' Allons mourir ' and dance gaily off to her death.

Her art always made for beauty. I have seen many actresses agonise through the last moments of ' La Dame aux Camélias ' with heartrending fits of coughing and sick-room symptoms in full play.

Sarah passed lightly and mercifully over these details and struck an infinitely deeper and more touching note by the portrayal of an overwhelming happiness.

The change that came over the face of the dying woman when she heard of her lover's coming was a nightly miracle to which I never got accustomed. I have often watched it from the side, at about four yards distance, but it was no trick of the stage.

There was first a quick look at the bearer of the news, then the haggard face began to glow, the skin tightened all over it, smoothing away every line and giving an effect of transparency lit from within, the pupils of the eyes dilated, nearly covering the iris and darkly shining, the rigid lips relaxed and took soft childish curves, while from them came a cry that close at hand sounded no louder than a breath yet could be heard in the uttermost corner of the theatre. The frail body seemed to consume before our eyes in the flame of an unbearable joy and to set free the glorified and transfigured spirit.

But what need is there to sing the praises of Sarah Bernhardt, the actress ; to chronicle her tours and her triumphs ? Have not these things been inscribed, if not in letters of gold, at least in letters of printer's ink half a foot high upon the walls of the world ? Yet, though as artist she belonged to the public, her home life was very much her own and was passed in far greater privacy and seclusion than those of most English players who constantly show themselves in Society. Off the stage, most of her thoughts and affections were centred upon one beloved object, her son, Maurice, in whom her happiness began, continued and ended, and whom she had done her very best to spoil, from his childhood upwards—so far succeeding that he had no notion of the value of money or of the possibility of doing without anything which for the moment he happened to want.

To any hints as to such imperfections in the character of the paragon she would turn a deaf ear. " You must not blame Maurice," she would say. " It is not in the least his fault. That is how I have brought him up."

And truly, from her point of view, her bringing up was not unsuccessful, for he gave her what she most wanted from him, a great and devoted love. Even after his marriage he would come every day to see her ; if she were in England he would come over to her once a week ; he never forgot the little courtesies and attentions that were so dear to her, and I doubt whether she could have had a son who would have better satisfied her or given her greater happiness.

The rest of her home circle was patriarchal ; uncles, cousins, nieces appeared and reappeared ; there seemed an endless supply of them, and for them there was always open house in the Boulevard Pereire.

Her marriage in 1881 with a handsome Greek, Jaques Damala, had not been a success from the first, and very shortly after the wedding the happy pair had discovered that if they were to remain happy they must cease to be a pair as soon as possible, so each had gone his and her different way and for many years practically ceased to exist for each other.

I remember one spring morning in Paris, finding Sarah poring over patterns ; yards of chintz and strips of brocade surrounded her.

" Come and look," she cried. " I'm having my bed-room done up : what colour shall I choose ? "

" I like white for a bedroom," said I.

" White ? " said Sarah, in tones of deep amazement, " *white ?* "

" Well, why not ? " I asked.

" White ! " repeated Sarah, who seemed unable to get over the suggestion. " Why, it would be ridiculous. People would *laugh*. They would find it absurd ! "

" I didn't know the chintz had to be allegorical," I said. " What would be the proper thing then ? "

" I was thinking of this pattern of violets," said Sarah, who had of course made up her mind before asking advice. " Or this with the bunches of lilac."

" But," I began, " I don't see why lilac——"

" It's mauve," said Sarah. " Mauve and violet are half mourning, and if a woman of my age is not a widow she ought to be."

I wonder whether she recalled this speech when, less than two years afterwards, I helped her to carry her heavy crêpe cloak and bonnet under which she seemed extin-guished up to the violet room.

Sarah Bernhardt was hardly one who would be expected to shine in a domestic capacity, yet her kindness, care and patience during the last year of her husband's life could hardly have been excelled, and the more credit is due to her because the circumstances of his illness were especially calculated to alienate her sympathy. She hated weakness and had a horror of drugs, an almost morbid dread of surrendering self-control—and poor Damala had become a slave to morphia.

Latterly, he only seemed normal when under the influence of the drug, yet Sarah thought he was improving ; she fought hard to help him, and I felt that the shock which his sudden death undoubtedly was to her had been much increased by her sense of failure.

She told me that she had felt sure he was overcoming the habit ; she believed that she had been herself or sent to every chemist in Paris forbidding the sale of morphia to him, and he had finally become so much better that he was starting on a journey to Greece to see his mother.

On the last night before his departure, Sarah had started for a short tour in France, feeling that all was well with him. The next day she was recalled by the news of his death, and on unfastening his luggage, all ready packed for the journey, she found—stores of morphia. In spite of all care and supervision he had secreted enough to poison a regiment.

I had always liked poor Jaques Damala and got on well with him. He had been brought up in England and spoke English without a trace of foreign accent, and I really believe that it was the Englishman in him that attracted Sarah, who always had the most genuine love for England and the English ever since they, as she expressed it, ' let her alone.'

On her famous first visit to London with the Comédie Française she had not been let alone, but had seen English Society from the hunted lion's point of view and had found it very perplexing.

Many years afterwards she spoke of it to me : we were driving down the Knightsbridge Road on our way to see Burne-Jones, whose work Sarah loved. As we passed the Albert Hall she stared at it in vague recognition, then burst out laughing. " Ze la-ast R-rose of Somaire," she murmured.

I saw no connection between the Albert Hall and roses, last or otherwise, and asked for an explanation.

" That is what I recited—in English—at that dreadful-looking place when I was first in England."

" Recited—the Last Rose of Summer—but whatever for ? "

" I don't know," said Sarah thoughtfully. " People

did not seem to care what I recited so long as I recited something. I didn't understand it—and I'm sure *they* didn't—but everybody was delighted. I *was* so unhappy on that first visit : I hated it."

" Hated it ? " I exclaimed. " I thought it had been such a triumph. Why, it was the Year of Sarah Bernhardt : the Comédie might not have existed ; Coquelin, Got, Croizette, Mounet Sully might all have stayed at home. Everyone went to see Sarah, and if she did not appear they yelled for their money back."

" Yes," said Sarah, " I know now that they meant to be kind, but I didn't understand ; it was so different—I thought they were all trying to insult me. As you know," she went on, " in France and in most other countries, we artists—the Bohemians—live in a world of our own. No Society woman in Paris would think of asking me to her house except as an artist, and I should not ask her to mine. When I arrived here in England I had invitations from all sides, many from strangers who had no introduction to me. I thought—there must be some mistake—these people did not understand that I went my own way and that my way was perhaps not theirs. If they had made this mistake I would correct it. Whenever I went to any of these functions I took my little boy with me and always had myself announced as ' Mademoiselle Sarah Bernhardt and her son '—but nobody minded, not a bit. They crowded round and stared. I felt that they did not care for my art —for my work—but only wanted to stare because I was very thin and horrible stories were told about me. I was miserable."

" But—now ? "

" Now all is well. I have my own friends here in London as in Paris ; I am *chez-moi* and I am happy. The English are so faithful ; if they love you it is for always. That is unlike the Parisians—you may be doing your best work, but they will suddenly tire of you, and then the only thing is to leave them for awhile."

Certainly Madame Sarah was now prepared to be

pleased with everything English, even approving certain picture exhibitions to which I escorted her with grave doubts.

"We have things as bad as this in Paris," she said soothingly. "Quite as bad. Worse." And she was right.

For Burne-Jones's work she developed the greatest admiration and used to make expeditions with me to his studio. The admiration was mutual, for Sarah's pale face with its shadowed eyes and slow, mystic smile, the hieratic pomp of her golden robes, stiff with jewels, her garlands of jewelled flowers, her girdles of turquoise, opal and agate, seemed to come straight from the wonderland of romance which the artist loved to paint. She was, as Ellen Terry once said, more a symbol than a woman ; she was the wan, flame-robed queen of his ' Laus Veneris,' she was Morgan-le-Fay, and he was delighted to meet her among the, to him, completely uninteresting surroundings of nineteenth-century London.

In letters to me he always alluded to Her (spelt with a capital letter) in wildly exaggerated phrases and terms of ecstasy, but, though he could never refrain from such touches of burlesque, his joy in her art was very deep and genuine. Here are a few examples :

"Will you give the enclosed to the Supreme and Infinitely Glorious One, kneeling as you give it. She is not to dream of troubling to answer. Who am I, great powers, that she should take a moment's trouble ! "

"Yes, Wednesday will do lovelily and I'll be with you at 7, and She has but to fix her own time about Briar Rose and it shall be my time and everybody else's time."

"Tell me how long She stays and how long is to be seen and worshipped in this new play—for go I must though I shall be ill for a week after it."

"Even if I were free to-morrow I don't think I could meet Her at lunch.—I cannot speak French even to a waiter and what could I say to her ? "

" No, come with Her and gently interpret what She says to me
—and I will gape open-mouthed and be quite happy. AND AT THE
LAST MOMENT LET HER CHANGE HER MIND AND ALTER
THE DAY OR HOUR. ON NO ACCOUNT IS SHE TO BE
BORED OR TIRED BUT TO HAVE EVERYTHING HER OWN
LOVELY WAY AND AT A MINUTE'S NOTICE."

Sarah had a great desire to have her portrait painted
by him and sent me the following letter hastily scribbled
from Paris after one of her tumultuous departures from
these shores.

MON CHER GRAHAM,
Je suis désolée de n'avoir pu aller les jours que je vous avais
promis vous rendre visite. J'ai eu tellement à faire qu'il ne me restait
pas une minute. Je le regrette beaucoup mais je me console un peu
parceque vous allez venir à Paris. Voulez-vous me rendre une service, mon cher Graham. Je voudrais avoir mon portrait par Burne-
Jones. Voulez-vous lui demander ce qu'il me prendrait d'argent pour
le faire. Ce me sera une très grande joie de conserver et de laisser à
mon fils une œuvre de cet artiste de génie. Je compte sur vous pour
cette délicate commission. À bientôt. Je vous serre bien fort vos
deux mains. À bientôt.

Votre grande amie,
SARAH BERNHARDT.

I did my best as commission agent, but nothing came
of it. Burne-Jones hated painting portraits and, sooth to
say, painted them very badly ; only succeeding when he
found a sitter easily translatable into his ideal type.

I pointed out that Sarah especially lent herself to such
treatment ; that, if he so willed, she would sit to him as
the Empress Theodora, completely covered with jewels
from head to foot. He was visibly shaken by this vision
and promised to think of it, but his thought never materialised, much to my regret.

The portrait could hardly have failed to be interesting.
Not long afterwards Madame Sarah gave a further proof
of her partiality for things English by accepting and
putting into rehearsal Oscar Wilde's ' Salomé.'

Wilde had written the play in French, but with no

particular actress in his mind, and he and I had often talked over its possible production together.

"I should like," he said, throwing off the notion, I believe, at random, "I should like everyone on the stage to be in yellow."

It was a good idea and I saw its possibilities at once —every costume of some shade of yellow from clearest lemon to deep orange, with here and there just a hint of black—yes, you must have that—and all upon a pale ivory terrace against a great empty sky of deepest violet.

"A violet sky," repeated Oscar Wilde slowly. "Yes —I never thought of that. Certainly a violet sky and then, in place of an orchestra, braziers of perfume. Think— the scented clouds rising and partly veiling the stage from time to time—a new perfume for each new emotion!"

"Ye-es," said I doubtfully, "but you couldn't air the theatre between each emotion, and the perfumes would get mixed and smell perfectly beastly and—no, I don't think I care for the perfume idea, but the yellow scheme is splendid."

However, when Sarah accepted the play and was to put it on at once during her short London season, there was no time for the yellow scheme and she had to do what she could with the material ready to her hand. I was called in to help and advise.

"We must contrive it all somehow out of the 'Cléo-patre' costumes," said Sarah. "We can arrange and alter and get quite a good effect, I'm sure; but some day I hope to produce the play properly."

The Cleopatra dresses proved very useful and all was going well. For Sarah I had designed a golden robe with long fringes of gold, sustained on the shoulders by bands of gilt and painted leather which also held in place a golden breastplate set with jewels. On her head was a triple crown of gold and jewels and the cloud of hair flowing from beneath it was powdered blue.

"C'est la reine Hérodias qui a les cheveux poudrés de bleu," Oscar had read, to be at once interrupted by Sarah,

SKETCH OF THE AUTHOR by SARAH BERNHARDT
Drawn in Paris, 1888

" No, no ; Salomé's hair powdered blue. I *will* have blue hair ! "

This dress, stately, almost priestly, and indeed partly suggested by the sacerdotal robes of Aaron, seemed to me to express that royal ' Salomé, fille d'Hérodias, Princesse de Judée,' but when I saw the play given as an opera, Salomé ran in and out of her palace half naked, in the flimsy muslins of an Eastern dancing-girl.

" By the by," said I to Sarah. " The dance."

" What about it ? "

" I suppose you will get a *figurante* to go through it, won't you ?—veiled, of course, and with your blue hair ——"

" I'm going to dance myself," said Sarah.

" *You* are going to dance the Dance of Seven Veils ? "

" Yes."

" But—but how ? "

" Never you mind," said Sarah, with her enigmatic smile—and to this day I cannot imagine what she intended to do. For, alas, our labours were vain and ' Salomé,' banned by the Censor, was never seen upon the boards.

It was curiously thoughtless of Oscar Wilde not to have applied earlier for a licence which, in those days, he should have known was very unlikely to be granted, and Sarah, thinking of her wasted time and trouble, felt no little indignation. She had no notion that the play was yet in the balance or would not have undertaken the production, and the verdict of the Censor came as a complete surprise to her ; nevertheless, she put aside her wrath to condole very kindly with the poet in his disappointment.

Now, for a time I will take leave of Madame Sarah in one of her happy hours.

In 1907 she was ill, she began to feel her marvellous powers failing her ; in 1908 she discovered the cause and underwent an operation in Paris.

On her next visit to London I called on her with a friend and, missing her, was coming down the stairs of the hotel when I saw the well-known figure in advance of me. " There she is," I said, but my friend looked incredulous. " That is not Sarah Bernhardt—that is a young girl." Nevertheless it was Sarah.

That night I saw her in ' Phédre ' at her very best, wonderful as ever before, and I went round to speak with her after the play. Many old friends were with her, Jean Richepin—whose play, ' Le Chemineau,' was then running at His Majesty's Theatre—Georges Clairin, and others.

I stared at her, my astonishment absolutely banishing my manners. " But—but it's ridiculous," I blurted out.

" Yes," said Sarah, gravely looking at herself in a long mirror. " Yes, it's ridiculous. That is the word. I can hardly believe it yet. I feel that I have been summoned before le bon Dieu and he has said to me, ' Well, Sarah Bernhardt, you have been a very good girl on the whole —you have made the most of your time—you shall have your youth back again.' "

For there she stood, the slender, pathetically lovely Phædra of old, a miracle for all men to see.

ON our return from abroad my mother took a house in Rutland Gate, where she 'lived very happily ever after' like the good folk of fairy-tale, and I went back to Albert Moore, in whose studio I spent two more years of steady work.

I was gradually promoted until I began to be of a little use to my master and entrusted, to my deep satisfaction, with the making of certain flower and drapery studies for his pictures.

His ideas of housekeeping were still unchanged, the spiders and the cats rollicked unreproved, but I was now accustomed to them and minded them no more than he.

My dog, Mouton, who always came and went with me, was a new feature in the establishment, but luckily he and Moore's dog, Fritz, struck up a surly friendship, so all was harmony.

Those were very happy years for me ; at the studio the kindly dogs and the gentle, earnest Albert Moore, and at home the delightful companionship of my mother, of whom in earlier days I had never seen enough, owing to her many ties. She had a mind richly stored with knowledge but eternally youthful ; we were in absolute sympathy although we disagreed upon almost all subjects, this making for lively discussion and the truest friendship.

She was very popular, and between what she called my 'artist lot' and her more solidly respectable circle we had a heterogeneous collection of friends who interested and amused both us and each other.

" I can't think how all your 'mixed varieties' shake down so well together," someone observed to my mother. " Many of them wouldn't speak to each other anywhere else."

" Really ? " said my mother placidly. " Well, when people come to my house I expect them to behave themselves—and they do."

I think it was in '87 that I first made the acquaintance of Oscar Wilde at the studio of a friend, though I had known him well by sight for years.

He was not often to be found in studios, for, despite his attitude as the Apostle of Art, he did not really either care for or understand pictures, a fact that painters very quickly found out. He could and did talk bravely of them before the laity, but before artists he was perforce silent —and he did not like to be silent. He was the *littérateur* before all, art was literature to him, life was literature, and, in the end, he gave a literary touch even to death by murmuring, " Doctor, I fear that you are encouraging me to die beyond my means."

He was an artist in words only : in line, colour or music his taste was merely a cultivated one and by no means impeccable ; though in a letter to me he once stated a preference for the Art of Painting, only, I think, in order to turn a phrase gracefully.

" I wish I could draw like you," he wrote, " for I like lines better than words and colours more than sentences. However, I console myself by trying now and then to put ' The Universe ' into a sonnet. Some day you must do a design of the Sonnet, a young man looking into a strange crystal that mirrors all the world : poetry should be like a crystal ; it should make life more beautiful and less real." .

As conversationalist he was brilliant. He had both wit and humour, a combination not often met with, and being tempered with humour, his wit was never unkind. When, in little newspaper skirmishes with Whistler, the latter became excited and, whipping the buttons off the foils, lunged with the point, Wilde was helpless : he would not wrangle in public, rancour and bitterness amused him not at all ; among his numerous entities he was a gentleman.

A born *raconteur* he certainly was, the only one I have ever met. His stories seemed to grow naturally out of the general conversation and not to interrupt it ;

their length was not perceptible and his hearers did not realise how long they had been silent.

One day the world was especially black for me. I had violent toothache and so bad a cold that I could not go to the dentist, who had kindly consented to drop in upon me 'after hours' and relieve me of my tooth. For him I sat waiting, a mass of aching sneezing misery, when the door opened and 'Mr. Oscar Wilde' was announced.

I suppose my expression was eloquent, for Mr. Wilde at once said, "You're not pleased to see me."

"The person does not exist whom I should be pleased to see," I snapped. "I hate everybody and wish they were dead!"

"Just so," said Mr. Wilde, seating himself comfortably.

"I said that no one but the dentist was to be admitted," I wailed, "but that's a new man and I suppose he thought——"

"*What* did he think?" cried Wilde, for once genuinely moved. "D'you mean he thought that I—*I*——?"

I nodded.

"But—but I don't look like a dentist, do I?"

"O, I don't know," said I, soothingly. "Perhaps in the half-light you might pass——"

"Don't!" cried Wilde. "It's awful. I feel as if I *were* a dentist! Let's talk about something else."

And then happened a really wonderful thing. Oscar Wilde could not bear sick people, he would not have crossed the road to see one if he could help it, but—I really think to convince himself that he was not a dentist—he started talking and telling stories so brilliantly that for an hour and a half on end I laughed without ceasing, and when the real dentist arrived I had no toothache and no cold left; I had laughed them away.

I particularly loved his obviously apocryphal histories of undoubtedly non-existent friends or relatives.

His 'well-known facts' and 'perfectly true stories' I

received with a certain amount of hesitation, but when he began a tale with—" Did I ever tell you about my cousin Lionel ? "—or " I was only yesterday thinking of that strange thing that happened to poor Uncle Theodore " —I realised that I was in for a ' good thing ' and felt sure that from beginning to end the flow of the narrative would be unruffled by any breath of veracity.

These tales would often be direct improvisations ; one could sometimes see them coming and even detect their source of suggestion in surrounding objects ; sometimes they would be told to create a desired atmosphere, some-times to gain time.

On one occasion he was staying with me for a few days in the country, where he was like a fish out of water. We had been for what I considered a short stroll and were coming back through a wood, Wilde curiously quiet and toiling along with an expression of deep discomfort. Suddenly he brightened.

" Let's sit down," he said.

" What for ? " I enquired.

" Well, what do people usually sit down for ? "

" You can't be tired," I said, sternly. " We have been no distance and we can't sit down now. We shall never get home if we do."

" I shall never get home if we don't," said Oscar, seating himself with an air of finality. " Do sit down. Look here—if you'll sit down I'll tell you a story. Did I ever tell you about George Ellison and the Palmist ? "

" No," said I, " and I don't know George What's-his-name."

" O yes, you do," said Oscar. " You must. Well——" And the story began which was afterwards worked up into ' Lord Arthur Saville's Crime.'

On another day I found him talking very nicely and feelingly to my mother about his Aunt Jane.

" I didn't know you had an Aunt Jane," said I.

Wilde looked at me sadly. " No," he said, " I daresay not. She was a very old lady, I hardly remember her myself. But I am sure that I have often told you about Aunt Jane's Ball."

" Never," said I.

" Aunt Jane, poor Aunt Jane," he repeated, very slowly, I suppose giving himself time to visualise Aunt Jane, who was quite evidently new-born within the last two minutes.

" Poor Aunt Jane was very old and very, very proud, and she lived all alone in a splendid, desolate old house in County Tipperary. No neighbours ever called on Aunt Jane and, had they done so, she would not have been pleased to see them. She would not have liked them to see the grass-grown drives of the demesne, the house with its faded chintzes and suites of shuttered rooms, and herself, no longer a toast and beauty, no more a power in the county-side, but a lonely old woman who had outlived her day.

" And from year to year she sat alone in her twilight, knowing nothing of what passed in the world without. But one winter, even Aunt Jane became aware of a stir in the air, a wave of excitement sweeping over the neighbourhood. The New people were coming into the New house on the hill and were going to give a great Ball, the like of which had never been seen. The Ryans were enormously rich and—' Ryans ? ' said Aunt Jane. ' I don't know the Ryans. Where do they come from ? ' Then the blow fell. The Ryans came from nowhere in particular and were reported on good authority to be ' in business.'

" ' But,' said Aunt Jane, ' what are the poor creatures thinking of ? Who will go to their Ball ? ' ' Everybody will go,' Aunt Jane was assured. ' Everybody has accepted. It will be a wonderful affair.'

" When Aunt Jane fully realised this her wrath was terrible. This is what things had come to in the neighbourhood then—and it was her fault. It had been for her to lead ; she had brooded in her tent when she should have been up and doing battle. And then Aunt Jane made her great resolve.

"*She* would give a Ball—a Ball the like of which had never been imagined : she would re-enter Society and show how a *grande dame* of the old school could entertain. If the County had so far forgotten itself, she herself would rescue it from these impertinent interlopers.

"And instantly she set to work. The old house was repainted, refurnished, the grounds replanted ; the supper and the band were ordered from London and an army of waiters engaged. Everything should be of the best—there should be no question of cost. All should be paid for ; Aunt Jane would devote the rest of her life to the paying ; but now money was as nothing—she spent with both hands.

"At last the great night arrived. The demesne was lit for two miles with coloured lamps, the hall and staircase were gorgeous with flowers, the dancing-floor smooth and shining as a mirror.

"The bandsmen were in their places and bowed deeply as Aunt Jane, in a splendid gown and blazing with diamonds, descended in state and stood at the ballroom door.

"There she waited. Time went on, the footmen in the hall, the waiters in the supper-room began to look at each other, the band tuned up two or three times to show its zeal, but no guests arrived.

"And Aunt Jane, in her beautiful gown, waited at the ballroom door. Eleven—twelve—half-past twelve.

"Aunt Jane swept a deep curtsy to the band. 'Pray go and have your supper,' she said. 'No one is coming.'

"Then she went upstairs and died. That is to say, she never again spoke a word and was dead in three days. And not for some considerable time after her death was it discovered that Aunt Jane had quite forgotten to send out any invitations."

Oscar Wilde's telling of the tale was admirable ; his attitude as affectionate nephew well sustained, his grief chastened but genuine.

My mother was quite affected. "Poor, dear woman,"

she said as he left the room, " what a comfort it is to feel quite sure that she never existed."

When committed to paper, his tales lost much of their charm, and I think that most of his written matter is too imitative to be long lived.

It was as if he said to himself before sitting down to write, " This story shall be by Hans Andersen, this by Flaubert, this by Maeterlinck." He never tried the effect of one by Oscar Wilde.

In his plays he gave his originality more rein, except with regard to plots, in which he seemed to take no great interest ; he did not care how ancient or stage-worn a situation might be ; what his characters did was of little moment, what they said was everything. I well remember, on the first night of ' Lady Windermere's Fan,' the effect upon the audience of the stream of whimsical, elusive flippancies, dialogue far more artificial than the most ponderous stage talk, yet seeming natural because of its novelty. It amused and amazed.

I had seen Wilde on the day before and had found him full of a new idea. " You have your place for the *première* ? That's right. Now I want you to do something. Go to Such-and-such a shop and order a green carnation buttonhole for to-morrow night. No, I know there's no such thing, but they arrange them somehow at that shop ; dye them, I suppose. I want a good many men to wear them to-morrow—it will annoy the public."

" But why annoy the public ? "

" It likes to be annoyed. A young man on the stage will wear a green carnation ; people will stare at it and wonder. Then they will look round the house and see every here and there more and more little specks of mystic green. ' This must be some secret symbol,' they will say. ' What on earth can it mean ? ' "

" And what does it mean ? " I asked.

" Nothing whatever," said Oscar, " but that is just what nobody will guess."

And certainly, what with the green carnations and an

elaborate burlesque speech by the author, in which he congratulated the audience upon their performance and remarked upon the super-excellence of his play and how much he had enjoyed it, the production, apart from its real merit, achieved a *succès de scandale* which launched it on the fair tide of popularity.

One day Oscar Wilde came to me all enthusiasm about a new play which he was writing.

" It's wonderful," he said. " It is in French."

" Why in French ? "

" Because a play ought to be in French. It opens like this " ; and producing some notes he read aloud to me the first few pages of ' Salomé.' One was ill prepared for Wilde's serious moods, they were so rare : as I listened I decided that this could not be the result of one of them.

What he was reading was a burlesque of Maeterlinck, very clever, very delicate, but nevertheless a burlesque.

" Comme la princesse Salomé est belle ce soir ! " read Oscar, chanting the phrases with great satisfaction. " Vous la regardez toujours. Vous la regardez trop. Il ne faut pas regarder les gens de cette façon—il peut arriver un malheur."

By this time I thought I was safe and laughed approvingly. Oscar looked enquiry. "That's a funny bit," said I, with a complimentary chuckle, " it's exactly like——"

" Like what ? "

" Like Maeterlinck, of course : didn't you mean it to be ? "

" How perfectly odious you are sometimes," observed Oscar in his spoilt-child voice—and lo, I had made a great mistake. He had been reading his *magnum opus* and I had found it funny. I was out of favour for some little time, but I have never been able to alter my opinion. Take Maeterlinck and Flaubert from Wilde's ' Salomé ' and what remains ?

Not very much except a distortion of the legend which seems to me to spoil its pathos and interest. Salome, the schoolgirl, just home for the holidays, showing off her accomplishments at her mother's bidding, all unwitting of what ' that one dancing of her feet ' would bring forth, is an arresting little figure ; Salome, the wanton, dancing away the life of the man who scorned her and gloating over his severed head, is a theatrical commonplace.

Yet so firmly has Wilde's version of the story taken hold upon the public imagination that it is now widely accepted as Holy Writ. Though why holy ?

It has been interesting to me to note how, in the years that have passed since his death, the memory of the real Oscar Wilde has faded and has been replaced by a strange simulacrum, half invented by the curious, half dictated by the man himself.

In course of time his self-estimate as the Lost Leader of Art and Culture in England, set forth in the pages of ' De Profundis,' has come to be adopted as history.

" I was a man," he wrote, " who stood in symbolic relation to the Art and Literature of my age. Few ever hold such a position in their own lifetimes and have it so acknowledged."

Few indeed, and of those few most certainly Wilde was never one. His ' serio-comic ' position as High Priest of Æstheticism was won in drawing-rooms by means of persistently making a fool of himself, a method which to him must have presented many difficulties and which he dropped altogether after a few years of youthful high spirits.

But the opinion on Art of the set before which he had posed was a negligible quantity, and the reputation when won actually stood in his way as a serious writer and prevented a wide acknowledgment of his great natural gifts.

Among the workers he was never welcomed wholeheartedly as one of themselves. The painters, as I have said, would have none of him as a critic, literary men regarded him with suspicion, first as a desultory amateur, then as an incurable plagiarist, and much of his delicate and charming work was not accorded anything like its full meed of praise.

All this is now forgotten, and with it the boyish good-humour, the almost child-like love of fun, the irresponsible gaiety and lightness of touch in which lay his unquestionable charm ; the nimble-witted Irishman has vanished with the fastidious stringer of lovely words upon long melodious phrases, and gradually has been evolved a sinister figure, half sinner, half saint, unrecognisable to anyone who had known him, a creation of pure fiction, wholly foreign and mythical.

Stirred by the hopeless tragedy of his end, imagination has worked backwards from it, fashioning a being fit for so sombre a fate.

The actual Oscar Wilde is no longer remembered.

As I stood with Ellen Terry in the studio of Epstein, the sculptor, before the tomb to be erected to his memory in Père Lachaise, a ponderous crag of stone whereon a huge Sphinx, at once Deity and Monster, with crowned head and wide unseeing eyes, rushed blindly forward upborne upon mighty wings, the incongruity struck me with such force that, before I was aware, I had laughed. The most ephemeral of triflers weighed down by all the gigantic symbols of Eternity, the mouse crushed beneath its mother the mountain.

THOUGH for many years I had worshipped from afar and had been, so to speak, brought up in the shadow of the Lyceum Theatre, it was not until a memorable evening in the winter of '87 that I first met Ellen Terry.

I was at a dance, and I remember that it was a dull dance, and I was making preparations to leave it when there was a sudden stir at the door—something was happening—something in the nature of a sunrise.

At the entry stood a golden figure which seemed actually to diffuse light, the golden figure which I had first beheld in the palace of Belmont.

A fairer vision than Ellen Terry, then at the zenith of her loveliness, cannot be imagined : she shone with no shallow sparkle or glitter, but with a steady radiance that filled the room and had the peculiar quality of making everybody else invisible.

From after experience I feel sure that she was in act of whispering to her hostess, " Now don't you bother about me and I'll just slip in without being noticed and sit down somewhere "—a feat which might have been performed with equal ease by the sun at noonday.

Somehow or another I got myself presented and indeed, though I did not at the moment realise it, the meeting must have been arranged by Providence expressly for my benefit, for neither before nor after have I ever again seen Ellen Terry at a dance—except at her sister's house, which does not count.

Though I could only secure a few words I at once fell completely under the matchless charm of her personality ; the stuffy room and the jigging music faded, leaving only Ellen Terry, who might have stepped in from some dim garden, her arms full of lavender and lad's-love and bringing with her a freshness, a breeze from the open sky.

What was it that made her so unlike any other actress ; why had the stage left no mark upon her, for never was woman less stagy or artificial ? I think it was because, at the most critical and receptive age of nineteen, when most young players are working up towards their first success and living wholly in the world behind the footlights, she left the stage and gave what would be considered her best years to a real life, away in the country, far from theatres and all concerning them.

During these six years, which I have often heard called the lost years of Ellen Terry, she lived through those emotions which she was to portray later on ; she knew great happiness and keen suffering, glad tranquillity, fear, loneliness, and even actual want ; she learned in her sorrow to creep close to the heart of Nature and to draw from it help and comfort, in her joy to turn to Nature for an answering smile.

That quiet but eventful time was very sacred to her. She spoke of it seldom, to me not at all during the first years of our friendship, but I know that it was often in her thoughts, and later on, especially when we were together in the country, perhaps jogging along the lanes in a donkey-cart or sitting in the spring copses among the bluebells, she would often say, " This is like Harpenden days," and would tell me tales of those hidden years which had so developed her character and her art. Most of the tales were sad, yet like Sophie Arnould, she held in loving memory ' *les beaux jours quand j'étais si malheureuse.*'

Often, during that period, she had felt the pinch of poverty and had not known where to look for supplies. She had sat up many a night doing copies of elaborate architectural drawings for which, when finished, she would get a guinea, and this fine work, done by very insufficient light, strained her eyes and produced a weakness in them which ever afterwards troubled her.

One dismal evening, she told me, everything had looked unusually black. She had been alone for many days, funds were very low, she was ill and anxious. She had harnessed the little rough pony and driven to meet the last train, hoping that someone, half expected, would come by it and put an end to the fears and the loneliness.

But the last train played her false as it had often done before, and she drove back through the dark lanes wearied out in body and brain. She would not trouble about supper, she would creep into bed and rest—rest was all she could think of. She would go straight to bed—but there was the pony. The pony must be unharnessed and rubbed down, and though she wanted no supper, the pony must have his. So the weary girl led the weary pony into his stall and made him comfortable ; shook up his bed, gave him his drink of water, and finally, raising herself on tiptoe, began to pull down his supper of hay into the manger from the rack above her head. As she did so, out of the hay and straight down her back fell a mouse.

We have heard of the patience of Job, but it is not on record that the patriarch at the supreme crisis of his afflictions had a mouse down his back. Had this been so we might have heard less of his patience. It was the Thing Too Much : the girl's brave spirit for once was conquered. Never had she been so tired, never so unhappy, never so utterly alone ; here was the darkest hour of her life—and she had a mouse down her back. It was her nadir. Never, before or after, did she touch the misery of that moment.

On another night, returning from one of those forlorn expeditions to the station, her lamp had gone out and the night was pitch dark. In a lonely lane a man's rough voice suddenly called out some obviously useless question. She answered shortly, heard the rough voice mutter, " My God, it's a gal ! " and the next minute a man had sprung into the cart beside her—she felt his hot, whisky-laden breath on her cheek.

Drawing back as far as she could, she clubbed the whip and brought down the handle with all her might upon the place where she judged his head ought to be. It was evidently there—for after a minute's pause something dropped heavily upon the road and she, whipping up the pony, fled away into the darkness.

She never heard anything more of the matter, so the man must have quickly recovered, but he probably remembered his meeting with the ' gal ' in the dark lane for some time to come.

A third dismal tale was of returning home through a wood, late on a dark night, ill and nervous, starting at the snapping of a twig or at the tall shadows cast by her lantern. As she reached the middle of the wood a shining object in her way attracted her attention ; she lowered the lantern and found herself looking into the bright eyes of a large frog. Behind him sat another frog, also solemnly staring, beyond him still more ; she was in the midst of a circle of frogs which swarmed over the path in all directions. When she had thoroughly taken in these details she dropped the lantern, which immediately went out, leaving her in pitch darkness.

Even afterwards, in broad daylight, she was never able to make up her mind as to what she ought to have done. If she stepped forward—no, that did not bear thinking of. But the way back presented equal difficulties. What she finally did was to feel about for a clear space and then to sit down and wait shiveringly through the long hours of darkness until dawn began to steal between the branches and the frog party broke up.

Against the misery of this enforced vigil may be set the joy of another, entered upon willingly.

She had been talking with one whose opinion carried great weight for her and he had objected to some trivial remark as unworthy.

" That thought is small," he had said, " and you should have no room for small thoughts. Thought should be great."

" How can I make my thoughts great ? " asked Ellen Terry. " What must I do ? "

" For one whole night," he said, " you must lie out in the fields alone and watch the sky from dusk to dawn."

So all night long the girl lay on the short grass of the common looking up into the great mystery of the night.

No sleep came to her, but the stillness and the awe and the beauty sank into her and brought rest and knowledge.

The wonderful pageant of the heavens passed over her from its rising to its setting, the moon drifted away behind the coppice and the stars shrank and grew pale in the dark hour before the dawn, but the watcher still lay there, wide-eyed and happy, until in the grey of the morning she crept to her room and fell asleep.

What she had learnt that night she could not tell ; she could not remember, but she *knew*, and the knowledge remained with her. What she had learnt was something of proportion, something of rhythm, of reverence, of melody —she could not formulate, only feel, but the memory never faded, and all through her life she found courage and peace in a vision of stars passing across the sky above Fallows Green.

And I think it was then that she first fell in love with night, for, though golden Portia and dazzling Beatrice might suggest the sun at his height, yet Ellen Terry was a daughter of the night, happy in its shadow and mystery and loving the moon with a strange ecstasy which I have never met with in another.

She was weary, the moon rested her ; she was sad, the moon consoled her ; she was anxious, the moon gave her peace ; like the Princess Daylight of the fairy-tale she seemed to wax and to wane with it, and only at the full of the moon was the true Ellen Terry at her very best.

The moon magic stayed with her all her life, and I have a letter in which she rejoices that her youngest grandson is able to share it with her.

"—Good Lord, that November moon ! I had to pull little Teddy out of his bed one night so that he should not miss the teeming loveliness. His face in the pale light I shall never forget. The delicacy of it—so grave and so adoring ! His morning reading has been a great bond between us, but the Moon—He made me promise to wake him up once a month to see the sight. . . ."

Yet I know that, however sympathetic might be her companion, the moon spell always drew her back to Harpenden and Fallows Green. Once, in the after-years, I was sitting with her in an orchard under the full moon : she had been silent for a long while, quietly content and peaceful.

Suddenly I turned to look at her, thinking she spoke. Beside me sat a girl of eighteen or nineteen, the wistful face, half child, half woman, which we know in the pictures of Watts, gazed up at the moon between the apple branches, the lips moved in whispered speech.

I got up softly and left her—three are always an awkward number.

It is seldom given to any of us to step back across the years and to re-live even a few moments of the past, yet Ellen Terry experienced something akin to this in 1912.

Her thoughts had been dwelling much upon early days —I think the moon must have been unusually bright and near the full—and she felt a sudden longing to revisit the place of memories. She would go by herself that she might walk alone with her dreams and reconstruct old times out of what she might find left of old places.

She found much, for the world had stood very still at Harpenden, the countryside had escaped development and 'improvement' and still kept its rustic quiet and peace.

She passed along the well-remembered lanes, repeopling the farms and cottages with the folk of the past, now, she supposed, all swept away : she had been very young in her Harpenden days and the neighbours had seemed to her, for the most part, well stricken in years.

A farm gate stood open and she looked along the path into the dim old house. This used to be—ah, yes— Thrales's. The Thrales, two old men and a still older sister, had lived there—all that were left of the famous Thrales of Streatham.

They had fired the imagination of the young Ellen Terry. Here were undoubted Thrales. Not exactly the right Thrales perhaps, but still Thrales—and old—and if they had not personally known Doctor Johnson and Sir Joshua and Mrs. Siddons, or made Sophy Stretfield cry for

ELLEN TERRY

Pastel study by THE AUTHOR, 1891.   (Irving's " Ellen in Heaven")

the benefit of Fanny Burney, one could pretend they had, which would be very satisfying.

But the Thrales had proved uninspiring. They were heavy and slow, admitting to vague ' papers ' concerning the family stored in an attic, but taking no interest in them.

They were wholly bucolic, had gone back to the land for good, and were far less alive than dear, bright, dead and gone Mrs. Thrale of Streatham.

No, it must be confessed that the Thrales had conspicuously failed to make good from the Dreamland point of view ; still—the gate was open—no one was about— Ellen Terry would look once more into the low, dark kitchen.

As she passed into its shadow she seemed to leave the present outside. Within the room all was unchanged. The old furniture stood in the old places, the old clock ticked in the corner, but the big old Thrale men no longer strode about ; the house was silent and empty—she started as she realised that it was not empty.

There, on a chair by the fire sat what seemed the oldest thing of all : shrivelled and bent it sat there ; its claw-like hands folded, its eyes fixed curiously upon her, the shadow of what once had been a woman.

The two gazed at each other silently until from the old, old creature in the chair came a far-away voice. " Well, Nelly," she said.

" Well, Miss Thrale," whispered Nelly, for Ellen Terry had vanished, leaving little Nelly from Mackery End standing there half afraid of the dim room and the shadow in the chair.

The old woman sat still, looking across the gulf of the years which to her seemed the space of a day and a night. She had, as the neighbours said, ' touched her hundred ' a few days before and Time had passed her by. So Nelly had run in again. She had been in yesterday, had she not ? So why——?

Old Miss Thrale still gazed, searching her memory.

What was Nelly doing in her kitchen again so soon?
Suddenly her face brightened.

"You want to see the Tiger?" she said.

"The—the *Tiger*?"

"Yes," said Miss Thrale. "You may run upstairs
by yourself and look at it."

Ellen Terry gasped slightly. She had been searching
for the Gate of Dreams, and behold it stood wide.

"The Tiger? Upstairs?" she faltered.

"Yes," said Miss Thrale, more sharply. "*You* know
where it is. In the cupboard on the landing."

In the cupboard—of course! The long-forgotten
Tiger, once escaped from a menagerie and shot by one
of the Thrales as it prowled along the lane! The long-
forgotten cupboard where its stuffed but fearsome presence
lurked, mysterious and mothy!

"I don't think I'll look at the Tiger to-day, thank you,
Miss Thrale. I only wanted——" But it was evident
that Miss Thrale took no further interest in what was
wanted.

The spark of recognition had leaped up quickly, to be
as quickly extinguished; the little scene from the long-
ago was played out and Ellen Terry passed softly out again
into the sunlight and the world of To-day.

All her life the atmosphere of the open country was
about her: though she never played the part upon the
stage, her favourite rôle in private was The Country Girl.
For the town and all the town could give she cared not a
jot, she delighted in her friends but hated what is called
Society, she loved companionship but shrank from the
crowd and contrived a thousand ways of escape from it.

She had a collection of odd little cottages in unlikely
places within reach of London and was perpetually disappearing into one or another of these burrows.

The first one to which I was admitted was a tiny public-
house on the outskirts of Uxbridge, on the road leading
to Chalfont St. Giles, and thither I was bidden one day in
early spring for 'a breath of fresh air.'

The Audrey Arms stood in a row of cottages and next to another little ' pub ' which sold much better beer and drew most of the custom. Ellen Terry was obliged by her lease to keep the business going, but had established a reputation for ' swipes ' at the Audrey Arms which filled the coffers of the establishment next door. Only one customer dropped in during my visit when we were at luncheon in the bar parlour and I stepped out to serve him. It was my sole experience as potman and I trust that I gave satisfaction and good measure.

Later on I was admitted to other retreats : the funny little cottage in Kingston Vale, the Tower Cottage, Winchelsea, a house built into the ivied wall of the ancient Town Gate, and, best of all, the lovely old farm at Small Hythe, with its huge timbers and cool low rooms full of the scent from a great bed of Madonna lilies which blew through and through the knot holes of the wooden walls.

The perfect simplicity of Ellen Terry's life and mind was in curious contrast to the exotic complexities of her great sister artist, Sarah Bernhardt, but I noticed that, in their relations to each other, while Sarah knew little or nothing about Ellen, Ellen understood Sarah completely and, as a natural result, liked her greatly.

Once, during a performance of Sarah's, I was taking the air outside the theatre for a minute. The play was ' L'Aiglon,' during which I often required air. I was still under the golden spell of Sarah, impressed by the solemn ritual that surrounded her, the bowing servitors, the *jeune premier* in waiting to lead her from the stage ; I was reflecting that I had never met anyone else outside the classic drama who required to be ' led.'

Bump ! A large basket collided abruptly with my back ; behind it was the lovely wistful face of Ellen Terry.

" What have you got there ? " I enquired.

" Eggs," replied Miss Terry, as if it were the most natural thing in the world for England's leading actress to struggle along Charles Street at eleven p.m. laden with eggs. " I'm out early. Is Sally B. dead yet ? "

I gathered that she wished to know if Madame Bernhardt had finished her last act and replied in the negative.

" Then let's try for the back row of the pit."

We obtained admission for ourselves and the eggs and found Madame Sarah by no means moribund but still haranguing the ghosts in the interminable vision scene.

At its close we went round to see her and she enquired where we were sitting. " In the pit," said Ellen Terry. Madame Sarah was really shocked. That a sister goddess should watch her from the pit pained her : what, she wondered, were goddesses coming to in these levelling days. She would give us stalls—a box. Ellen Terry didn't want a box. " *Il faut que nous*—go on, you tell her," she said. " We've left the eggs in the pit and we *must* go back," said I in the French tongue.

Madame Sarah was accustomed to my French and sometimes understood quite a lot of it, but now she looked hopelessly at me. " Eggs ? " she repeated vaguely, and really seemed relieved when we left, evidently anticipating a mental crisis.

A woman friend of Ellen Terry's, who knew her perhaps better than anyone else, once gave a wonderfully true description of her.

" She is like a garden of spring flowers," she said, " a garden without a hedge round it. And cheap excursion trains come in and the trippers swarm over the paths, stubbing up the flowers and strewing the grass with orange-peel and ginger-beer bottles. We think that the garden can bloom no more, but next morning there is not a footmark on the grass, not a flower disturbed, not a single drop of dew brushed away."

OUR LADY OF THE LYCEUM

OF Ellen Terry, the actress, Our Lady of the Lyceum as Oscar Wilde used to style her, what a series of wonderful pictures lives in the memory. Ophelia, a pale shadow with bright hair, the perfect Portia, effulgent, golden, Camma of 'The Cup,' beautiful exceedingly, but too frail for the great scene of denunciation in the Temple of Artemis, Juliet, Viola, Beatrice, Imogen, a very pageant of fair women shown in the likeness of one fair woman.

Who shall say which part became her best?

As Portia I think she must have realised almost everyone's ideal—she *was* Portia; as Beatrice she realised something so far above *my* ideal that I could hardly recognise the character, for I have the bad taste not to admire Beatrice.

For the (in my eyes) noisy, pushing, unmannerly, Messinine minx Ellen Terry contrived to substitute a wholly delightful creature whose bubbling and infectious high spirits were never allowed to hide her gentle kindliness and well-bred grace of manner.

From what she evolved her I have never made out; I cannot find her in the play, even with the aid of the crib supplied by Miss Terry, but I hope that my blindness is at fault and that Shakespeare really wrote the part as she played it.

Many people said that her Beatrice was a foretaste of what her Rosalind might be, and surely this supports my theory, for what has Beatrice in common with 'heavenly Rosalind'? Dear me, how intensely Rosalind would have disliked the woman!

About the Lady Macbeth of Ellen Terry there was much diversity of opinion because she did not conform to the accepted Siddons tradition, but her view of the character was an entirely legitimate and logical one and supported by every line of the part. Driven on by love and ambition for her husband she determines at all costs to sweep away the one obstacle that bars his way to power;

she sees no further than the murder of Duncan and until
this is accomplished she is steel and adamant, allowing
no thoughts of pity or honour to weaken her purpose.
The murder done, her strength fails ; she cannot support
Macbeth in his lying tale or act out the scene of hypocritical grief ; she faints and is carried away and thence-
forward is but a weary, broken creature, flashing into
action for a moment at the interrupted banquet but
almost at once sinking back into apathy.

I can hear now the dull hopelessness of Ellen Terry's
voice as she mechanically answered Macbeth's, " What is
the night ? "—

" Almost at odds with morning, which is which."

while from her throne she watched the chill dawn-light
creep into the hall of feasting.

While she was studying the part a copy of the play was
lent to her annotated by Sarah Siddons and she was
much interested to find that the great actress had cut
out the swoon after Duncan's murder as ' too terribly
hypocritical,' her theory being that the faint was feigned
in order to show the grief of the hostess. This, of course,
may be the right reading, but Ellen Terry's led more
naturally to the rapid breakdown of mind and body
which followed the crime.

One note by Mrs. Siddons recorded what must have
been a marvellous effect. Against the great apostrophe
to the spirits of evil in Lady Macbeth's first scene she had
written, ' All this in a whisper.'

" Would it not be wonderful and terrible ? " said
Ellen Terry. " Of course it ought to be in a whisper
but *I* couldn't do it. There would be no use in my
trying. I have to get at it another way—but the whisper
is *right* ! "

She was always more than ready to admire another's
work. As Lady Macbeth her appearance was magnificent :
long plaits of deep red hair fell from under a purple veil
over a robe of green upon which iridescent wings of beetles

glittered like emeralds, and a great wine-coloured cloak, gold embroidered, swept from her shoulders.

The effect was barbaric and exactly right, though whence the wife of an ancient Scottish chieftain obtained so many oriental beetles' wings was not explained, and I remember Oscar Wilde remarking, " Judging from the banquet, Lady Macbeth seems an economical housekeeper and evidently patronises local industries for her husband's clothes and the servants' liveries, but she takes care to do all her own shopping in Byzantium."

As Queen Katherine, Ellen Terry again measured herself against the greatest of the Kembles and again was found by many to be wanting in force and weight.

In this play, both she and her great fellow-actor seemed to be a little misplaced ; Irving's Wolsey was a magnificent representation of a haughty Prince of the Church, but history gives us a very clear outline of Wolsey's appearance and personality and it is in direct opposition to Irving's. The great actor's pride, which seemed a consuming flame, was the pride of Lucifer, the rebel archangel, not the pride of the Ipswich butcher's son ; his ascetic face was that of a religious fanatic, pale with fasting and spiritual strife ; Wolsey loved good living and display, he was very much a man and a man of the world.

Irving's great moment, for me, was when, in his first passing across the stage, he turned and looked for a long moment at Buckingham. How Buckingham survived that moment I could never understand—I used to feel quite anxious for Johnston Forbes-Robertson. Luckily, in the part of Buckingham, the actor is unhampered by historical tradition. Buckingham may have been like a mediæval saint whose beautiful face above his black death robe recalled an exquisite early Italian carving in ivory, whose grand voice, ringing out between the strokes of the passing bell, drew all hearts towards him—he may or he may not. But Forbes-Robertson's Buckingham, possessing all these advantages, challenged no comparison and his scene of farewell was the triumph of the production.

Always nervous on a first night, Miss Terry was more than usually so in 'Henry VIII' and suddenly swept in upon me on the very day of the production in a highly distraught condition exclaiming, " I've just come in to tell you that I'm going to break down to-night. I can tell you the very line—it's in the scene with the two cardinals. I'm going to dry up—dead ! "

" But if you know the line—why dry up ? "

" I can't tell you why, but I know I shall," she said. And she did.

Her Cordelia captured all hearts. Lovely and gracious, she *was* Cordelia as she had been Portia, though I regret to say that, when studying the character, she wrote ' FOOL ' in large letters against the young lady's refusal to admit her love for her old father. Yet I am not sure that it was not as Imogen, the last great Shakespearean part played by her at the Lyceum, that she outdid all former achievements. Her scene of joy, on receiving the false letter, a joy so great that sorrow must needs be close behind, was absolutely overwhelming ; it moved to tears.

It is of course as a Shakespearean actress that her name will live, yet those who truly loved her unique genius will perhaps recall her most often as Olivia—the Olivia of Goldsmith. Here was a character after her own heart— so much like herself that, as she has told me, before going upon the stage, she had but to think herself back into certain periods of her own life to become the actual Olivia. Pretty Olivia, laughing with the Squire under the old apple-tree in the Vicarage garden, Olivia on the eve of her flight dividing her poor possessions among her dear ones and taking the farewell which she must not speak, Olivia in the wayside inn, looking with innocent eyes at her betrayer, unable to take in the brutal meaning of his words, Olivia at every turn of her pitiful little story lived and breathed before us.

In many of these parts she dominated the play or at least shone at Henry Irving's side with an equal lustre, but there were other minor rôles in which it was interesting to watch her loyal support of her great colleague and her capacity for making something out of nothing.

From a technical point of view it is almost more instructive to see a fine actor or actress in a bad part than a good one, and I never realised the art of Ellen Terry more clearly than in the part of Rosamund in Tennyson's ' Becket.' The character fairly puzzled her as she studied it.

" I don't know what to do with her," she said to me. " She is not there. She does not exist. I don't think that Tennyson ever knew very much about women, and now he is old and has forgotten the little that he knew. She is not a woman at all."

But she did her best for Rosamund and played her for all she was worth and more.

I was particularly struck one night by her absolute identification (for the moment) with the character.

In the last scene Rosamund sees the murder of Becket in the cathedral from a gallery above and rushes down a stairway to kneel beside the body. Behind the scenes, Rosamund gained her watch-tower with the help of a ladder which led to a little platform overlooking the stage.

I had come in to arrange with her some plan for the next day—we were going somewhere to show somebody something, I recall, but memory gives no further details.

She was already on her perch waiting for her last entrance and I climbed the ladder and sat with her quietly discussing our business when I asked some question and received no answer. I looked round and found Rosamund de Clifford beside me, pale and breathless, her eyes fixed and full of a gradually growing horror, deaf and blind to everything but the mimic murder on the dark stage below. The dying words of Becket floated up—" Into Thy hands, O Lord, into Thy hands "—she clutched my shoulder tightly, seeming to struggle for speech which would not come, until at last a long gasping cry broke from her lips as she tottered forward and began to run down the steps. Even as she ran the moment of identity with Rosamund passed, and Ellen Terry whispered back, " Missed it again ! I never can *time* that cry right."

' Fair Rosamund,' as represented by her, was indeed fair. She looked her loveliest, especially in the rich gown of her first entrance, a wonderful, Rossettian effect of dim gold and glowing colour veiled in black, her masses of bright hair in a net of gold and golden hearts embroidered on her robe.

I wonder what a leading lady of the present day would think of that dress, could she examine it closely. The foundation was an old pink gown, worn with stage service and reprieved for the occasion from the rag-bag. The mysterious veiling was the coarsest and cheapest black net, the glory of hair through golden meshes was a bag of gold tinsel stuffed with crumpled paper, and the broidered hearts were cut out of gold paper and gummed on. The whole costume would have been dear at ten shillings and was one of the finest stage dresses that I have ever seen.

Lucy Ashton in ' Ravenswood ' was another small part which in Ellen Terry's hands became a great one ; the almost wordless mad scene was of her very best, and deeply moving.

Her effects seemed so natural that it was difficult to believe they had ever been studied and I remember that she herself was surprised to find how exactly she repeated her performance each night. One evening, after the scene at the Wolf's Crag in which Lucy is seized by a fit of half-hysterical laughter at the excuses made by Cabel Balderstone for her frugal entertainment, Henry Irving came up evidently much annoyed.

" Why did you alter the laugh ? " he asked. " It put me out altogether—I was waiting for you to finish."

" I laughed as usual," said Ellen Terry.

" No, you didn't," said Irving. " You always say Ha ! ha ! seventeen times—you only said it fourteen times to-night."

" I knew nothing about those seventeen Ha ! ha's ! "

said Ellen when telling me about it. " It was pure luck my getting the same number every night. I try to time the laugh, of course, but as to how many Ha ! ha's !——Now I am *sure* to get it wrong ; I shall see Henry standing there counting."

' Ravenswood ' also dwells in my memory as the play in which I very nearly appeared with Miss Terry in an unrehearsed scene.

At the close of the last act, the craggy coast disappeared for a few moments in gloom, the stage, strewn with rocks, the dead body of William Terriss and other objects of interest, miraculously cleared itself, and when the shadow lifted the final tableau was revealed—the incoming tide rippling over the Kelpie's Flow under a sky full of the glory of dawn.

It was a wonderful illusion ; the empty stage looked limitless, the scene was almost entirely a transparency, the effect being produced by the gradual turning up of concealed lights.

Lucy Ashton had died distraught, to the keen distress of the audience and her own complete satisfaction. It was one of the few scenes in which she really admired herself and she now stood, bunching up her trailing satin robes, quite unwearied and full of the youthful desire to be where she ought not to be and to see what was not intended for inspection.

" Let us watch the change to the Kelpie's Flow *on* the stage," she whispered to me. " It's so interesting to see how it all works. We can hide behind that rock."

We hid. The play was ending, the lights began to fade ; Edgar of Ravenswood had ridden off to his fate and the witch woman's prophetic chant rang out in the shadows.

> " He shall stable his steed in the Kelpie's Flow
> And his name shall be lost for ever mo——"

Darkness fell and things began to stir curiously ; trees and rocks developed strange activity and slid silently away in all directions. Hayston of Bucklaw's dead body glided by, skidding comfortably along on a sliding plank. As it passed, the corpse giggled audibly and remarked, " Look out. Your rock's going next."

Our rock ! Our solid, immovable rock in whose shelter we crouched ? Impossible. Nevertheless, after a preliminary shiver, our rock got into motion, sailing slowly across the stage bound for the far-distant O.P. wings. Other smaller rocks which would have masked our retreat had already deserted us—in another moment the deceased Bride of Lammermuir in all the glories of her wedding toilette would be discovered sitting in the middle of the Kelpie's Flow !

We did our best, and the progress of Miss Ashton and friend on all fours across the Lyceum stage must have been an impressive sight which was at any rate much appreciated by the late Bucklaw, who had drifted into haven and was now sitting up, absorbed in our Odyssey and trying to shout advice in a whisper. It was a race between us and the rock and a close one at the finish but luckily ending in a dead heat. " Where—where was my train ? " panted Lucy Ashton.

" Most of it was in my mouth," I puffed—I was very hot and dusty ; " the rest was bunched up between my knees."

" Thank goodness that Henry went straight up to his room," exclaimed Miss Ashton piously, and I thanked goodness from a full heart.

One of the most beautiful scenes ever put upon the stage was in ' Ravenswood ' ; a dell in a spring coppice where sunbeams sifted faintly through the tender green and where the Mermaidens' Well bubbled up amidst sheets of bluebells. It was by Hawes Craven and was an almost perfect illusion as well as an admirable background for figures. It was repainted and used again as the hawthorn brake in ' King Arthur,' but at the loss of much of its original charm.

For the ' King Arthur ' scenery and costumes Irving

had gone to Burne-Jones, who made lovely and elaborate designs for both.

Ellen Terry was so absolutely of the legendary period, those mythical, mystical days which never were and never could have been, that her Queen Guinevere had been looked forward to for years : when it came it was a disappointment.

It was not her fault ; she looked lovely and played well.

It was not precisely the author's fault, for J. Comyns Carr had pieced together a very workmanlike frame in which to set the series of Burne-Jones pictures which formed the real attraction of the play. It was the fault of Tennyson, whose ' blameless king ' of the Idylls has taken such root in the public mind that Mr. Carr no doubt feared to dig him up.

Unfortunately, a blameless Arthur knocks all meaning out of the Arthurian legends, and Arthur became Fortune's fool upon whose haloed head unmerited misfortunes were heaped by a freakish Providence, while Guinevere, no longer the instrument of Fate, was merely a frisky matron, ' no better than she should be.' No awkward questions were raised as to the parentage of Modred, he had apparently ' just growed,' like Topsy, and Johnston Forbes-Robertson, as Launcelot, played and looked Galahad to perfection.

Under these circumstances there was little chance for Guinevere and it is curious how little I can recall of the whole production beyond Irving's figure in black armour, which seemed as though it had stepped from the canvas of Burne-Jones.

One would have thought that this ideal knight and the two ' blessed damozels,' Ellen Terry and Sarah Bernhardt, would inevitably have been seized upon as models by the Painter-in-Ordinary to the Court of King Arthur ; but, as far as I know, he never made even a sketch of one of them. It is even more strange that Ellen Terry, who was the accepted type of the Pre-Raphaelite School and an embodiment of all the romance and glamour of their favourite literature, should never have been painted by any member of the band.

Yet she has been fortunate in her painters ; the Watts studies have caught much of the wistful charm of her girlhood, and the splendid Sargent portrait (Lady Macbeth) will be an enduring memorial of her maturity.

Irving secured the ' Lady Macbeth ' and it hung for many years in his room at the theatre, in company with his own portrait by Whistler, which chance had delivered into his hands.

One evening he announced with some diffidence to Ellen Terry that he had bought a picture : he knew that picture dealing was not in his line and, as a rule, consulted her before committing himself.

Ellen looked anxious. " A picture ? "

" Yes. As I was passing a frame-shop I saw that thing that Whistler did of me—Philip of Spain—do you remember it ? "

" I should think I *did*. Well ? "

" Well, I thought I'd ask the price and the man said a hundred pounds."

" A hundred pounds ? "

" Yes. Was that too much ? "

" A hundred pounds ! There weren't any *other* Whistler pictures in the shop, were there ? "

" O yes, lots. I didn't look at 'em—I only wanted the portrait."

All the next day Ellen Terry was hopelessly busy but on the day after she flew to the frame-shop : not a Whistler canvas was to be seen—the great chance was lost.

In spite of his luck, Irving never cared for the ' Philip ' picture. Applauded for his cleverness in finding and buying it, he conceded it a place in the Beef Steak Room at the Lyceum but never hesitated to say that he thought little of it. And, from his point of view, he was right. He had no concern with it as a design and did not value its tone and quality : he regarded it solely as a portrait and as such it is of little importance. It is a mere rub in

158

of the wonderful face, a fine start as to tone and with promise of character in the expression but hardly carried further than the preliminary stage. Irving was a bad sitter, impatient and uninterested, and this may have had something to do with the incomplete state of the picture. Whistler demanded full measure from his models both of time and patience and certainly would not have got much of either out of Henry Irving.

Ellen Terry, on the contrary, was a good sitter, her love of art and real understanding of pictures giving her far more sympathy and consideration for the artist than is usually accorded to that downtrodden person.

I myself victimised her several times, though only once—from an unexpected sitting—did I get anything like a satisfactory result.

On one dark, foggy morning a ring had come at my studio bell. I opened the door—there stood Ophelia, wraith-like in the mist, an aureole of pale hair clinging about her face and shoulders.

" I've washed my head," announced the apparition, resolving itself into Ellen Terry. " May I come in and dry it ? All the fires at home seemed to have gone out," she continued, as she drifted into the room, " and I remembered that you usually have a good one so—here I am. You haven't got a model, have you ? "

" Yes," said I, " if you don't mind being one."

" No, I don't mind," said Ellen with resignation : she knew the ways of studios and seldom escaped from one without paying toll, " but you must let me sit by the fire so that my hair may dry."

So she sat by the fire and her hair dried beautifully and I made a pastel study which, by happy accident, turned out a good likeness, catching a rapt expression which I had tried for before but never succeeded in fixing. Irving used to call the head ' Ellen in Heaven,' and there was something appropriate in the title, though she had but been drawn to the skies by a warm fire and the satisfactory drying of her hair.

159

When that ceremony was at an end and my sketch finished, she rose to go.

" I don't sit badly, do I ? " she said. " I daresay I could have made something as a model. Are there men painting away behind each of those doors ? " she enquired, as we came out into the dark passage. " Do I know any of them ? "

" You know Phil Burne-Jones—the end door," said I. " None of the others, I think."

" Then I shall call on them and see if they'll engage me," said Ellen firmly, and rang the nearest bell.

" No, no. Go away ! " bellowed the artist, bursting forth for a second, then slamming the door.

I coughed discreetly.

" Pooh, he didn't look at me. That doesn't count," said Ellen, moving to the next bell.

" Perhaps this one *will*," I murmured, " and what are you going to do then ? "

But the door was already open.

" Please, do you want a model ? " said Miss Terry.

" No," said the man, peering at her in the dimness, " that is—here, you'd better come in."

The model hesitated, then came inspiration.

" I ought to tell you that I only sit for Scriptural subjects," she observed. " The Infant Samuel and so on."

She posed and I thought we were lost, the Infant Samuel was most attractive ; but luckily the light was dim, the poor man missed his chance and casting a distrustful look at the infant, hastily shut himself in.

" He was rather better," said Ellen hopefully.

" *He* thought you were a bit off it," said I. " Goodness knows what the next one will think."

She rang at a third door with no result.

" I can't get hold of this one," she complained, applying herself afresh to the bell.

" No more can the police," I observed. " He has been ' wanted ' for the last three weeks."

Ellen seemed suddenly discouraged.

"I don't think I'll try any more of them," she said. "They don't seem very interesting so far—perhaps I had better stick to my present job."

And I agreed with her.

SEEING much of Ellen Terry and being often about the Lyceum Theatre, it must naturally have followed that I knew Henry Irving well. I wonder. With Ellen Terry, the actress and the woman were two separate entities ; one saw them and thought of them clearly apart. I knew her Beatrice, her Imogen, her Portia, and I knew besides one who was all of them yet none of them : they were her shadows and she the reality.

Of Irving I knew a melancholy figure that was Hamlet, a courtly, exquisitely mannered gentleman who was Doricourt after some years' tutelage to the Vicar of Wakefield, a freakish mischievous being who was Macaire or Alfred Jingle, a genial comrade, ' hail fellow, well met ' with all men who was Iachimo (on his best behaviour) and Fabian de Franchi, a magnificent host who was Wolsey : but Henry Irving—did I ever meet him ? I cannot be sure.

His art was his life—his soul. He had vowed himself to it by a pact as awful as that between Faust and Mephistopheles ; like Peter Schlemihl, he had sold his reflection ; the mirror of memory gives back a score of counterfeit images, but of the true Irving, the dweller in the innermost, hardly a trace.

Far more could be learned of Henry Irving by watching his nightly performance than by talking to him for hours. In his assumed character he was anxious to give expression to everything ; as himself he was careful to tell nothing.

His artistic life was one long struggle towards perfection ; fault after fault he conquered, one by one he laid by his mannerisms, line by line he modelled the beautiful, sensitive face that he had evolved from his original immobile and rather ordinary features. To the hour of his death he worked incessantly, his whole career was a progression and those who witnessed his last performance probably saw him at his best.

This surrender of self to Art gave an intensity to his work which, to my mind, placed it far beyond the achievement of any other actor ; in fact, I have always divided actors artistically into two classes, Henry Irving—and the rest, but it also brought isolation. Art was before everything ; he gave his goddess all that she demanded and had but little ' small change ' to throw away upon everyday life. He was popular and a man's man, loving in his few hours of leisure to chat over a cigar and to see familiar faces round his table, but for intimate friendships he had no time and no need. He was self-sufficing.

"Henry is very fond of you," once said Ellen Terry to me.

"Henry?" I exclaimed, in astonishment. "Henry doesn't care twopence about me. He doesn't *mind* me ; that's all."

"Well, he certainly doesn't mind you," said Ellen, adopting the amendment with unflattering swiftness, " he wouldn't have you about the theatre and in his room if he did. He doesn't mind you a bit."

So we left it at that. Henry didn't mind me. I am proud to remember it.

This satisfactory attitude he adopted from the beginning, for upon my introduction to him by Ellen Terry he immediately asked me to supper. It was at the last moment, somebody else had probably failed him, but I prefer to look upon the invitation as the dawn of his ' not minding ' me, and the picture of that first supper at the Lyceum—the bright, candle-lit table among the shadows of the old Beef Steak Room—the beautiful ivory face of the host against the dark panelling—remains in my memory. Round that pale face, which seemed to absorb and give out light, the rest of the scene grows vague and out of focus, save for another pale face on the wall beyond, the passionate face of Edmund Kean as ' Sir Giles Overreach.'

Mr. and Mrs. (afterwards Sir Squire and Lady) Bancroft were there, Walter Pollock and his wife, I think Bram

Stoker, Irving's acting manager, and of course my sponsor, Ellen Terry.

Why do I remember nothing more of this, my feast of inauguration, but the fact that the room was very hot ? This remains with me as instancing Ellen Terry's quickness at the uptake. Those of the theatre are as a rule insensible to stuffiness and I gasped in silence for some time but at last leaned across to her and murmured tentatively, " By the living jingo——" to which she at once replied, " So am I. For goodness sake, Henry, let's have a window open."

Is it necessary to remind a generation which despises the classics that the context, instantly supplied by Miss Terry, may be found in ' Lady Wilhelmina Skegg's ' remark in the *Vicar of Wakefield* that ' by the living jingo she was all of a muck of sweat ! '

Walter Pollock, who was a frequent guest at the Lyceum suppers, was famous for a wonderfully exact imitation of Irving with which he used to delight convivial gatherings. Irving was curiously sensitive to ridicule, doubtless in consequence of his early struggles, and greatly disliked caricatures of his delivery and style, but, coming to hear of Pollock's performance, one evening paralysed him by suddenly saying, " Now let us have that imitation of me that everybody is so fond of."

" O, I couldn't—I——" stammered the unhappy mimic.

" Go on, go on," said Irving. " Here," handing him a book, " read a page of this imitating me."

Pollock meekly took the book and began in a half-hearted and shamefaced way, then, warming to his work, finished in his best manner amidst the usual applause.

Irving waited till the laughter had ceased and then said slowly and with perfect sincerity, " My boy, I never heard you read so well before in my life ! "

It must sometimes have struck his imitators that, while raising a laugh at his expense, they were pronouncing many words correctly for the first time.

At one of the Lyceum gatherings a man was insisting that, as a rule, English was spoken correctly, that mere pedantry of diction was not elocution, that, in fact, he could and did pronounce English perfectly himself. " Say something to me," said Irving quietly. " Say anything. I will engage that you make a mistake in every line."

The gentleman, who had a fine voice and fancied himself as a reciter, began—" There was a sound of revelry by night——"

" Stop," said Irving. " What did you say ? "

" There was a sound of revelry——" repeated the reciter.

" Ah," said Irving. " What's revulry ? "

" Why—rev'lry," said the perplexed reciter. " You know what it means."

" There's no such word," said Irving. " Listen." And in his clear-cut, staccato utterance he gave the line— " There was a sound of re-vel-ry—by night." The word ' revelry ' danced and glittered, the word ' night ' fell like a pall. The reciter recited no more.

The best imitation of Irving that I ever heard was from Sir Arthur Pinero : it was not imitation but reproduction and was given from the point of view of admiration, not of ridicule. It was no caricature but the actual voice and speech of Irving, with the beauty and subtlety keenly observed.

Sir Arthur was saying how, when he was playing the Second Murderer in ' Macbeth,' he used nightly to be so appalled by the horror conjured up by Irving's voice in some lines addressed to him that he found it difficult to go on with his part.

> "—and with him,
> Fleance his son, that keeps him company,
> Whose absence is no less material
> Than is his father's, must embrace the fate
> Of that dark hour."

These lines he repeated like an actual echo of the great actor ; the voice white and flute-like on the word Fleance, giving for the fraction of a moment a picture of youth and innocence, then deepened and veiled, turning to a sort of muffled roar on the concluding phrase, the last two words rolling on and on in ominous reverberations.

Like much great and original work, Henry Irving's acting was an easy mark for the critic's arrow. As an artist he resembled Rossetti, in that he came to his task fully equipped with genius and imagination yet lacking the power of self-expression : unlike Rossetti, he had infinite patience and by sheer hard work he gradually brought the technical side of his art to something very near perfection.

When, as a boy, I first saw him he was already at the head of his profession, but even then would occur passages of self-conscious stiffness in his performance that were almost grotesque, yet—like a faulty sketch by Rossetti— arresting, suggestive, intensely interesting.

His personality was so strong that though his reading of a character might be challenged, it could never be forgotten : you might be unable wholeheartedly to accept (let us say) Irving as Shylock, but you nevertheless saw Shylock as Irving for the rest of your life.

How well I remember his Romeo in 1882 ; a part in which he was generally admitted to have failed. No one had a good word for his Romeo and I, bowing to my elders and betters, took it from them that it was bad. But—it spoiled me for all other Romeos. I have seen handsome Romeos, young Romeos, nicely behaved and altogether attractive Romeos, but no other absorbing and fascinating Romeo, above all no other Italian Romeo.

Everything about the slender man with the pale olive face and burning eyes was Italian ; the dreamy languor of the opening scenes, the flaming intensity of his first glance at Juliet, drawing her eyes to his as by the spell of a mesmerist, the blind fury of rage in which he fell upon Tybalt, like nothing but a wild cat or an Italian boy, the stony calm with which he received the final stroke of fate, the news of Juliet's death, when in a moment of silence the youth grew to a sorrow-stricken manhood, all were essentially and typically Italian. In one scene he failed as he always did when a similar call was made upon him. Strong emotion breaking out in torrential speech he never could portray ; his voice grew weak, he spoke slower instead of faster, words became inarticulate. He failed in Romeo's ' banishment scene ' with the Friar just as he failed in Shylock's scene with Tubal and Macbeth's outburst at the banquet ; the very keenness of the imagined passion hampered its utterance. The audience often laughed at this scene as Englishmen are wont to laugh at any display of strong emotion—they would most certainly have laughed at the real Romeo. Irving's despair was too real, it went beyond the border-line of art.

His attacks of self-consciousness, though they almost disappeared before the end of his career, often led to his doing himself scanty justice on first nights. At the Lyceum it was known that ' the Governor ' was on first nights either at his best or worst. If the last rehearsal had not been quite satisfactory, if he were anxious about the production as a whole, he forgot himself and was at his very best, playing easily and with complete self-control. If, on the contrary, all was well and he had only himself to consider, a strange paralysis sometimes descended upon him, extinguishing his voice and stiffening his movements.

A sad example of first-night failure was his long-contemplated and deeply studied King Lear.

At a dress rehearsal Ellen Terry had objected in the tent scene to some purple drapery which struck a harsh note and spoiled a fine colour scheme. " Don't tell me about these things *now*," Irving had said, straining under the burden of his tremendous part. " Afterwards, if you like, but not now. You've put me out—I shan't get back into the part to-night."

On the night of production he failed to make himself heard ; he seemed to miss the pitch, his acting was superb but his words were inaudible.

At the end of the play he came before the curtain and

167

made his usual short speech of thanks, each word falling clear cut as crystal from his lips and reaching the remotest corners of the theatre : as he bowed and retired a gentleman in the gallery called out, " Why didn't yer speak like that before ? " It voiced the feeling of the house, there was an unmistakable murmur of assent.

Irving came up to Ellen Terry, who had realised his failure and was greatly distressed. " What did that man mean ? " he asked. " Have I not been speaking distinctly ? "

" I couldn't hear a word you said from start to finish," confessed Ellen, who knew that she would be cross-examined until she told the truth.

" Good God ! But—but why didn't you *tell* me ? "

" Because you particularly asked me not to speak to you during the performance."

And so it fell out that Irving's ' Lear,' one of his most memorable impersonations, was recorded as a failure and will always be so remembered. It was a deep disappointment to him, all the more as he knew that his performance was good, nay of his very best. I saw the play again on the fifth night and Irving's rendering was magnificent, its pathos terrible.

I can still see him, weary and half dazed, sitting up on his couch and staring at the daughter he had banished as she bent tenderly over him. " You are a spirit, I know —when did you die ? " he whispered, and I can almost weep now when I recall his voice.

I have said elsewhere that he did not much care for or understand pictures, but when the artist touched a dramatic chord with mastery he responded to it at once.

Madox Brown's ' Cordelia's Portion,' a print of which hung in his dressing-room, he had always admired immensely and when he came to produce ' Lear ' he founded his conception upon the Lear of Madox Brown and induced the veteran artist to advise on the mounting and to make sketches for it. The result was fine ; sombre and austere throughout until the final heartrending scene of the old king's death beside the body of Cordelia, which was enacted amongst flowery down-lands where white chalk cliffs towered out of a sea of dazzling blue under skies full of pitiless sunshine ; a daring and most poetical touch which seemed to isolate the two tragic figures and to intensify the darkness of their doom.

When Irving was studying ' Lear ' he went to Boscastle in Cornwall, then a tiny village with one old-fashioned inn, where I joined him for three or four days.

He was absorbed in his work and though he seemed to love the wild coast and the evening rambles by the sea— I remember a wonderful night of moonshine when all the grass along the cliffs was starred with glow-worms green as emeralds—and though he enjoyed talking with the fisherfolk and hearing their tales of secret caves where the seals lay hidden, yet his thoughts were never long away from Lear.

Once, during a walk when we were discussing some totally different subject—probably dogs—he stopped and, gazing fixedly at me, demanded, " Where am I going to get that feather from ? "

" Feather ? "

" Yes. *You* know—when I say ' This feather stirs. She lives.' What am I doing with a feather in my hand ? Where did it come from ? Did you ever see Lear acted ? "

" No," said I.

" That's a pity : you might have remembered. I saw in a book that Macready used to pluck the feather out of Edgar's helmet, but I can't do that."

" Why not ? " I enquired.

" Why not ? Why if I started plucking feathers out of Terriss the whole house would roar. What *can* I do ? "

We sat down and became gradually aware of feathers, quantities of feathers, lying about on the grass.

" Here are feathers," said Irving slowly. " Any amount of 'em—and the scene is by the sea—just like this. I'll have a feather tacked to the stage cloth just where I kneel beside Cordelia ; then I can pick it up and—there I am."

He gathered up a few feathers thoughtfully.

Next day I found him near the same spot, his hand-kerchief full of feathers.

" I'm going to keep them and use them in ' Lear,' " he said, displaying his take. " I shall like to feel that they were picked up by the sea—real seabirds' feathers."

I inspected the collection. " Ye-es," I said regret-fully. " But you know, those are all *hens'* feathers. They've blown out of that yard—somebody has been plucking a fowl."

" Ah," said Irving with one of his curious staccato grunts, and emptied his handkerchief. The feathers had lost their powers of inspiration—why could I not have held my tongue ?

A queer little incident during the run of ' Lear ' remains in my mind from its sheer incongruity.

" Graham," said Cordelia one evening to me as we stood together at the wings during the last act, " why do men always spit on their hands when they are going to take up anything ? "

" They don't," said I, " at least, only labourers hand-ling a spade or a navvy gripping a pick-axe. I assure you it's not usually done."

" Well," said Cordelia, " you come and look at Henry."

It was almost time for his last entrance, bearing the body of his murdered daughter, and the said daughter began to get ready, stretching herself at full length upon a table that she might be the more easily gathered up.

King Lear swept down from his dressing-room and stood beside her, waiting for his cue. As it came he tossed his arms aloft in a wild gesture, uttering the old king's mad wail, " Howl, howl ! " then, stooping over Cordelia, whispered, " Now then—ready ? " carefully spat upon both palms, rubbed them hastily together and, shouldering his burden, trudged with it on to the stage.

HENRY IRVING IN CORNWALL
Hitherto unreproduced photograph taken by THE AUTHOR

It was oddly comic—the grand figure and the homely, rustic gesture. It must have been a throwback to some Cornish farmer ancestor.

In long and trying rôles such as Lear or Macbeth his great reserve of strength, unimpaired until within the last eight or nine years of his life, stood him in good stead. He never had ' off' nights, never walked through a part but always played for all he was worth.

" Henry simply does not understand ill health," Ellen Terry once said to me. " If I am ill he is very kind and polite, but he never believes that there is anything the matter with me."

Very few of his parts seemed to tire him. Hamlet was a strain—he gave so much to it—and he dropped it from his repertory comparatively early ; after playing Lear for fifty nights he recognised that a longer run would have been barely possible, but ' The Bells' always exhausted him to an alarming extent, and it is possible that his continuing to play Mathias against doctors' orders may have hastened his end.

' Louis XI,' with its long and terrible death scene, which left the audience horror-stricken, seemed to affect him not at all. At the fall of the curtain he would rise up perfectly fresh and slip at once out of the part as he would have put off a coat, while out of the death trance of Mathias he could come half dazed, cold, breathless and trembling. It used to surprise me when seeing him at the wings or in his dressing-room during ' Louis XI ' to note how little ' made up ' he was : except for a waxen pallor and two ' blacked out' teeth he looked much as usual. On the stage he was completely transformed but the change lay almost entirely in expression, and in the final agony the mean and cunning lines would melt from the face, leaving it ghastly but beautiful.

He was often criticised as old fashioned for not ' going with the times ' and producing plays of the moment, but he paid small heed to his advisers, and his choice was made from a perfectly clear mental standpoint to which, as a great artist, he was surely entitled. About that time, under the banner of the giant Ibsen, the introspective, morbid-erotic drama was coming into fashion, in which subjects usually discussed in private were threshed out at length upon the stage before a blushful and embarrassed house.

Irving was old fashioned in that he was essentially normal and healthy minded, and in a normal man the instinct of reticence is as strong as is in a madman the desire to strip himself in public. I remember speaking to him of a French poetical play with a wonderful man's part in it. He became interested. " Tell me some more about that," he said. " Tell me the story."

I told it as best I could—some parts were a little difficult.

" Yes," he said at last. " Yes, but—that's a horrible story."

" So's Macbeth."

" But Macbeth isn't disgusting. I don't believe that the public wants disgusting things. Anyhow, it won't get 'em from me."

He was taken to see a rising actress in a great Ibsen rôle which had won for her a sudden fame. She had previously engaged herself for an Australian tour and efforts were being made to cancel the contract that she might follow up her success in London. " If that's the sort of thing she wants to play she'd better play it somewhere else," was all that Irving would say.

Ellen Terry has put upon record that he did not care to see others act ; did not, as a rule, appreciate the acting of others.

I found this true on the few occasions when I have watched a play with him : his eye was all over the stage, nothing that was wrong escaped it. I remember seeing Ada Rehan's in many ways brilliant Rosalind with him from a box, but was not helped in my enjoyment by the stream of comments, ejaculations and questions which flowed from him.

" What's that sort of fishing-net affair—with the light *straight* upon it—meant for ? "

" That's atmosphere," said I—I knew the effects of Mr. Augustin Daly. " It lends mystery to the back cloth."

" Good God ! " said Irving. Then—" Look ! Look at those huntsmen dancing along on their toes to the music ! Does he think he's doing comic opera ? "

Miss Rehan's performance only provoked the remark, " How long d'you suppose those silk tights would last in the forest ? " and the entrance of the Duke's pages to oblige with a duet, two highly coloured ladies in yellow wigs and ' panto ' principal boy costumes, tripping gaily in polka step, was the final blow. " *Good* God ! " said Irving for the last time and quietly evaporated.

Ellen Terry told me of an unfortunate occasion when she had induced him to see Frank Benson's Hamlet. He had perceived the thought and hard work that had been put into the performance and had commended some points highly. " Benson would be so pleased to hear you say that," she had pleaded. " Do go round and tell him yourself. You have really liked some of it, haven't you ? "

" Yes, yes," said Irving. " Yes, certainly, of course I'll tell him." But unhappily he had been *really* interested ; there was one question that he really wanted to ask, and when brought face to face with Benson he asked it at once. " Now tell me, my boy," he said very kindly, taking his arm. " Tell me. Why *do* you play Hamlet ? "

I think he was really fond of Sarah Bernhardt, but I never once heard him speak of her acting. He always seemed pleased to meet and talk with her, though as he had no French and she hardly any English, conversation was carried on under difficulties.

Sometimes, when they met at social functions where each was equally bored, they would carry me off to a remote corner, plant me between them, and converse through me with great animation. Sarah I could interpret glibly enough, but Irving's part in the dialogue used to tax my scanty French vocabulary to the utmost—and beyond, and I was not helped by his impatient ejaculations—" Well—why don't you tell her ? Go on—*tell* her."

Ellen Terry's daughter, Edy, once had the luck to overhear them earnestly discussing finance and retrenchment : they were both so excited that the gift of tongues had been vouchsafed them and they talked volubly. " You get money," Sarah was repeating with emphatic gestures. " You see ? You—get—*money*."

It must have been a wonderful moment : the two supreme spendthrifts lecturing each other on economy.

Irving, like Sarah, was quite unable to keep money ; it flowed like water through his fingers, though, unlike her, he had few expensive tastes.

On his productions he spent unsparingly yet not recklessly and the actual cost of some of his most effective ' sets ' would surprise a modern manager ; but first and last, the greater part of his earnings went back into his theatre. The rest he gave away, lavishly, without stint, almost without thought. He would have liked to walk down the Strand scattering gold in handfuls to either side, like Aladdin.

If he were served at an hotel with a luncheon that pleased him he sent the cook a five-pound note, the waiter's tips were golden ; it was magnificent—or ridiculous—as you pleased.

Ellen Terry took the latter point of view and, in the days when the Lyceum coffers were growing light, she tried to reason with him.

" It's so unnecessary," she urged. " Waiters don't expect sovereigns."

" They seem pleased enough to get 'em."

" But it's so extravagant : you ought to economise."

" Pooh."

She played her last card. " Henry—it's vulgar."

" *Vulgar ?* "

" Yes. It *is* vulgar to go about behaving like a crowned head or a prince in a pantomime."

" Ah." Irving was struck by the idea and perhaps the

next waiter only got fifteen shillings, but on the morrow all was as before.

" And it *is* aggravating," said Ellen to me, " to see Henry sitting upstairs in an hotel handing sovereigns to anyone who comes into the room, while his friends are holding a council downstairs to save enough of his money to pay for his own funeral."

But when the end came, his last rites were such as no wealth could have won for him : when he passed to his rest in Westminster Abbey beneath the pall of glittering laurel, his country felt that the honour was fitting, and as years go by his figure emerges from the past more and more clearly, lonely in its greatness and already among the Immortals.

THE supporters of Irving at the Lyceum for the most part formed a stock company which seldom changed, but from time to time several ' leading juveniles ' came in to take up important parts. Of these temporary stars the most regular in its appearances was William Terriss.

Fairy godmothers galore had evidently flocked to Terriss's christening bearing every gift to fit him for an actor's career : they bestowed upon him a handsome face, a graceful well-knit figure, a splendid voice, a wonderful sense of the stage ; but hardly had the last of them decreed that he should speak his lines most beautifully than a mischievous sprite popped up and added—" But he shall not understand a single word of them."

His reply to Irving who had asked him the meaning of a line in ' Much Ado About Nothing '—" O go along, Guv'nor ; it's poetry, isn't it ? "—exactly defined his attitude towards the Arts, an attitude which enabled him to give some Shakespearean passages with great effect, by strict attention to the sound and no appreciation whatever of the sense.

He always gave his friends the credit of sharing his ideas on the subject of Shakespeare and poetry in general.

Once, at a revival of ' The Merchant of Venice,' he was standing in the wings beside Ellen Terry, who was nervous about her words and anxiously thinking them over before going on. " What's the matter, dear ? " asked Terriss—all women were ' dear ' to that large-hearted man.

" Nothing," muttered E. T., turning away.

" Not well, dear, eh ? Feeling a bit done up ? "

" No."

" Anything wrong at home ? "

" *No.* Go away, do," snapped the victim, at bay.

Good-natured Terriss stared at the unwonted rebuff, then a light broke. " *I* see, dear," he said. " It's that damned Portia. I never could stand her jaw myself."

It was always interesting and instructive to hear Terriss discourse on Shakespeare. It is usually difficult to get at people's real opinion of the Bard ; his great name awes them into a respectful silence. Not so with Terriss.

I remember getting a note from him during a performance of ' King Lear,' asking me to come round to his dressing-room during an interval. I found him sitting on a big dress basket against which he was idly drumming his bare heels. There was something oddly comic about his appearance as Edgar. Ragged, half-naked, with masses of tangled hair falling to his waist, he still suggested a pink and white pantomime fairy. He looked pretty—and ridiculous—and most attractive.

" Well ? " said he hospitably.

" Well," said I. " You wanted to talk about something ? "

" Not a bit, dear boy," said Terriss. " I saw you in front and you always go round to see the Guv'nor or Nell and never come and see *me*, so I just thought I'd send a line."

" I see," said I, perching cautiously on the basket beside him. " Going well to-night, isn't it ? "

" As well as you can expect," said Terriss thoughtfully, sticking out his lower lip which made him look under fourteen. " It's a damned dull play, you know, dear boy. Damned dull. Heavy as—as anything. *I* do my best to lighten it up a bit, but——" He sketched a despairing gesture indicating the impossibility of providing adequate ' comic relief' to ' King Lear.'

" I saw you doing it," said I, with combined truth and tact.

" It doesn't do to take all this stuff so slow, you know," went on Terriss. " If you've *got* to say it, get it over. People pretend they like it but they yawn their heads off."

He was one of the kindest of creatures, always ready to cheer and comfort anyone in distress and, as he was quite unhampered by any regard for probability or veracity, he often succeeded.

177

One evening Ellen Terry came to the theatre much frightened about her mother who had suddenly been taken ill. Terriss was at once to the fore with words of comfort. "Don't you bother, dear," said he, as they waited together at the side. "*She'll* be all right, you'll see."

"But I feel so anxious," said Ellen. "I can't help being afraid that she has had a slight stroke."

"Stroke," cried Terriss cheerfully. "What's a stroke ! Look here, dear ; you know *my* mother." Ellen nodded. "Fine, healthy old lady as you could see, isn't she ? "

"Yes."

"Well, *she* had something *like* a stroke. In a bath-chair for months, she was, with her head hanging over the side and her face all crooked."

"O, Terriss ! "

"Give you my word. And now—look at her ! "

Ellen was greatly cheered and relieved and went through her evening's work without difficulty. A short time afterwards, meeting one of Terriss's sisters, she referred to the conversation. "Your brother was so kind when I was troubled about mother," she said. "He told me all about *your* mother."

"*My* mother ? "

"Yes—about the stroke and the bath-chair."

"Bath-chair ? "

"Yes—and her head hanging over the side and——"

"Mother has hardly had a day's illness in her life," said the outraged daughter. "She has never *been* in a bath-chair. What could Willie have been talking about ? "

Nevertheless, Willie had talked to some purpose. It was always quite impossible to be angry with him.

Though curiously modest about his many real accomplishments and talents, he loved to pose for imaginary characters quite at variance with his own : it was the true actor's love of impersonation and stage effect.

We were walking together one day down Kensington High Street, deep in matter-of-fact conversation—I remember the subject still ; it was incandescent gas.

Though too glaring for a living-room would it not do very nicely in his hall with one of those rose-coloured globes—here he caught sight of his bus drawn up outside Barker's and leaped upon it. He climbed to the top still talking of gas, then, seeing admiring glances fastened upon him in recognition, his manner changed.

"Good-bye," he chanted, leaning low over the rail, the pathetic stop in his magnificent voice pulled out to the full. "Good-bye, and—God bless you, my dear, dear boy!"

I regret to remember that I failed him. Memories of Mr. Vincent Crummles parting with Nicholas Nickleby—'Farewell, my noble—my lion-hearted boy!'—thronged upon me and I laughed till I cried.

But Terriss never minded being laughed at; it was one of his lovable characteristics.

As an actor he was of the greatest value in certain parts. Poetry was beyond him; as the lovesick Orsino in 'Twelfth Night' he was ridiculous, as Claudio in 'Much Ado About Nothing' he looked and played like a 'principal boy' in burlesque, with his grand voice and gallant bearing he could rattle through Don Pedro and Mercutio very bravely, and he was a fine Henry VIII and Henry in 'Becket,' but in two parts he was supreme and unapproachable, Hayston of Bucklaw and Squire Thornhill. Both of these characters he accepted at their own valuation and played them from their own point of view as fine fellows, good fellows, whose hearts were in the right place and whose little lapses were not only excusable, but only to be expected.

His speech to the betrayed Olivia—'But if you *want* to go home, Livy, why don't you *go*?'—struck the exact note; it was no villain casting off his victim, but a bored child who didn't want to play any more. You felt no impulse to pistol the Squire nor even to kick him, but merely to slap him and put him in the corner. With a less enthralling Olivia it would have been dangerous—it was so disarming.

179

He had led a roving life by land and sea, had in his own person played wild and romantic parts before he assumed them on the stage, and there remained something of Thornhill and Bucklaw about him in private life. One could not help regarding him as a wilful, rather stupid, high-spirited, charming child. When he was good his face lighted up with the sunniest of smiles, when he was naughty the pouted lips and lowering brows of a sulky boy recalled the sculptured Antinous, whom in fact he closely resembled.

Still young and beautiful at fifty, he died by the knife of a maniac, Time having proved quite unequal to dealing with him. It seemed a fitting end to a career of adventure, and Ellen Terry summed him up with genuine sympathy and understanding when she said to me—" Poor dear Terriss—I do hope that he lived long enough to realise that he was murdered. How he would have enjoyed it ! "

Terriss was by far the best foil to Irving of the Lyceum young men ; his rough-and-ready, hit-or-miss style emphasised the subtleties of the great actor, though Johnston Forbes-Robertson and Alexander were much better able to appreciate them.

George Alexander I first saw as County Paris in 'Romeo and Juliet,' looking a mere boy and very handsome. He came back to the Lyceum for ' Faust,' taking up the name part at a day's notice and much against his will, as he had, on the first night, made a big hit in ' Valentine,' a smaller but more effective rôle.

To go through the long part of Faust with so little preparation was rather an ordeal for the young actor, and it was not made easier for him by Ellen Terry, who, finding the love scene in the garden interrupted by Faust's references to his book—to which he clung as a shipwrecked sailor to a spar—suddenly snatched it from him and flung it away, remarking, " Never mind the words. Just say ' Ma-a-argaret ' whenever I leave off speaking and you'll be all right." He *was* all right, but I suspect that, with his usual thoroughness, he had taken care to be almost word perfect.

He always took any suggestion from Ellen Terry gratefully and in good part—even to the introduction into his person of a long hat-pin at an emotional moment in 'Macbeth' with the whispered comment, "You ought to be *feeling* this part a little more, Alec."

They always understood each other, and when he left the Lyceum, she, and Irving also, took the greatest interest and pleasure in his successful career as a manager.

"It angers me," she once said to me, "to hear people talk of Alec's luck. If they worked as he does *they* would have luck. Nearly all the things that most managers leave to their staff he does himself; he looks into everything and neglects nothing—and then they call his success 'luck'!"

His Faust was charming—one realised how good it was when someone else played it. I saw Terriss in it afterwards—a rollicking swashbuckler. Alexander never forgot that he was the learned doctor miraculously rejuvenated; he was quiet, thoughtful, observant.

Once, during the run of 'Faust,' that run and the careers of two great actor-managers might have been cut short. At the close of the first scene dense clouds of vapour rolled from the ground and Mephistopheles, seizing Faust, flew up with him through the mist. One night, as they rose into the air, something—I forget what —went wrong with the little moving platform that wafted them skywards and the Demon and the Doctor fell off into space, luckily landing on the stage not many feet below them. Had they fallen down the open trap into the depths of the under stage—well, it would have been a pity.

George Alexander and I saw much of each other during 'Faust' and formed a lasting friendship; I was made free of his cosy though microscopic house in Park Row, Albert Gate, and passed with approval by his wife, who was—though she would not for worlds have had it known—a remarkable woman.

In a world of dangerous and designing women I think the greatest fraud I ever met was Florence Alexander. She posed as, and succeeded in looking, the charming simpleton, the pretty, empty-headed butterfly, flitting from tea-party to tea-party and raffling rubbish all the day at every opening bazaar. To further aid her schemes Providence had given her just the face she would have chosen, the face of an intelligent but frivolous kitten. (I painted a fairly good portrait of her myself, but her best is by Sir Joshua Reynolds, who called it ' Mrs. Abington as " Miss Prue." ') Beneath this innocent mask lurked a strong personality ; clear-headed, long-sighted, infinitely patient and tactful, an untiring worker and a firm friend, wise, brave and generous.

She was of the greatest use to her husband, both at home and in the theatre, and his marriage with her was the best of his many good strokes of Fortune. Throughout his life she was his chief helper and adviser, and in a letter to me only a few days before his death he wrote—" Florence has simply been an angel through it all."

Her tiny Park Row home was a model of comfort, though its proportions were a trial to her hospitable soul, and her feats as a hostess were really remarkable considering that four guests filled the house and five crowded it to inconvenience.

Here I came to close quarters (in the most literal sense) with many interesting people, but what I most enjoyed were occasional Sunday evenings when Irving would come alone and chat quietly in the little dining-room. He liked his *jeune premier* and had early penetrated Florence Alexander's disguise, esteeming her highly.

Sometimes he would come to supper there with J. L. Toole, the old comedian, Irving's closest friend and comrade of past years ; and in Toole's company a new Irving would appear, or rather, I suppose, an old Irving reappeared, an almost boyish creature, mischievous and cheery.

As they talked of old times they would become more and more the young men of those bygone days, and I remember, when walking away with them down a deserted Knightsbridge after one of these evenings, feeling like a reverend senior between two lads chuckling over their escapades.

They were recalling how, arriving very late at some provincial town, they had only had time to hurl themselves into a fly and drive straight to the theatre, getting into their stage costumes and making up *en route* ; and they dwelt with boyish delight upon the amazement of the driver when, in place of two respectable tourists who had entered his cab, there emerged a bibulous comic countryman and a villain of the deepest dye, who had apparently made away with his original fares and annexed their luggage. Actors both, I think that, unconsciously, they realised the excellent contrast that each was to the other—Irving's pale, tragic mask beside dear old Toole's irresistible low comedy grin—and even in private life could not resist putting some delightful acting into their scenes together.

Faust and Macduff were Alexander's two best chances at the Lyceum and he was admirable in both. It is said to be impossible to fail in the latter part, though I have seen the feat accomplished and by a fine actor, but Alec's Macduff was especially convincing. Perhaps his Scotch blood aided him here as it certainly did in other matters, for he had a considerable amount of the shrewdness that comes from North of the Tweed: his business capacities were undoubted and he sometimes had an almost uncanny insight into the characters and capabilities of his fellow-men.

" I wonder, Alec," said I once, " why So-and-So is thought so much of. He always makes a mess of any job he takes up. *Is* there anything in him ? "

" Nothing whatever," said Alec. " But you see, he has failed in everybody's particular line, therefore everyone feels very kindly disposed towards him."

It was so simple, yet it had never struck me.

When he left the Lyceum and went into management,

it was Alexander who gave me my first commission to 'dress' a play.

It was a little curtain-raiser called 'Fool's Mate,' and I have forgotten all about it save that the date was 'Queen Anne' and the hero was played by Fred Terry.

I have had to 'dress' Fred Terry several times and it has always been a real pleasure, not only because his fine figure lent itself gallantly to picturesque garb, but chiefly because he wore costume with a sense of style and period by no means common to all actors. He also was a Lyceum young man for a brief season, and I well remember his Sebastian to his sister's Viola in 'Twelfth Night,' a wonderful translation of Ellen into the masculine. He played it again twenty-five years later, to the Viola of his own daughter Phyllis.

Johnston Forbes-Robertson appeared every now and then in Lyceum productions, though he never became a member of the permanent company. I seem to have known him nearly all my life and yet to have seen very little of him : we were good friends when we met, but we met seldom. His Claudio and especially his Buckingham were memorable performances, but his chief triumphs were won under other banners than Irving's.

As a manager he did much to uphold the Lyceum traditions, and with great success. There came to him indeed, as to most managers, a short period when Fortune refused to be wooed, and, talking to him when he was bringing out 'The Passing of the Third Floor Back,' I found him in the depths of gloom.

"*I* believe in the play," he said, " but no one can tell how the public will take it. Anyhow, it's my last card and if it fails I shall change the title to 'The Passing of Johnston Forbes-Robertson.' "

That it did not fail, but ran until for sheer weariness he could play it no longer, is still a theatrical tradition. It broke dangerous ground, but was an interesting experiment and well deserved its popularity.

It would be discourteous to take leave of the Lyceum

without paying homage to its real master—Fussie. Fussie was a fox-terrier. All the intimacy that Irving withheld from mankind he lavished upon dogs : dogs—or perhaps latterly, *a* dog—were the link between him and humanity. If you liked dogs—more especially if dogs liked you—if you got on well with Fussie and took a real interest in his rheumatism, Irving would suffer you almost gladly ; and that is about as far as most of his friendships went.

Fussie had originally belonged to Ellen Terry, but Irving had won his heart through his stomach (he was a greedy dog) and he gradually became his property or, more correctly speaking, he became Fussie's property. Never were his master's thoughts long away from Fussie, even in the toil and stress of his hardest work. I remember there was once talk of a wonder-working oil, a ' sure cure ' for rheumatism, and Irving sent for two bottles, one for Fussie and one for my dog, Mouton, who was also a sufferer. Perhaps the oil possessed all the virtues claimed for it, but it also possessed a smell so appalling that, on its arrival, I dispatched it there and then to an invalid friend at a distance.

The bottle reached us just on the eve of a most important production, and when we next met, Irving stood upon the stage, after the fall of the curtain, playing the host to one of those brilliant first-night gatherings for which the Lyceum was famous.

Distinguished Guests were thronging up—each must have a word and a smile—but, as I slipped past, he stopped me with a gesture and carried on a conversation under great difficulties which shaped itself more or less thus. " Did you—how d'you-do ?—get the seal oil ? " I nodded. " Did it—how are you ?—glad you were able to come—didn't it——? " I was able to supply the missing word and nodded still more violently.

" Yes, it *did*. Something awful. Didn't yours ? "

" Awful—yes, wonderful play—so glad you were pleased—you wouldn't rub *that* stuff—*how*-d'-ye-do ?—into your dog's leg, would you ? "

185

My dog, Mouton, had a cult for Irving and was very jealous of Fussie, behaving to him with frigid politeness but always trying to divert Irving's attention to himself. Once he had accompanied me to a dancing lesson given at the Lyceum, and was sitting quietly at the prompt entrance watching the gyrating class when Irving and Fussie walked on to the stage and stood awhile, absorbed in each other as usual.

The neglected Mouton sat in his dark corner till he could bear it no longer, when, rising slowly on to his hind-legs, he walked thus erect straight across the stage, looking over his shoulder at Irving and softly growling at Fussie, who had no parlour tricks and who watched the performance with amazement and contempt.

On one terrible occasion, when the Lyceum company was going to America, Fussie, starting with his master, was left behind at Southampton in the hustle of embarkation. Days after he turned up, dusty and footsore, at the theatre, then in the hands of Mary Anderson, and was of course recognised and received with due reverence by Barry, the stage-door keeper.

Irving thought that he must have found his way back by following the railway lines, and this theory was confirmed when, on a later American tour, the hapless Fussie was again left behind at the New York station when the company set out for San Francisco. His master discovered the loss almost at once and the train was held up, when a small white object came into sight plodding steadily along the line. Fussie had started for California.

'ARRANGEMENT in black and brown, Miss Rosa Corder.' I remember the picture in '79 at the Grosvenor Gallery and have always thought it by far the best of what Whistler called his ' black portraits.' More subtle in quality than the ' Sarasate,' in every way superior to the overrated ' Lady Meux ' and ' Comte Robert de Montesquiou,' more complete than the lovely ' Fur Jacket,' it eclipsed its most serious rival, ' Le Brodequin Jaune—Lady Archibald Campbell,' in its grave dignity and noble beauty.

A fair woman, in a black jacket and long black skirt, stands in profile against a black background holding in her right hand a plumed hat. Nothing could be more simple, yet it is one of the world's great pictures. When I first saw it in the Grosvenor Gallery I knew neither Miss Corder nor Whistler, but the portrait was one day to introduce me to both.

Its original owner was a certain C. A. Howell, a mysterious and fascinating Anglo-Portuguese, around and about whom has collected a perfect Arabian Nights' Entertainment of tales true and untrue ; the hero himself being, I think, chiefly responsible for the untrue ones.

He had in his time been almost everybody's bosom friend and usually their private secretary. The secretary-ships always came to an abrupt end owing to financial complications ; the friendships often lingered surprisingly long. He always seemed to have been extraordinarily attractive to ' portable property ' such as pictures, furniture, and bric-à-brac ; they flew to him, and adhered, as the steel to the magnet.

No one knew what he possessed or did not possess, nobody could exactly remember when or why they had bestowed upon him various *objets d'art*, and he had several times excited curiosity by pseudo-posthumous sales to which his bewildered friends had flocked in the faint

187

hope that their long-lost and half-forgotten treasures might come to the surface—which they seldom, if ever, did.

One day I received a hurried scrawl from Ellen Terry —" Howell is *really* dead *this* time ! Do go to Christie's and see what turns up."

I went ; and apparently people had become weary or distrustful of Mr. Howell's abortive demises, for the sale was poorly attended and a valuable though very miscellaneous collection fetched low prices.

Among the pictures two stood out as masterpieces and both were by Whistler, the ' Rosa Corder ' and the ' Crepuscule in Flesh Colour and Green—Valparaiso,' that dream of opaline dusk falling on phantom ships becalmed in an enchanted sea. They were each equally beyond my reach, but, in a spirit of adventure, I recorded two absurd bids—bids so futile that I did not trouble to go to the sale. When I heard that both the wonderful things had been knocked down to me I was as much amazed as delighted.

A few days afterwards I received a letter from Whistler. " I am told," he wrote, " that you have acquired the two paintings of mine that were offered at the Howell sale the other day. This being the case, you will perhaps pardon my curiosity to see them hanging on your walls and my desire to know the collector who so far ventures to brave popular prejudice in this country."

" The collector "—it sounded so important—and elderly. I had been brought up by Albert Moore in the knowledge and love of Whistler, but had never met him, and now I felt very young and uninteresting and quite sure of proving a disappointment.

However, I was in for it ; Whistler was coming to luncheon, my mother had taken to her bed in a sudden attack of shyness which she called a slight chill, and I was left alone to face the Great Man in much perturbation and a thick yellow fog.

I had of course heard tales of his sarcasm, his pitiless

wit, his freakish temper, and by the time he arrived was on the point of developing a slight chill myself.

But behold, instead of the Whistler of legend entered a wholly delightful personage, an *homme du monde* whose old-world courtesy smoothed away all awkwardness and who exercised an almost hypnotic fascination such as I have met with in no one else.

I knew him for Whistler by the restless vitality of the dark eyes ; there was the dapper figure, the black curls, the far-famed white lock, but of the scoffer, the Papilio mordens, not a trace.

We seemed to slip into a sudden intimacy : it may have been partly owing to the fog which walled us round with thick darkness, swallowing up all sights and sounds from without and leaving us curiously alone in the lamp-lit room.

This first impression of a friendly Whistler was, I am glad to say, never effaced ; I seldom came across the fretful satirist of ' The Gentle Art of Making Enemies.' This work was certainly held by the author in high esteem ; he once read nearly the whole of it aloud to me at a sitting with the greatest enjoyment, but his delight in it was mischievous rather than malicious, and the Enemies, having served their turn, seemed if not forgiven, at least forgotten. The man whom I knew was courteous, kindly, and affectionate and showed a lovable side to his nature with which he is not often credited.

The meeting between the painter and his masterpiece, ' Rosa Corder,' was quite touching. He hung over her, he breathed softly upon her surface and gently stroked her with his handkerchief, he dusted her delicately and lovingly.

" *Isn't* she beautiful," he said—and so she was.

" And what else was in the sale ? " he asked, when he could tear himself away from Miss Corder.

" Well," I said, considering, " there was a most lovely lacquer bed—black lacquer with a curious canopy."

" Like this ? " asked Whistler, sketching a great oval in the air.

189

"Just like that," said I.

"That's mine!" cried Whistler. "I never *could* remember where that bed was. He would never *let* you remember where your things were. What else?"

I went through a list of objects that had pleased me, Whistler thoughtfully docketing them—"That was Rossetti's—that's mine—that's Swinburne's"—and so on. He seemed not in the least put out at the loss of his property, all ill-feeling being merged in admiration.

"He was really wonderful, you know," he went on. "You couldn't keep anything from him and you always did exactly as he told you. That picture," pointing to 'Rosa Corder,' "is, I firmly believe, the only thing he ever paid for in his life : I was amazed when I got the cheque, and I only remembered some months afterwards that he had paid me out of my own money which I had lent to him the week before."

The portrait, it appeared, had been a commission from Howell, and Whistler instanced his prompt acceptance of the same, with little or no hope of payment, as an example of the man's strange influence ; but a still stronger influence must have been the pure and noble face of the sitter, her clear-cut profile and gentle dignity of bearing.

Some years after I became possessed of the picture, Ellen Terry asked me to a box at the Lyceum, saying that I should there meet a friend. When I arrived, a lady sat in the box alone ; someone unknown to me yet strangely familiar—the small head—the grave, delicate face—of course! Had I not left her at home half an hour since, and here she was at the theatre—Rosa Corder, but little changed since she had sat for the great portrait.

She had posed for it, she told me, some forty times, standing in a doorway with the darkness of a shuttered room beyond her ; long sittings, lasting on two occasions until she fainted, and at last she had refused to go on with them. A painter herself, she could see that the picture was complete and that further work upon it would be dangerous, so she took courage and struck for freedom.

That she gained her point without much opposition shows that Whistler must have been satisfied with the picture himself. He had carried the head much further than was usual with him, but with no loss of breadth, and had achieved a wonderful likeness full of admirable characterisation.

I met Miss Corder several times after this first introduction and always with great pleasure : she had a beautiful stillness, as of one who through much sorrow had found tranquillity. She was a great lover of animals and they returned the compliment with interest. My dog, Mouton, had a *tendresse* for her almost equalling his appreciation of Henry Irving and would sit close beside her, on her very skirts if he could manage it, whenever he was in the room with her. She used to stay from time to time with Ellen Terry, and in the April of 1904 I heard from that kind friend that she was dead.

" Poor Rosa Corder," she wrote, " she has gone—somewhere—out of this world. I often think of her wonderful pale hair which lay upon the ground several inches when she was standing up. I liked her greatly. I don't know for certain the date of the Whistler picture, but think it was about 1869."

How far resemblance in the portrait went beyond that of mere form and feature I discovered by accident.

I found a friend of mine, a sporting soldier, to whom art in almost any form was a sealed book, studying the picture with deep interest.

" Like it ? " I asked, in surprise.

" Yes," said he. " That woman's a horse-breaker."

" No, she isn't," said I, " she's a painter."

" Well, anyhow she knows a lot about horses," he persisted, " and she lives among 'em."

Once at a rehearsal Sir James Barrie, impatient at the impossible subtleties demanded of the players by the producer, called out to an actor—" Mr. ——, I want you to cross from left to right silently conveying to the audience that you have an aunt at Surbiton."

The actor did not feel equal to the task : how had Whistler conveyed to my friend that Miss Corder lived at Newmarket and painted race-horses ?

The Master was so far satisfied with our tête-à-tête luncheon that we made a day of it. The fog still rendering most objects invisible, he suggested that such an opportunity of viewing the Academy should not be missed, so we repaired thither, the appearance of the Arch Enemy within their gates fluttering the dove-cotes of the Forty not a whit ; thence we went to the New English Art Club, then the stronghold of what Whistler called the ' Steer-y-Starr-y-Stott-y lot ' in elegant allusion to the chief painters' names, and finally parted on the best of terms.

I knew that his easy acceptance of me was due to friendship for Albert Moore, with whom he had discussed me ; nevertheless, I felt not a little elated, and from that time we saw much of each other until, some years later, he deserted London for Paris.

He was then living in a little house in Cheyne Walk with a large garden behind it. He was perpetually changing houses and each house was to serve as a subject for new and charming schemes of decoration, but, as a matter of fact, these schemes were never carried out.

Once in the house, he distempered the dining-room walls lemon yellow, hung the Six Projects (lovely sketches for pictures that never materialised), laid a white cloth upon the table and placed thereon a centre-piece of ' Old Blue ' which was his most cherished possession—and then fell to work and forgot all about the rest of the house wherein one stumbled up uncarpeted stairs and sat upon unpacked crates. But the yellow dining-room was a dream. A little peat fire always burned on the blue-tiled hearth, the Projects sparkled on the walls, the room seemed full of warm spring sunshine.

The front and back drawing-rooms on the first floor were used as a studio and were all that a studio should be—very bare—very untidy—very dirty, yet made beautiful by the glimpse of the river from two tall windows.

Here I used often to come when light was fading and he could paint no more; we would sit in the blue twilight that he loved and he would talk, sometimes fantastically, capriciously, his thought alighting for a moment on a subject, like his sign-manual, the Butterfly, extracting a sip of what I am bound to confess was not always honey, and flitting gaily on to the next. But on one subject, his Art, he never jested; when he spoke of that he was always in deadly earnest. He was usually a pitiless critic of his own output and would day after day wipe out work which to anyone else would have appeared perfect.

On one or two memorable occasions we turned out the studio together, going through the many canvases stacked against the walls, and I had brief glimpses of pictures almost complete, some of them, to my eyes, among his best work, which I have never seen or heard of again.

One in particular I remember: a girl in black, painted I think from his sister-in-law, Miss Phillip, standing by a table covered with a white cloth on which were silver tea or breakfast things. It was a large canvas, about the size of the 'Rosa Corder,' and at that moment most beautiful.

Another wonderful 'rub in' on an even larger scale was a full-length figure of Venus, running with wide-flung arms and flying tresses up a beach of golden sand from a sea of pale turquoise. A small version of the design was among the cherished 'Projects,' but the large picture, as far as it went, was even finer: it was the most poetic treatment of the well-worn subject that I have ever seen. Here was no languid nymph posing in an unseaworthy shell, no conscious bather struggling with her back hair, but the incarnate Joy, born of the sunshine and the dancing foam.

Even as he showed it to me I realised that at no time in his life could he ever have carried that picture to a finish; to paint a life-size nude figure to satisfy himself would always have overtaxed his frail physique and powers of draughtsmanship—but I wonder what has become of that lovely, half-realised dream.

He frequently spoilt his work by trying to take it beyond a certain point and then, as a rule, destroyed it ruthlessly ; though in his last two or three years this critical faculty deserted him to a certain extent, and I have seen adorers, during that late and brief day of popularity, bending in reverence before ' little masterpieces ' which formerly would never have survived their hour of birth. The delicate hand had grown weary, the drawing (never a strong point) had gone all to pieces, and the execution was weak.

But when I first came to his studio these days were still far off. He would often go on painting after I arrived, and I would watch breathlessly while the magician wove his spells. In his painting there was no mechanical process, no laying of an elaborate foundation, as with Albert Moore. He painted direct upon a dark ground—very slowly—each brushful of delicate colour laid on and left, the next very slightly overlapping but not mixing with it. The picture began to grow at once into the effect desired ; it was, as he loved to say, ' finished from the first,' though over it, when perfectly dry, were painted many other pictures until he succeeded in pleasing himself.

Doubtless by this means he obtained freshness and spontaneity, but there was one drawback. Paint in course of time becomes transparent and the dark ground beneath must gradually appear through it, dulling the superimposed hues. During the years that the ' Rosa Corder ' was in my possession I noticed a perceptible difference.

Whistler, when he met a picture again after a long separation, always saw the change, yet not even to himself would he acknowledge the cause. He would order varnishing and, in many cases, cleaning—cleaning as a picture dealer understands it—and under this treatment some of his best work has suffered severely.

He at once ordered ' Rosa Corder ' into dock for repairs, and with a sinking heart I saw her carted off to the 'restorer.' Two days later I visited her in hospital and the operator, showing me a small corner of the canvas, said triumphantly, " There ! And the whole picture will 'come up' just like that."

" The whole picture will come home with me at once," said I, and ' Rosa,' after a thorough dusting and under a light coat of varnish, returned home none the worse.

I do not think that other people's pictures interested Whistler much. Nothing would induce him to praise where he saw no merit, though when he could say an encouraging word to a friend it seemed to give him real pleasure. Once—only once—he really liked a painting of mine, a small portrait of Sarah Bernhardt, and I remember him carrying it about the room, putting it in various lights and ejaculating at intervals—" No, but I say—eh ?—isn't it—eh ?—isn't it—pretty ? "—and the word ' pretty ' was not used opprobriously. But such moods were unusual.

Albert Moore was about the only living painter for whose work he expressed unqualified admiration, but he had never cared to acquire an Albert Moore. Moore *did* possess a Whistler, but he kept it in a dusty corner with its face to the wall.

As a fact, I have never known a painter anywhere near the front rank who could see much merit in work upon other lines than his own. Whistler could find nothing to admire in a portrait by Sargent. " Is he still doing that brown stuff ? " he would enquire if I came to him from Sargent's studio. The superb decorative quality of Burne-Jones's designs escaped him altogether ; he could only see the mechanical painting and the early Italian *pastiche*. For Burne-Jones, Whistler's pictures might have been blank canvas—the lovely, limpid brush-work, the delicate mystery wrought their charm for him in vain. Sargent, always broad-minded and kindly, perforce admired the technical perfections of Whistler's best works, but I think they gave him little pleasure : the artistry, the creative touch that distinguishes a picture from a clever life study, weighed but lightly with him.

The truth is that no great painter cares much about pictures painted by other people : catholic appreciation would seem to be a second-rate quality.

I, always hopelessly second-rate, often found myself in difficulties with Whistler over this point. He would have his friends and disciples ' leave all and follow him,' and he knew me to be compassed about with guilty entanglements elsewhere ; though I tried to keep them discreetly in the background they were always turning up. On the whole he bore with them wonderfully.

Once, I remember, we had taken Mrs. Whistler to call on Albert Moore and were walking away from his house together when I prepared to say good-bye and turn Hammersmithwards.

" What are you going down there for ? " asked Whistler, suspiciously.

I braced myself. " I'm going to see Burne-Jones."

" Who ? "

" Burne-Jones."

" O—Mister Jones " (this curiously pointless gibe never palled upon Whistler). " But what on earth are you going to see him for ? "

" I suppose, because I like him."

" *Like* him. But what on earth do you like him *for* ? *Why* do you like him ? "

He had now faced round barring the way, his little cane rapping angrily on the pavement. Why did I like Burne-Jones ? There were so many reasons and I could not stand in the middle of High Street giving them all to Whistler. I took the first that occurred.

" I suppose—because he amuses me," I said feebly.

" Amuses you ? Good heavens—and you like him because he amuses you ! I suppose "—with rapid deduction—" I suppose *I* amuse you ! " Another rap of the cane and a fiery glance. Here was an impasse. If I said yes—yet on the other hand, if I said no——

" Don't tease him, Jimmy," said Mrs. Whistler. " Surely he may choose his own friends."

Whistler suddenly and lightly touched my hand. "He doesn't mind, do you?" he said with one of his rare smiles. Though he laughed much he seldom smiled, the carefully studied sardonic grin being merely a stage effect and counting for nothing. When he smiled he was irresistible : I felt that he had apologised and sworn undying friendship, though I am sure that nothing was further from his thoughts. The memory of Burne-Jones's evidence against him in the Ruskin trial always rankled. Truly this had been a great mistake, but the primary error was the calling of Burne-Jones on the case at all, a craftsman in an entirely different branch of Art. They might as well have called Grinling Gibbons or Benvenuto Cellini. Whistler himself as a critic of Burne-Jones's work would have been of equal value.

In spite of occasional encounters of this sort our good fellowship flowed on very peacefully, though I sometimes noticed attempts to trouble the waters by friends unknown who had probably fared less well. Once, during a visit to Paris, Whistler had begun a portrait of Sarah Bernhardt, but I fancy it went little beyond the first sitting : Sarah had arrived late, had failed to keep appointments, and had been unable or unwilling to give the artist the allegiance that he required from a sitter. On his return he was talking over the incident with me when suddenly he paused.

"By the by," he said, "someone told me that *you* had asked her not to sit to me—had said that it would not be worth her while and had advised her to get out of it."

"Really?" said I, rising and preparing to be cast forth into outer darkness, "and what did you think of that?"

"I thought nothing about it," said Whistler. "I have never thought of it again till now. Of course I knew you hadn't."

So the little shaft of malice missed its mark—but what a pity that the portrait was lost to us : the mysterious

Sarah, interpreted by Whistler, should have proved a masterpiece.

Another selected sitter who failed to appreciate the honour paid to him had been Disraeli. Whistler had long wished to paint that remarkable man, whose bizarre appearance appealed strongly to him as a subject, and he had tried through many channels to attain his desire, but in vain.

One day he had come upon the longed-for model sitting alone in St. James's Park, apparently absorbed in thought. Even Whistler experienced an unusual sensation which he recognised as shyness in the strange and sinister presence, but plucking up his courage, he plunged boldly in, endeavouring to recall himself to the mystic Prime Minister and finally making his request. The Sphinx remained silent throughout ; then, after an icy pause, gazed at him with lack-lustre eyes and murmured, " Go away, go away, little man."

Whistler went, and with him the Great Poseur's chance of immortality on canvas. He shortly afterwards graciously assented to sit to Millais, who produced—nothing in particular to everybody's entire satisfaction.

After Whistler left the house in Cheyne Walk to set up in Paris I of course saw him less frequently, but we kept up a fitful correspondence and he always came to see me on his visits to London to arrange his exhibitions. He was most particular as to how his works should be shown and always, if possible, designed and supervised the decoration of the room ; the slightest divergence from his plan counting as a heinous offence.

During his brief reign as President of the British Artists of Suffolk Street he devised for the Gallery a very quiet scheme of grey-brown with just a hint of gold here and there, but while it was being carried out he was perforce absent for a few days. On his return he found that gold was being used freely, to the complete undoing of his design, but the artist in charge, much disappointed at his President's disapproval, explained that there *was* the gold, and, in his opinion, it ought to be used.

" After all," continued the well-meaning man, " you're *using* gold in the decoration, so I don't see why——"

" Look here," said Whistler patiently, " suppose I'm making an omelette and you come along and drop in a seagull's egg. I'm *using* eggs, but—see ? "

I hope that the British Artist saw, for Whistler was really an authority on omelettes and indeed on cookery in general, and perhaps I should quote one of his golden rules as a guide to housewives.

" I can't think why people make such a to-do about choosing a new cook," he would observe reflectively. " There is only one thing that is absolutely essential. I always ask at once, ' Do you drink ? ' and if she says, ' No,' I bow politely and say that I am very sorry but I fear that she will not suit. All *good* cooks drink."

The flitting to Paris with all his household gods was necessarily something of an upheaval, and in the bustle of departure Whistler, always impatient of tedious formalities, omitted to pay his last quarter's rent. This I learned not long afterwards from an acquaintance who was estate agent for a large London property and who was bewailing to me the unbusinesslike habits of painters as tenants.

" Now *you* are a painter," said he. " Do you know anything of a man called Whistler ? "

I thought that he was being lightly humorous and attempted a like jocularity. " I seem to have heard the name before," I said. " Haven't you ? "

" No," he replied in obvious innocence. " And I don't know where a letter will find the man. He has taken away his furniture and there is nothing left in the house but a big screen with some sort of blue daub on it and a few pictures. I suppose they would not be of any value, would they ? "

I gasped. The lovely and beloved screen that stood in the yellow dining-room painted with a great nocturne in blue and gold, the river and the night sky, dreamily

blue, and twinkling orange lights ! And the ' few pictures '
—what were they ?

I cannot now recall the exact brand of lie that I told
to the trustful enquirer—whether it was merely a negligible,
white affair that a trifle of purgatorial flame will set right,
or whether—but the thought is depressing and, anyhow,
it had to be done.

I then hastened to Whistler's frame-maker, who was
also an old friend of my own, and besought him to remove
the screen and the pictures (among which was the well-
known ' St. Mark's by Night ') at once to his store-room
while I made my confession to the Master by letter. But
never could I tell him the whole story. To lose his
pictures would have been trying but by no means so heavy
a blow as to learn that Lord ——'s solicitor had never
heard of him.

On the sad return to England after the Paris years I
do not like to dwell. Mrs. Whistler had become alarm-
ingly ill, and when she was brought home the end was
already close at hand. Her husband, who was devoted to
her, would not acknowledge the hopelessness of the case :
he shut his eyes to it and would talk to me of schemes for
the future, of houses to be taken, of studios to be looked at,
all to be done ' when Trixie was better.'' And yet he
knew—and I knew—and he knew that I knew. He now
looked old for the first time, and after the dreaded blow had
fallen was never the same man again.

He wandered for awhile to Lyme Regis and other
places and I heard of him from time to time from a kind
friend of his and old school-fellow of mine, Arthur Studd,
who was much with him ; but he finally drifted back to
Chelsea and Cheyne Walk, to a house which never took
on any Whistlerian atmosphere, a house that I hated at
sight and whose hideous brass door I never passed without
a sense of discomfort. Here I remember but few meetings
and not one that did not leave me sad. Once he seemed
almost himself ; he had been writing one of his old, freakish letters and was chuckling over it as of old, yet a note

was unfamiliar. He looked ill, but—there was something else. He read me the letter with glee, challenging approval. " Well ? Eh ? Well ? How's that, d'you think ? " I hesitated. It was too long, too laboured, all was said in the last sentence and the involved paragraphs leading up to it should have been cut out. " Eh ? " still said Whistler, and I still hesitated.

Miss Phillip, his sister-in-law, made some excuse to brush by my chair. " Don't tell him *now* if you don't like it," she whispered. " He has been over it all the morning and he's so tired."

So tired. Yes, that was it. He was tired—tired at last. Certainly the two most vital people that I have ever known were Whistler and Sarah Bernhardt. Life was to them an art and a cult, they lived each moment consciously, passionately. I had seen the painter after a day's struggle with a picture, the actress after a hard evening's work, come to a momentary halt from physical exhaustion, yet it was as the halt of an engine at a station—the imprisoned energy still throbbed and panted to be off again. This was different : Whistler was ' so tired.' I only saw him once again.

A YOUNG painter, after two years in the Paris studios, had come to London and had been making a round of the theatres. Apparently he had not been impressed and was holding forth upon the English Stage to a gathering of artists in most uncomplimentary terms.

" But," he said, " what surprises me most is that you *have* an actress—a really great actress who could hold her own in Paris or anywhere—and you don't seem to know it."

Whistler had just come into the room and was listening : he now stepped forward to the young man who was a stranger to him. " You are speaking of Nellie Farren, of course," he said. " Yes, you are quite right, but that's a secret ; very few of us know it and we keep it strictly to ourselves."

Nellie Farren. The name sounds to me like a laugh —the echo of many delightful laughs. I suppose it is now necessary to state that Nellie Farren was what was then called a Burlesque Actress and was Principal Boy at the Gaiety Theatre.

The Gaiety Burlesques were not achievements to be remembered with pride ; puns stood for wit, jingling rhyme carried along dull dialogue, the productions were upon the ordinary pantomime lines, and the costumes quite peculiarly ugly. But—they gave us Nellie Farren. Kate Vaughan, the exquisite, floated through them, vaporous, dreamlike ; Edward Terry, grotesque as a Gothic gargoyle, had a quaint and original comic force ; but it was the genius of Nellie Farren that held together those feeble extravaganzas, and when she left the stage it became at once apparent that they were beyond human endurance.

But Nellie seemed pleased enough with them ; content to make pleasant little bricks without a particle of straw, to lend wit and sparkle to dull lines by her humour and charm. After all, she was doing something that nobody else could do and that must always be amusing.

" How on earth," I once asked her, à propos of her performance in ' Ariel,' a more than usually idiotic work, " how on earth did you suddenly give the thrill—make a ' spirit pass before my face ' in the middle of that nonsense with nothing to help you ? "

Nellie meditated. " Well, you see," she said, " I've played the *real* Ariel heaps and heaps of times and sometimes I got thinking myself back into the real play. Then —well, I suppose what you mean happened *then*."

And I suppose it did, for she had reversed the usual progression from burlesque up to Shakespeare and had worked from Shakespeare down to burlesque—but how much she brought with her !

She had never been able to cure herself of the habit (early acquired) of serious and intense acting, and she moved through the ogling, posturing Gaiety crowd a living soul amidst a bevy of wax dolls ; her vitality and keen intelligence were like an open window in a heavily scented room.

She loved her public, the ' Boys of the Gaiety,' for their loyalty and genuine devotion to her, but I think that sometimes, and in secret, she longed for wider fields to conquer. She looked forward almost pathetically to the occasional tours round the suburban theatres where she could count upon audiences who cared to see acting, and for them she would put forth all her powers.

I have seen her at Islington lift the burlesque of ' Jack Shepherd '—or rather the part of Jack—by an extraordinary projection of her personality into high comedy and most moving drama ; the prison scene, the breakdown in the ' flash ' song and the change of the swaggering young rascal into a terrified, whimpering boy, were unforgettable.

On this plane she could do what she liked with her audience ; she held them between her hands, their laughter and their tears were hers.

She always loved the part of Jack Shepherd as ' giving her a chance,' but when, after her retirement, the actress who succeeded her failed in it she was genuinely distressed. " Poor, dear girl, why didn't she come to me ? I could have shown her how to do it." With due deference to both ladies, I doubt it.

Nellie Farren was the adored of artists ; grave and reverend seniors like Poynter and Burne-Jones would troop off like boys to applaud her ; yet she was never seen in studios, seldom to be glimpsed at any social function, Bohemian or otherwise.

I had long bowed before her and had several times applied to people who ' knew everybody ' for an introduction. These great creatures of course all knew Nellie —or said they did—but no introduction was ever forthcoming.

At last I thought of applying to a hard-working, ' useful ' actress. " Want to know Nellie Farren ? " she said at once. " All right. Take you to see her any day."

So, permission being granted, we one afternoon presented ourselves.

A tiny figure rose to receive us, trim and upright, garbed in an awe-inspiring costume of black velvet with a long train. It might have been a chatelaine of old giving audience to pilgrims from afar, but the wide-open, child-like eyes of Nellie Farren looked quizzically at me as she said, " Well, here I am. And I've smartened up a bit for you, too. Look at this." She revolved to show her sweeping draperies. " But I know you'll be disappointed all the same."

There she made a mistake. The real Miss Farren after the Nellie of the Gaiety was like a charming original drawing after a highly coloured copy. The yellow curls had vanished with the dazzling pink and white complexion, but the wonderful little face, twice as expressive in its innocence of ' make up,' the plentiful brown hair flecked with grey, and the slight touch of old-world dignity, formed a far more compelling picture. Brilliant as was the Boy Nellie, the quiet charm of the little grey lady held its own without the aid of limelight.

I cannot recall much that passed during that first interview, but I remember that Miss Farren became rather
puzzled by the dates of some of my theatrical recollections.
I was not, in truth, very ancient and there was still much
of the ' scrubbed boy ' about my appearance, but my
mother, who was an ardent theatre-goer, had begun my
dramatic education on my fourth birthday and I had a
retentive memory.

We passed down the ranks of the Farrens, discussed the
early Gaiety burlesques and the still earlier Lydia Thomp-
son period, and touched on the reign of the Bancrofts at
the Prince of Wales's ; then Miss Farren produced Buck-
stone and I countered with Phelps.

" Phelps ! " exclaimed the lady, staring at me in
wide-eyed amazement. " Phelps ! But he was *my* master
—he taught *me* ! " Then in a hushed whisper that was
irresistibly comic—" Gracious goodness, child—how ever
old *are* you then ? "

Perhaps out of reverence for my supposed grey hairs,
Nellie Farren graciously admitted me to her friendship and
consented to sit to me for a portrait which was started not
long afterwards.

I had hesitated between the dainty dame of private
life and the radiant Nellie of the boards, but she threw in
her vote for the latter ; that was the only Nellie Farren
with whom the public had any concern, and consequently
that was the Nellie to be recorded.

" I must ' make up ' for it, of course," she went on,
entering into the scheme with zest now that she was
committed to it, " and I'll put the wig on at home before
I start. It's such a business tucking away my own hair
under it : you see, I've got so much ; I can *sit* on it."
The next day she arrived at my studio, yellow-headed and
chuckling.

" Look at the cabman," she laughed, drawing me to
the door. " He's an old friend and comes round most
mornings to see if I have a job for him—I call him ' Darkie.'
When I turned up just now with clouds of golden hair

bursting out of my bonnet in all directions you should have seen his face ! Look at him now—he doesn't think it becoming." And certainly Darkie had an air of respectful but distinct disapprobation.

During the sittings that she gave me I tried from time to time to express to her what she stood for to the tribe of artists who delighted in her work ; even hinting delicately at the cult for those beautifully modelled supports which were the joy of draughtsmen.

"I should have thought," said Miss Farren with austerity, "that there were enough legs to be seen at the Gaiety without bothering about mine."

"But you must know that yours are different," I urged : it was a subject upon which I felt strongly, and I went into details. Miss Farren gave her attention.

"You mean—they're slender and straight—with straight knees, like a boy's."

"Yes, like a boy's ; except for the boy's puppy joints and big feet."

"I see," said Nellie. "Then—perhaps that explains something that rather puzzled me. Someone brought a French painter on to the stage one evening (funny lot those Frenchmen) and introduced him to me. I don't remember his name, but I believe he was a bit of a swell. Well—all he could say to me was, ' Ah, Miss Farren, if I might paint your legs.' I didn't like it. I said, ' Look here, young man, I've been on the stage some time and there are people who will tell you that I know my business—and if all you can find to look at when I'm acting is my legs ——' The man seemed quite upset. Then you don't think he was trying to be funny ; you think he was in earnest ? "

"But of course he was," I assured her ; and I believe that thenceforth Miss Farren regarded the French nation with greater tolerance.

Certainly she was the only woman I have ever seen who looked well in the hideous traditional costume of ' principal boy.' I remember telling her of a remark made

NELLIE FARREN AS " RUY BLAS "
From an oil sketch by THE AUTHOR, 1902

by my mother after a visit to the Gaiety, where she had not admired the attire of the chorus ladies.

" Why do those poor girls make such dreadful sights of themselves ? " she innocently enquired. " Surely they might all dress *nicely*, like Miss Farren."

" But," I had objected, " Miss Farren only appeared to be wearing a pair of shoes, and a bit of muslin pinned on to her somewhere at the back."

" Dear me," said my mother, " now I remember, that *was* all. But she looked very nice and I should never have noticed it if I'd met her in Bond Street."

Nellie Farren laughed. " Yes, I remember that bit of muslin," she said. " When I tried on that dress at re-hearsal everyone called out ' Splendid ! ' but it seemed to me—well, rather——"

" I suppose it was," I admitted.

" So I got that bit of muslin and began to fasten it on, but they all shouted, ' Oh, you'll spoil it, Nellie,' and seemed so worried that I let it alone. But I was going to have that muslin, and I fixed it on so that it hung down at the back."

" It didn't hang down much," said I, remembering her flights across the stage, followed at a distance by the muslin.

" Didn't it," said Nellie comfortably, " well, I thought it did, so that was all right."

It always amused her to ramble back into the old Gaiety days and to recall their thrilling events of the utmost importance—such as the sad episode of Kate Vaughan's *chevelure*—" She came into the theatre one afternoon with all her hair a deep sea-green. I could only stare and say, ' Lor', Kate ! ' and she said, ' Yes, I know ; but it's all right at night.' And sure enough at night it was a beautiful brown. Then the wig man said, ' You'll excuse me, Miss Vaughan, but if you go on using that stuff, every hair on your head will come off,' and "— in an awful whisper—" it *did*."

Such stories never disturbed my firm belief that Kate

Vaughan never really existed. She was a floating mist, a drifting moonlit cloud, a phantom born of melody and rhythm, and, I am quite sure, evaporated nightly at the wings when the music ceased. To imagine Kate Vaughan eating her dinner, or putting on her boots or blowing her nose was an obvious impossibility. She was not a burlesque actress and made no attempt to become one : when, as Morgiana, she poured the boiling oil into the jars containing the Forty Thieves, she might have been pouring out cups of afternoon tea. She said, in effect, to her audience, " This bores me extremely and I suppose it bores you, but I'm going to dance again later on and then you'll be pleased."

Nellie Farren, on the contrary, lived in her parts. She was altogether a child of the theatre ; the world outside hardly existed for her and she knew little that happened in it.

I was one day showing her a picture by Rossetti which recalled an old and long-forgotten memory. " Rossetti," she said slowly, " it's a long time since I heard that name. He used to be a clever sort of man. Did he get on ? "

" My dear," I explained, " he got off some time ago. He has been dead for years."

" Rossetti." Nellie repeated the name thoughtfully, evidently quite unaware of its claims to immortality. " I suppose it's the one I mean. A queer fellow—was going to marry a red-haired girl."

" That's it," said I.

" They wanted to adopt me," said Nellie.

" Good gracious," I gasped.

" Yes, that's what father said," she continued. " He thought it an odd way to start married life—especially as they seemed to have no money. Of course he wouldn't give me up, but I often used to go with him and sit in the painting-room. Is the red-haired girl dead, too ? "

" Yes," said I.

What would have happened if father had given Nellie up and she had gone to be a daughter to the morbid, overwrought ' girl with red hair ' and her wondrous husband ; her clear-cut common sense in that house of dreams and shadows, her matchless vitality thrown against that painted arras of mediævalism and mystery ; above all, her delightful sense of humour allied to Rossetti's delightful sense of humour ? The result might have been surprising.

Rossetti always wanted the best of everything, so it should not have surprised me that he had contemplated the annexation of Nellie Farren. Her tales of the theatre held so much interest for me that I once asked her why she did not write her reminiscences.

" Why ? " said Miss Farren. " Well, because I've always noticed that as soon as anyone writes his life there's an end of it—he's dead. Take poor Toole, for instance."

" But Toole's alive," I objected.

" No, he isn't," said Nellie sadly. " Look at him."

I thought of the pathetic, aged figure that once had been that most cheery of laughter-makers—and agreed with her. Poor Toole was not alive.

" But Toole is pretty old," I suggested.

Nellie looked at me suspiciously.

" You're not asking how old *I* am, are you ? " she said. " I've never told anybody that yet and I'm not going to begin ; but this I will tell you. When I was about twenty-four, mother was sitting ' in front ' one night ; and when I came on her neighbour said, ' Wonderful old thing, isn't she ? She's fifty-six and has got twelve children.' But whatever my age may be, I'm not dead and don't want to be—so I shan't write my life."

There was probably never a more individual actress than Nellie Farren : she held her audience by sheer force of personality, and I think she often looked for this power in vain among the generality of actors.

" They don't put enough *into* it," she once said to me.

" Don't work hard enough, do you mean ? " I asked.

" No, not exactly that," said Nellie. " That's not much good by itself. D'you remember young Lonnen ? "

I nodded. A clever, grotesque young actor who had

made a hit with his Irish songs. " Well, *he* worked if you like ! Heavens, how that poor child sweated at it—literally, I mean. When he'd been on the stage for five minutes he might have been running five miles. I used to talk to him about it. ' For goodness' sake, boy, go slow,' I told him. ' You can let 'em have it just as well without bursting yourself like that. Take it easy.' But he couldn't. I suppose he wasn't strong enough, poor lad."

Towards the end of Miss Farren's reign, a change had come over the Gaiety burlesque, showing a certain falling off in fun and in all-round acting, but a decided gain in beauty. Fred Leslie, a comedian of peculiar charm, replaced Edward Terry, Sylvia Grey succeeded Kate Vaughan the peerless, but avoided comparison by her originality and girlish freshness : she was an exquisite dancer.

Nellie Farren alone remained unchanged ; in no way did her natural force abate. The American tour, which set its mark upon Leslie—he went an actor and returned an entertainer—affected her not in the least, though it gave her a unique experience. The Americans had not cared for her, had not recognised her delicate art : it was the only time in her life that she had not been beloved and it left her puzzled and not a little angry. She knew her own value ; knew that she had given of her wonderful best, and, feeling it rejected, made no secret of her opinion of the American public. Australia and the Australians she loved, though there she met with the mishap that ended her stage career ; for during her last years she was almost crippled by rheumatism, brought to a crisis during her Australian tour by sleeping in damp sheets.

She never played again after her return to England, though the terrible scourge left no disfiguring traces : the trim figure was unaltered and she walked and moved as buoyantly—or as she expressed it ' boyantly '—as of old. Only her hands, contracted like little withered leaves, showed a mark.

" Why do you not act again ? " I once asked her.

" At any rate, why not appear at a matinée now and then ?
You would delight so many and you would look just the
same as ever."

" Yes," said Nellie. " They wanted me to play Sam
Weller last week, but I wouldn't. I know that people
would be kind, but I can't jump and run about now as I
used to, and they would look at me and say, ' Yes, it's
Nellie—but it *ain't* Nellie.' "

Perhaps she was right, but Nellie would always have
been Nellie, *quand même.*

Much as I loved her burlesque acting, I had often
longed to see Nellie Farren in a real part in a real play,
and once very nearly achieved my desire.

A great friend of mine, a doctor, was anxious to get
up a matinée in aid of his hospital, and I had applied for
help to Ellen Terry. Together we discussed the programme.

" I've got an idea," said Miss Terry. " We won't do
the usual variety entertainment, but something that people
will really want to see. We'll do a burlesque, played
entirely by serious actors, and then something serious,
played entirely by comic actors, and it will be really interesting to see what we make of it. We'll do Planché's
' Andromeda ' : I used to play a small part in it long
ago ; now I'll play Andromeda—and we'll get Julia for
Perseus ; she will look splendid. And Bram shall manage
for us."

Bram Stoker, the Lyceum manager, came in with
great enthusiasm.

" There's no use in getting a small theatre," he said.
" All London will come : we must take Drury Lane."

And so the wild idea grew. Beautiful Julia Neilson
accepted Perseus at once, William Terriss would play the
King ; Sylvia Grey had a part and, to my everlasting
self-satisfaction, chose me as her partner in a duet dance.
(I do not mind saying that my step-dancing was not bad,
because hardly anyone now living can say it was.) But
the great sensation was to be reserved for the after-piece

—the Trial Scene from 'The Merchant of Venice' : Shylock, Fred Leslie ; Portia, Nellie Farren.

I shall always regret that this scene was never acted ; for, alas, the whole scheme came to nothing. The play then running at the Lyceum had to be taken off and Henry Irving could not spare his leading lady or his manager from rehearsals. The experiment would have interested everybody and its collapse was a real disappointment ; though most of the kindly cast played for me in the ' usual variety entertainment ' which was perforce substituted, and I still have Ellen Terry's letter volunteering to open : I wonder if any great Star ever proposed such a thing before.

" You will probably find it difficult to ask anyone to come first on the programme ; they hate beginning—playing the audience in. So do put me down to open. I don't mind a bit—in fact, I shall be glad to get away early."

Anyone who has ever tried to arrange a Star Programme will understand what difficulties were thus smoothed away. George Alexander, with Marion Terry and the St. James's Company, played an act from ' Lady Windermere's Fan,' Terriss and Miss Millward made a gallant dash at Petruchio and Katherine, Ellen Terry and Martin Harvey played ' Nance Oldfield,' Sylvia Grey danced : I had indeed much to be thankful for, but I mourned and still mourn the lost Portia of Nellie Farren.

The Ellen of the Lyceum had a great admiration for the Ellen of the Gaiety and their friendship dated from many years back. I remember her telling me of a long-ago tour, during which she, her sister Kate (afterwards Mrs. Arthur Lewis), and Nellie Farren shared rooms together. Nellie Farren looked after the commissariat, Ellen shopped, and the ornamental and genteel rôle was allotted to Kate Terry on the strength of a smart new bonnet. But whenever either of the Nellies wished to make an impression she borrowed the bonnet, and Kate Terry stayed at home.

After Miss Farren left the stage I never again entered the Gaiety—it had become meaningless to me. In spite of my devotion to the Queen of Burlesque I had never been a ' Gaiety Boy ' in the accepted sense of the word nor joined the nightly queue that waited at the celebrated stage door to do homage to the chorus ladies : nevertheless, my one and only appearance ' behind the scenes ' at that theatre was decidedly unconventional.

I had joined a small class, which included Ellen Terry, her son and daughter and her sisters, Marion and Florence, for a few dancing lessons from Sylvia Grey—Miss Terry and I, I remember, performed a sort of Harlequin and Columbine duet, the effect of which she always spoiled by exclaiming, as she subsided gracefully into my arms, " Now then—hold up ! Twelve stone ! "—and we had all gone to the Gaiety one evening *en masse* to observe and applaud our teacher, as befitted good and diligent pupils.

Nellie Farren was away on tour and had left such a blank that perhaps we could not do justice to those gallantly struggling to fill her place.

As we left we found rain and storm without.

" Let's go out by the stage door," said Ellen Terry to me. " Then we have only to cross the road to the Lyceum."

So we wandered back into the rapidly darkening theatre and explored shadowy passages in search of a way on to the stage. At last, in almost total gloom, we met an attendant and tried to explain our wants. I suppose she misunderstood, but at any rate what happened was that she seemed to give us a slight push, a door in the wall suddenly opened, we fell headlong down three steps and fetched up on the floor of the Leading Lady's dressing-room, where we sat in a blaze of light blinking helplessly. The room seemed quite full of young gentlemen with beautiful shirt fronts, and the Leading Lady was attired in a short white petticoat and something else—I am a bachelor and don't know its name, but there are pretty pictures of it in advertisements and I fancy it has ribbons somewhere.

Before the situation had time to become embarrassing, she had stepped forward, picked us up, dusted us and made us welcome ; as if the entrance of England's greatest actress on her head were a nightly feature of her receptions. She talked to us gently until she saw that we were more or less right side up again, and then, taking up a little lamp and adding nothing to her costume, she conducted us across the pitch-dark stage and down the cold passages to the stage door, where, most graciously and sweetly, she bade us good night.

" Well," said Miss Terry, as we splashed across the mud, " that was the most perfect exhibition of manners that I have ever seen. I don't believe there's a Princess in Europe who could have done that ! "

" The Princess would have slipped on a shawl, I expect," said I meditatively.

" I know—and that would have spoiled the whole thing. What a duck she looked, didn't she ? I'm sure I don't wonder——"

We stopped, on the brink of scandal.

" What fools *we* must have looked," went on Miss Terry. " Did you see me dive in ? "

" I was busy diving myself," said I. " If she had not been so charming——"

" We should be sitting there *now*," said Ellen Terry with conviction ; and I really think we should.

Oᴺᴇ summer in the late 'eighties there appeared in
London a troupe of American actors known as the
Daly Company. They came more or less unheralded and
with little puff preliminary, but at once made a hit, and
it was soon apparent that of the four principals each one
was in his or her way a great artist. John Drew, the first
young man, with his quiet yet essentially virile method,
was a marked contrast to our comparatively soft juveniles;
his handsome, mask-like face which seemed to express
nothing would suddenly let through a sly twinkle like the
flash of a dark lantern.

James Lewis was a dry comedian of irresistible humour,
Mrs. Gilbert a charming old lady who raised the most
commonplace part into the highest comedy, and the Leading Lady was Ada Rehan—bewitching, elusive, irritating,
amazing Ada Rehan—an actress of such compelling
personality that she is impossible to describe.

And these four fine artists were set down before the
London public to play a series of 'roaring farces,' old-
fashioned even in those days, translated from the German
into American by Mr. Daly, the manager, and performed
by the loyal four as though they had been masterpieces of
wit and humour, which indeed in their hands they actually
became.

They were soon installed as prime favourites; London
laughed with them and loved them; but even their
warmest admirers felt a little anxious when it was rumoured
that they were to attempt Shakespeare. At length 'The
Taming of the Shrew' was actually announced. Well,
that was not very serious. 'The Shrew,' as usually performed, was little more than a rough-and-tumble farce
and these clever people might be quite amusing in it :
still, it was dangerous, and the first night was awaited
with some misgivings.

It opened much as had been expected. The acting
was rather rough, the accent a little disconcerting, the

production tawdry and commonplace. Then entered
John Drew playing Petruchio's odious first scene with a
delicacy and humour that robbed it of all offence and
seemed to bring in a new atmosphere.

Then a voice raised without, a pause of expectancy, and
there swept on to the stage a figure that will never be forgotten by any there present—Ada Rehan as Katherine
the Shrew.

What the wonderful pair did with the play ; how they
contrived that the brutal tale of the bullying, starving and
frightening of a virago into a spiritless drudge should
become the delightfully amusing love story of two charming people I have never been able to find out, but nevertheless, the miracle was wrought. Katherine was reborn that
night and took her place among her deathless sisters,
Rosalind, Portia, Beatrice.

Not a whit of her shrewishness did she spare us ; her
storms of passion found vent in snarls, growls, and even
inarticulate screams of fury ; she paced hither and thither
like a caged wild beast, but her rages were magnificent
like an angry sea or a sky of tempest, she blazed a fiery
comet through the play, baleful but beautiful.

And when the storm passed and in the last great speech
she showed her happy love, her voice took on an unimag-
ined music, the words fell softly, slowly, like the last drops
of a clearing shower, while all along, through gloom and
shine alike, she wove a thread of the most delicate comedy,
brightening and condoning the violent scenes with strokes
of humour and changing the termagant's final humiliation
into the birth of her truer and nobler self.

It was revelation. Had Katherine ever been played
before and will she ever be played again ? I wonder.

Soon after the production of ' The Shrew ' I met John
Drew at the house of George Alexander, and both he and
Mrs. Drew became my very dear friends.

They then had rooms in Gower Street and used to
give little informal receptions to which their many admirers
crowded, but at first, I remember, Mrs. Drew was depressed

by what she considered the English frigidity. "My! They're cold," she exclaimed to me once when she had with difficulty sped her last guest.

"Cold!" I cried in real astonishment, "why they were all over you! I expected them to kiss you, and I rather think that one or two *did* kiss your husband on the stairs. What more can you want?"

But Josephine Drew could not formulate her wants; she only repeated, "My, ain't they cold?" until I began to feel quite chilly myself. I think, however, that the illusion was soon dispelled and she discovered that if, as a nation, we do not straightway take the stranger to our bosom it is not from want of accommodation in the said bosom, but rather from fear lest the visitor may not care for his quarters.

To these gatherings would usually come Mrs. Gilbert and James Lewis and his wife, but Miss Rehan, though an intimate friend, never put in an appearance, nor was she to be met at any other functions public or private : she remained behind the purdah, mysterious and aloof.

At the Easter following I was in Paris while the Daly Company was playing a short season there : the Drews and I were at the same hotel and we saw much of each other.

One day I came upon John and Mrs. Drew sitting in the court with a lady whom at first I did not recognise, a tall, rather sad-looking woman with a pale worn face and hair streaked with grey : almost before I was aware of it I had been introduced to Ada Rehan and we were all chatting together quietly, almost intimately.

I did not realise until some time later in what a happy hour that introduction had been effected. Ada Rehan shrank from meeting strangers, she was shy and (off the stage) intensely self-conscious ; her friends might have been reckoned on the fingers, but of these John Drew was one of the oldest and most trusted ; she was at rest sitting there quietly with him, she was amused by the bright ever-changing crowd and happily certain that no member of it noticed or recognised her. She was off her guard, and I think that from that moment she accepted me as a friend.

I had just come from Sarah Bernhardt's studio, where 'The Taming of the Shrew' as played by the American company had been under discussion. Sarah had asked for information, but did not obtain much. The few Frenchmen who had seen the play had gathered little from it and had been puzzled by the acting—they characteristically dismissed both as of no account. But, they rather grudgingly admitted, "The woman herself is superb, magnificent. It is to look at her that people go."

"Ah," said Sarah, "*succès de beauté*. I see."

'*Succès de beauté*.' I glanced at the pale, gentle face beside me, listened to the hesitating speech in sheer bewilderment.

How was it possible that this remote creature whose chief desire was to creep into a corner and hide herself could nightly flare forth into the incarnation of terrible vitality, the 'Tiger burning bright,' the flower of flame that was her Katherine the Shrew? I marvelled and still marvel, for I never solved the mystery of Ada Rehan, to which, I think, Augustin Daly alone held the key.

Mr. Augustin Daly, who shortly joined us and to whom Miss Rehan introduced me, was in many ways a most remarkable man. On first meeting him most people decided that he was a remarkably disagreeable one; afterwards some found that he could be remarkably attractive. But he was always remarkable, even in his clothes, which were remarkably seedy and vaguely 'wrong'—he looked like an itinerant photographer—and in his manners, which were remarkably bad. Still, there was a force about him, something dynamic and compelling, and even those who disliked him usually found themselves almost involuntarily doing exactly as he bade them.

That I was no exception to the rule soon became apparent as, shortly after we met, I undertook at his request—or, more properly, command—a task for which I had no reason to consider myself qualified.

During this visit to Paris Sarah Bernhardt had been most good natured and long-suffering in sitting to me, and my sketch-book was full of studies of the great lady, some the merest scribbles of momentary poses, others more elaborate portraits. Of this book Mr. Daly one day possessed himself and the contents apparently pleased him : at any rate he then and there asked me to dress a play for him.

" Have you ever designed for the stage ? "

" Only once," I confessed, " when I dressed a one-act play for George Alexander."

" Well, this is not a one-act play. I am going to pro-duce—mind, you must not breathe a word of this to anyone ; especially to no one in the Company——"

Mr. Daly's plans, great and small, were always pro-found secrets ; he loved to move in a mysterious way and to confide in no one. I took the required vow of silence, and with the air of a conspirator he proceeded to unfold himself : he was going to put on ' The Foresters ' by Alfred Tennyson, a play written round the Robin Hood legends and hitherto unacted and unpublished.

" But this will mean a big production," I stammered. " I don't think I can do it." I might have saved my breath : Mr. Daly had made up his mind and carried his point by sheer force of will.

He could entrust his one precious copy of the play to me for two days only, and in great excitement I read the poetic drama about which so many rumours were afloat : tales of its beauty and dramatic excellences, incredible hints of its having been submitted to Mary Anderson some two years earlier and by her unaccountably rejected. As I read, Miss Anderson's rejection became less and less unaccountable—but this was none of my business : I had been asked to dress the play, not to criticise it.

I did my best, and ' The Foresters ' proved the first of several productions that I costumed for Augustin Daly, but there was little satisfaction in the work. I never saw the scenery, the background for my figures, so could not judge of the finished picture, seldom saw a rehearsal, the plays being brought out in New York, and often found the completed costumes very odd travesties of the original designs. Mr. Daly had not the artistic knowledge to carry out a colour scheme or the sense of period to correct mistakes and had no reliable adviser.

He was always very pleasant to me, he showed me his gentler side, and I could have worked well with him could we have worked together, but the gulf of the Atlantic Ocean made collaboration difficult and the productions lacked unity.

' The Foresters ' met with great success in New York ; Daly sent me a triumphant cable and Ada Rehan wrote very kindly, congratulating me upon my work.

" ' The Foresters,' as you know, has been produced and so successfully. I wish you and the Tennysons could have been here on the opening night—that was the night to feel how successful it was. Now, of course, we shall have to reach expectation, which is always trying. I feel sure the Londoners will like it ; New York has gone wild over it. The costumes are very much admired, my first two most of all—and the fairies are really beautiful—all that you could wish. Is it not delightful to have all go so well ? "

But her high hopes for a London success were not fulfilled : London would have none of ' The Foresters ' and London was right ; the play was hopelessly weak, and the setting, though pretty, was crude in comparison to the finer London productions. Tennyson was not a playwright, and, but for Henry Irving, would never have been reckoned as such.

' Queen Mary ' made little mark, in spite of Irving's wonderful ' Philip,' but it is a fine play, the only good play that Tennyson wrote, and I often wonder why it is not revived by some middle-aged actress ; the reason I suppose being that no actress is middle-aged. ' The Cup ' succeeded through the grandeur of the Temple scene, the acting of Irving and the exquisite beauty of

Ellen Terry's ' Camma ' : Tennyson, however, disliked Irving's ' Synorix.' ' Becket ' contains fine passages but is not a fine play, though Irving's arrangement of it and superb acting made it appear so : yet the author left the theatre without a word of thanks or appreciation to the great actor who had done so much for him.

I never met the poet, though I used to see him occasionally driving about in the Haslemere neighbourhood, and wonder, of course respectfully, why, as he so much wished to avoid notice, he always dressed like George Cruikshank's ' Guy Fawkes.'

Luckily for me he did not see ' The Foresters.' In the scene of Maid Marian's dream I had tried to make the fairy vision grow almost imperceptibly out of its surroundings : the elfin figures were all in green, they were almost invisible in the green gloom of the forest, and as the dreamlight brightened and they moved out of the thickets their little white faces were like moonbeams, flickering through the leaves—at least I hoped so : that was the idea. When all was well forward Tennyson, who had apparently taken no interest in the proceedings, suddenly sent word that he wished the fairies to be gaily dressed in pink and blue, red and yellow. Maid Marian's (and my) dream of ' beechen green and shadows numberless ' seemed to be fading, unless—inspiration descended upon Mr. Augustin Daly—unless I never received the message.

" I shan't say a word about it," he decided. " Why should we spoil the scene ? " And we didn't.

The poet would not seem to have been a very inspiring master to work under or comrade to work with, but I never knew him personally and he may perhaps have been unfortunate in the stories of him that have survived ; for the most part records of snubs to youthful aspirants, rudeness to admirers who, though perhaps intrusive, were genuinely trying to show him respect and homage, and not very generous girds at brother poets. But here is a local Surrey legend which shows him in a more amiable though hardly more tactful mood.

At a garden-party, to which the Great Man had been decoyed, a timid lady was all unwillingly introduced to him. He seated himself beside her but spoke no word ; she was naturally tongue-tied. The silence was becoming oppressive when it was broken by the Bard, who remarked in deep tones, " Your stays are too tight."

" Oh," stammered the alarmed lady, " I—I *think* not. I——"

" They are," said the Bard. " I can hear them creaking."

It was too much : the unhappy lady leaped from her seat and fled like a hare. Later in the afternoon she saw with terror that the Poet was again shouldering his way towards her through the crowd : when he came within shouting distance he shouted, " I say." The victim, frozen to the spot, awaited him as the rabbit awaits the boa-constrictor. " I say—I was wrong. It wasn't your stays. It's my braces."

Here was at least the *amende honorable*, though coming in such questionable shape.

When Augustin Daly brought ' The Foresters ' to London John Drew was no longer among the players. A severe loss to the Company as a whole, to Ada Rehan it was catastrophe, for—to borrow a term from a sister art—John Drew as an accompanist stood alone. When playing ' opposite ' Miss Rehan as leading man, he worked for her so loyally, built up her effects so carefully and, in her ' big scenes,' effaced his own strong personality so cleverly, thus leaving the stage to her, that when he left her work became twice as hard.

Drew, I think, felt that he could advance no further with the Daly Company, which, with the development of Miss Rehan's genius, was becoming a one-woman show ; that if he was to have a career of his own he must carve it out for himself elsewhere ; so very reluctantly he cut himself adrift.

Daly, who could not understand such a defection, took it as a personal offence and insisted that Miss Rehan, who was his echo, should also be much hurt and affronted : she did her dutiful best, but, when not under the managerial eye, would relapse altogether and openly mourn for her old comrade. She herself told me—her sense of humour made the confession irresistible—that in their last performance together of ' As You Like It ' she, then supposed to be regarding John with cold aversion according to plan, had burst into tears on the stage as she placed the chain round his neck and had found great difficulty in going on with her part.

Ellen Terry with her quick intuition quite understood the situation and wrote to me from America, where she was touring :

" How is Ada Rehan ? I believe that she and I would be excellent friends if we could only meet for more than five minutes at a time. It seems odd that John Drew is downstairs—in the rooms below me in this Hotel—we have the same ' coloured gentleman ' to wait on us —but it was a doleful day for each, I should say, when John Drew and Ada Rehan ceased to act together—and *she* must miss it most—a woman would, I'm sure. If I didn't act with Henry he'd forget perhaps in a year (I wonder) but I shouldn't."

Though they hardly ever met after Drew's departure, the two were always anxious to hear news of each other and, when they were both in London, would hold communication in verbal messages through me. Once, when I was discharging my duties as go-between, a curious thing happened.

John had received news of the sudden death of his sister. It came to him as a great and unexpected blow, but characteristically he found time to remember the shock it would be to Ada Rehan.

" I wish you would go and tell Ada," he said to me. " Don't let her read of it first in a newspaper or hear of it casually."

Accordingly I went that afternoon to Miss Rehan's hotel and found her in good spirits and ready for a chat, but after we had talked for a little while there was a strange sound in the room, rather like the snapping of a violin string.

Ada held up her hand. " Hush," she said. " Did you hear that ? "

I nodded. She walked to the window and stood looking out, her back turned to me, for a long minute, then returned and sat down by me quietly. " Who is dead ? " she asked. " You have come to tell me that someone is dead."

" John's sister—Georgy Barrymore," I whispered.

We sat in silence until she said slowly—" An old friend. I knew that it was an old friend. I have heard that sound several times and always it has been followed by the news of an old friend's death. It is a sign for me. I always recognise it."

The strange thing was that the sound was undoubtedly real and as apparent to my ear as to hers.

The longer I knew Ada Rehan, the further our friendship advanced into intimacy, the less I could associate the actress with the woman. On the stage she was above all things the artist, her diction was exquisite, she spoke verse as I have never heard it spoken by another, the words melted in music and produced the effect of song, but without the aid of chanted notes or intoned phrases. If there was a fault it was the too great display of virtuosity.

And yet of all the work, the thought which must have been given to the creation of these vocal miracles Ada Rehan could tell nothing. She did not mind speaking of her work, she would discuss it with me gladly and openly, but—she had nothing to say.

She was a charming woman, though almost morbidly shy ; gentle, unworldly, intensely reserved, she in no way suggested the great actress, a fact not surprising in itself —the same might be said of Ellen Terry—but the surprise lay in the fact that she did not suggest the great artist, or indeed an artist of any sort.

She seemed to me to take but little real interest in the stage—I have seldom heard her discuss the performances of other actors or give an opinion upon a play. Music and painting interested her little ; she may have read, but I never found her doing so or heard her talk of books. Her taste in dress, surely part of an actress's education, was non-existent ; she would put on anything anyhow, with the result that when I first saw her in one of Mr. Daly's Americanised German farces in a costume of pillar-box red and a canary-coloured wig, the handsome young woman of six- or seven-and-twenty looked a charitable forty.

The curious charm, so triumphant on the stage, was still there in private life, but was more easy to analyse and revealed itself as the ripples of a delightfully quaint sense of humour on the surface of a nature deeply sad.

Gradually I found myself wondering—is this woman really a great, original actress or is she another's mouth-piece, an exquisite instrument played upon by a hidden musician ? Even in her acting I began to see strange incongruities.

In her Rosalind, a brilliant performance nobly con-ceived and carried out, would occur here and there pass-ages that took the breath away, so out of place did they seem ; passages of frankly vulgar clowning.

I suffered in silence, as became my insignificance, for some time, but at last, hearing so many criticisms from genuine admirers, I grasped my courage and spoke.

" Why *do* you do so-and-so ? " I demanded in some trepidation.

" Why do I ? " said Ada Rehan slowly, as if the ques-tion had never before occurred to her. " Why shouldn't I ? "

" Because it's wrong. It must be wrong. Rosalind isn't ashamed of her boy's clothes although for the moment she longs for her petticoats. ' What shall I do with my doublet and hose ? ' doesn't mean ' If Orlando sees my ankles I shall go home and destroy myself' ; it only expresses

225

her annoyance at having to remain a boy when she particularly wishes to be a girl."

" Ye-e-es," said Ada doubtfully.

" Well then, if you agree it's wrong, why do you do it ? "

Ada Rehan looked gravely at me. " Because I was told to do it," she said.

" By Mr. Daly ? "

" Of course by Mr. Daly."

" But—if he told you to do something that you knew to be artistically wrong, you wouldn't do it ? "

" Yes, I should."

" You *would* ? "

" Yes, and I should feel sure that he was right and I wrong."

" But you *don't* feel sure about this very point."

" Very well then," said Ada. " I should not feel sure —but I should do it all the same."

Here then were the clowning passages of Rosalind brought home to Mr. Daly, but against this discovery must be set the many and wonderful beauties of the performance.

Ada Rehan was not the woman to have invented the occasional vulgarities which marred her Rosalind's perfection, yet neither was she the woman to think out such miracles of melodious utterance as the speech of Katherine, " A woman moved is like a fountain troubled," or the even more marvellous ' Willow Cabin ' speech of Viola.

This last passage led to the only conversation I ever had with her in which she spoke of her technique with authority, but, curiously enough, while she spoke she grew less and less the Ada Rehan that I knew : I seemed to be listening to another voice beyond her. She was repeating a lesson.

I had asked her why she held back the applause at the close of this speech ; for her great efforts stirred the audience to the point of applause exactly as does a song.

" Why do you give the applause to Olivia there ? " I

had asked ; for it had puzzled me that Viola always ended on an upward inflection so that the public did not realise that she had finished before Olivia had spoken.

"Can't you hear?" said Ada. "That speech is a song and needs its few bars of accompaniment to finish it properly. See—it begins here with a recitative,

> 'If I did love you in my master's flame,
> With such a suffering, such a deadly life,
> In your denial I would find no sense,
> I would not understand it.'

Then a pause. Four chords—Olivia's words :

> 'Why, what would you?'

Then comes the aria :

> 'Make me a willow cabin at your gate
> And call upon my soul within the house.'

So on and on, working up to the end of the song :

> 'O, you should not rest
> Between the elements of air and earth,
> But you should pity me.'

Then again—very slowly—Olivia's four chords :

> 'You—might—do—much.

Then for the applause if you like, but those concluding chords must be heard or half the beauty is lost."

Now Ada Rehan, even if she had hit upon this idea, could not have formulated it, would never have put it into words. It was evidently a lesson well learnt, coming from the same source as her less admirable readings and making the elusive figure of Daly the more mysterious, for, as a rule, the cuts and inserted matter in his arrangements of Shakespeare showed quite unusually bad taste and lack of appreciation.

> "If music be the food of love, play on,"

sighed the love-sick Orsino, and the audience listened dreamily, lulled by the wondrous melody.

"Give me excess of it; that surfeiting,
The appetite may sicken and so die.
That strain again."

And whack, bang, we got the strain again, brayed out by
the full orchestra with song and dance contributed by the
Duke's private opera bouffe company, always grouped
about him and ready to oblige. The rest of the speech
was cut, quite judiciously from the common-sense point
of view, for dukes are probably accustomed to get strains
again when they give an encore and, if they wish to hear
music, are unlikely to talk through the performance. Still,
to many among the audience that cut was like a minor
operation.

I had costumed 'Twelfth Night' for the Company
and received several shocks when it was given in London
after having been produced as usual in New York. The
opening was a complete surprise. I had imagined the
sailors and the rescued maiden cast ashore on a desolate
coast in the dreary dusk of dawn and had contrived that
Viola's robe should seem wet and storm-tossed. They
turned up, bright and well groomed, on a beautiful afternoon at what appeared to be a fashionable watering-place
thronged with gaily dressed trippers who sang 'Come
unto these yellow sands' with a great deal of nice feeling.

But after all, it mattered little; as the spell of Ada
Rehan's Viola fell upon the house dresses and scenery
were alike forgotten: it was an evening of enchantment.

Besides 'Twelfth Night' and 'The Foresters,' I costumed for the Company 'Two Gentlemen of Verona,' the
fairy scenes of 'Midsummer Night's Dream,' a one-act
play by Clo Graves called 'The Knave,' and 'Cymbeline,'
which last was never produced.

I thought my designs for 'Cymbeline' rather good
and, as they never took shape upon the stage, am still
able to preserve this illusion.

I seemed to have settled down to be dresser-in-ordinary
(very ordinary, I'm afraid) to Mr. Daly when one day
arose what I cannot call a misunderstanding, as we under-

stood each other perfectly, but at any rate a temporary parting of the ways.

Just before leaving for New York, he sent for me and with his usual air of mystery revealed his latest scheme. He would produce ' Henry IV ' with Miss Rehan as Prince Hal.

Prince Hal, the swaggering young roysterer, ' *tout aux tavernes et aux filles* ' : it seemed a very unlovely idea. I knew the uselessness of argument, but would not lend my help to this misuse of Ada Rehan's genius. What excuses I made I forget, but I refused to dress the play.

Daly persisted ; my unwillingness seemed to make him the more determined to secure me, but for once I was firm and after a long and almost stormy scene made my escape, leaving the manager in his ' not angry but hurt ' attitude, hardly able to take in my unexpected rebellion.

He was to sail on the following day, so I felt safe, but next morning at a quarter to seven, while I was yet abed, entered to me a startled domestic announcing Mr. Augustin Daly.

" Waiting in the hall, sir. Says he *must* see you."

The habit of stooping to his lure without delay was strong in me : I huddled on a dressing-gown and descended, dishevelled and slipperless. He opened fire at once.

" I've only a minute. I've come to say that you *must* do the dresses. I wish it particularly."

I felt that I was in for the whole thing over again and sat down hopelessly on the bottom step of the stairs. Mr. Daly seated himself beside me and put forth his arguments *da capo*. This time he was not angry or hurt, but persuasive, insinuating, strangely fascinating.

I believe that if my bare toes had not been so cold I should have yielded gradually to the murmured spell— as it was I suddenly felt that he was trying to mesmerise me, to force his will upon me against my inclination and without my knowledge. With the coming of this idea to me the charm ceased to work : I knew quite well that

I did not want to dress the play—no, not even to design Miss Rehan's costumes if I would not undertake the whole—I intended to have nothing to do with it and managed to say so. Mr. Daly arose from the stairs and disappeared with a bang like the demon king in a pantomime.

He afterwards forgave me, and I should not have thought the incident worth remembering, save that it throws a tiny gleam of light upon his methods of extracting work and exacting obedience.

Whether he would ever have gone further with his plans for 'Henry IV' I do not know, but before anything more was heard of them he died quite suddenly in Paris, where he was staying on a holiday with Mrs. Daly and Miss Rehan.

It was a terrible experience for the nervous, sensitive Ada Rehan, and when I next saw her I remember her telling me how much she had been helped and sustained by Oscar Wilde, whom she and her party had come across accidentally a few evenings before.

She and the Dalys had been dining at a restaurant and, looking up, she had seen Oscar Wilde sitting with some men at a neighbouring table and looking at her tentatively. It was after the tragic shipwreck of his life; he was a wanderer and an exile, unrecognised by nearly all his former friends—and there he suddenly was, looking at her kindly and earnestly.

" I didn't know what to do," she told me. " Mr. and Mrs. Daly were with me and I could not tell how they would feel about it. You never *do* know with men when they are going to feel very proper and when they are not."

I agreed that the male sense of propriety was liable to fluctuations.

" And—*was* Mr. Daly feeling proper ? " I enquired.

" No," said poor Ada, " he wasn't. It was such a relief: if I could not have bowed I should have cried. So Mr. Wilde came over and sat with us and talked so charmingly—it was just like old times—we had a lovely evening. And then, only a few days later, Mr. Daly died. Arrangements had to be made and Mrs. Daly was not equal to taking them in hand. I seemed to be all alone, and so confused and frightened. And then Oscar Wilde came to me and was more good and helpful than I can tell you—just like a very kind brother. I shall always think of him as he was to me through those few dreadful days."

This was the last direct news of Oscar Wilde that I ever received, and I too am glad to remember him thus.

After Augustin Daly's death Ada Rehan was a changed woman; vague, purposeless, drifting she knew not whither.

I tried to get her to talk of future plans, of her art.

" I don't know what I shall do," she said helplessly.

" But of course you will act ? "

" I suppose so. I don't know. I feel somehow as if —as if I couldn't."

And the event proved that she was right ; Ada Rehan could act no more.

She appeared a few times in America in some of her old parts but with small success : she was brought out as Beatrice, a character that should have fitted her like a glove, and achieved complete failure.

She fell amongst friends, kindly but injudicious friends who encouraged her morbid dread of society and separated her from all her old comrades. Her health and spirits began to fail, and it was but the pale ghost of the once brilliant Ada Rehan that returned finally to America, where I have heard that some very gloomy phase of religious feeling darkened her later days until her almost unnoticed death.

Her career was a mystery which to me admits of but one explanation. Daly must have been a great actor who could not act. He was rough and uncouth, with harsh utterance and uncultured accent ; a singer without a voice, a musician without an instrument. But in Ada

Rehan he found his means of self-expression ; Ada Rehan with her quaint charm, her voice of music, her splendid presence and her gentle nature which he could mould to his will.

In real life they played the Trilby-Svengali drama of du Maurier's romance, and as Trilby's voice died with Svengali, so did Ada Rehan, the actress, vanish for ever after the death of Augustin Daly.

OF JOHN SARGENT

I N 1894 I blossomed into a Notable Personage myself:
it was a second-hand notability, a reflected aureole
but distinctly noticeable. I dined out in it for a couple
of seasons, and even now it sheds an occasional glimmer
upon an otherwise unillumined name. More or less by
accident, I became the subject of one of John Sargent's
most famous pictures.

Sargent was still a young man (nobody was very old
in the early 'nineties), and Tite Street, Chelsea, did not
as yet show the unending procession on its way to his
studio that thronged it in later days, but several distinguished clients had already passed that way and, as Oscar
Wilde observed to me, " The street that on a wet and
dreary morning has vouchsafed the vision of Lady Macbeth
in full regalia magnificently seated in a four-wheeler can
never again be as other streets : it must always be full of
wonderful possibilities."

Sargent's fame was approaching its zenith, though
sitters were still a little coy : his portraits were not
always quite what the subjects expected—they could
not feel comfortably certain of what they were going
to get.

" It is positively dangerous to sit to Sargent. It's
taking your face in your hands," said a timid aspirant ;
and many stood shivering on the brink waiting for more
adventurous spirits to make the plunge.

This was Sargent's great period, when he was not so
overtasked with commissions and was able to concentrate
upon the work in hand.

I had long wanted a portrait of my mother and was
lucky in persuading him to undertake it, though it was
perhaps not a complete success. My mother was a bad
sitter, she was shy and very loath, as she expressed it, to
' sit still and be stared at.'

Sargent could not reproduce her real self because
during the sittings he never saw it, although afterwards

233

they became good friends. Still, the portrait was a fine piece of work and a brilliant superficial likeness.

I was often commandeered to attend the séances, as my mother required support and considered that the casual woman friend worried the artist, in which opinion she was not far wrong.

Ada Rehan was sitting to Sargent at the same time, a large portrait of her having been commissioned by an American adorer, one Mrs. Whiting of Whitingsville, Mass. I remember the imposing name, as it seemed to fascinate Sargent, who became haunted by it and would chant it rhythmically as a kind of litany the while he painted, the ' Mass.' in very deep tones coming as a final Amen, in which I reverently joined.

Miss Rehan was another shy and reluctant sitter and, between the two, the poor artist must have had uphill work. Each, I think, found a certain comfort in the other's discomfort; they were comrades in misfortune and even shared certain studio ' properties,' Sargent borrowing from my mother her white feather fan for Ada to hold outspread while she glanced at the spectator over her shoulder.

The comic relief of the sittings was supplied by my dog, Mouton, who, well stricken in years and almost toothless, claimed rather unusual privileges and was always allowed one bite by Sargent, whom he unaccountably disliked, before work began.

" He has bitten me now," Sargent would remark mildly, " so we can go ahead."

Miss Rehan's sittings had been interrupted by a few final rehearsals of ' Twelfth Night ' before its production in London, but at last the evening arrived. I was ' in front ' with a friend, J. J. Shannon, then Sargent's most formidable rival among portrait painters, and had sent round a line to the Leading Lady asking to see her when all was over.

Almost from the start her Viola had enchanted the audience, but in the midst of her triumph, and success in a great Shakespearean rôle in Shakespeare's country meant very much to her, she found time to scribble a note and to send it to me.

Yes, come by all means. I have something particular to tell you about Sargent—something he said of you—you must hear it and, I hope, act upon it. Shall I tell you before your friend?—you must bring him. This evening is so nice—it has unnerved me a little.

Affectionately, ADA REHAN.

I felt puzzled and intrigued. What could Sargent have said of me, Sargent who so very seldom said anything of anybody? It was quite exciting. We presented ourselves in due course and found Viola rather overwhelmed by her great ovation, but still eager to impart news.

" Well, he's very anxious to paint you."

" Me ? "

" Yes. He wants you to sit to him ? "

" Wants *me* ? But good gracious, why ? "

" I don't know," said Ada, a little tactlessly. " He says you are so paintable : that the lines of your long overcoat and—and the dog— and—I can't quite remember *what* he said, but he was tremendously enthusiastic."

I did not wonder that Miss Rehan's memory had failed, but I was well able to supply the missing words. Sargent, I felt sure, had delivered himself thus—" You know—there's a certain sort of—er—er—that is to say a kind of—er—er—in fact a—er—er——" and so on and so on. He had not the gift of tongues, but that mattered little ; he was so well able to express himself otherwise.

No one had ever wanted to paint me before. Portions of me had been borrowed from time to time ; hands pretty frequently by Albert Moore, hands again by Poynter, quite a good deal by Walter Crane for immortals of uncertain shape and sex, but I myself, proper (I use the word in its heraldic sense), had never been in request. Even now, as far as I could gather, the dog and the overcoat seemed to be regarded as my strong points ; nevertheless, I felt very proud and—well, Sargent soon had three large canvases on hand instead of two.

235

Being but an amateur model, I was easily entrapped into a trying pose, turning as if to walk away, with a general twist of the whole body and all the weight on one foot. Professional models will always try to poise the weight equally on both feet and will go to any lengths of duplicity to gain this end.

I managed pretty well on the whole, but the sittings cleared up a point which had long puzzled me : why did models occasionally faint during a long pose without mentioning that they felt tired and wanted a rest ? One day the answer came to me quite suddenly.

I had been standing for over an hour and saw no reason why I should not go on for another hour, when I became aware of what seemed a cold wind blowing in my face accompanied by a curious ' going ' at the knees.

I tried to ask for a rest, but found that my lips were frozen stiff and refused to move. Hundreds of years passed—I suppose about twenty seconds.

Sargent glanced at me.

" What a horrid light there is just now," he remarked. " A sort of green——" He looked more steadily. " Why, it's *you* ! " he cried, and seizing me by the collar, rushed me into the street, where he propped me up against the door-post. It was a pity that Oscar Wilde opposite was not looking out of the window : the ' wonderful possibilities of Tite Street ' were yet unexhausted.

After the picture was well advanced it was laid by for a short time while the artist took a holiday in Paris, and when I started sittings again I found him much perturbed.

" I say," he began, " did you ever see Whistler's portrait of Comte Robert de Montesquiou ? "

" No," said I. " They never would let me see it while it was being painted. Why ? "

" Well, I'd never seen it either," said Sargent, " until I came across it just now in the Champs de Mars. It's just like this ! Everybody will say that I've copied it."

My old friend Robert de Montesquiou had been sitting

to Whistler while Sargent's portrait of me was in progress, but had shrouded the fact in all the romantic secrecy that his soul loved.

He was in England incognito (I cannot imagine why) and took much delight in gliding down unfrequented ways and adopting strange aliases ; visiting me by stealth after dusk with an agreeable suggestion of dark lanterns and disguise cloaks, though, as he was almost unknown in London, he might have walked at noon down Piccadilly accompanied by a brass band without anyone being much the wiser.

Whistler, who also loved to play at secrets, was equally clandestine, I, dutifully acting under orders, dissembled energetically, and Montesquiou was so wrapped about in thick mystery that no intelligent acquaintance within the three miles radius could possibly have failed to notice him.

And now the mystic portrait was on view in Paris, and Sargent had found it just like mine and feared that critics would agree with him.

And in truth a few people did make the remark, though there was really but little resemblance. Both canvases showed a tall, thin figure in black against a dark background, but the likeness ceased there and, as a picture, the Sargent was by far the finer. The Whistler was not of his best—the blacks were black, not the lovely vaporous dimness of the ' Rosa Corder ' ; the portrait was quite worthy neither of the painter nor the model, for the delicate moulding of Robert de Montesquiou's features was hardly suggested ; but Whistler was not then quite equal to the physical exertion of dealing with so large a canvas. He had started two portraits of Comte Robert, working upon them alternately, but as far as I know only one survived : it was the last large picture that he ever completed.

The Sargent, on the other hand, was of the artist's best period and he was painting something that he had ' seen ' pictorially and for some unknown reason had wished to perpetuate. Why a very thin boy (I then looked no more) in a very tight coat should have struck him as a subject worthy of treatment I never discovered, but he evidently had the finished picture in his mind from the first and started it almost exactly upon its final lines.

It was hot summer weather and I feebly rebelled against the thick overcoat.

" But the coat is the picture," said Sargent. " You must wear it."

" Then I can't wear anything else," I cried in despair, and with the sacrifice of most of my wardrobe I became thinner and thinner, much to the satisfaction of the artist, who used to pull and drag the unfortunate coat more and more closely round me until it might have been draping a lamp-post.

Even before the picture was finished its fame began to grow, and friends took to dropping in, anxious for a sight of it. Sargent's old friend, Henry James, whom I had known before very slightly, came several times and expressed high approbation.

The Henry James of those days was strangely unlike the remarkable-looking man of almost twenty years later, who was then himself painted by Sargent.

In the 'nineties he was in appearance almost remarkably unremarkable ; his face might have been anybody's face ; it was as though, when looking round for a face, he had been able to find nothing to his taste and had been obliged to put up with a ready-made ' stock ' article until something more suitable could be made to order expressly for him.

This special and only genuine Henry James's face was not ' delivered ' until he was a comparatively old man, so that for the greater part of his life he went about in disguise.

My mother, who was devoted to his works, used to be especially annoyed by this elusive personality.

" I always want so much to talk with him," she complained, " yet when I meet him I never can remember who he is."

238

Perhaps to make up for this indistinguishable presence he cultivated impressiveness of manner and great preciosity of speech.

He had a way of leaving a dinner-party early with an air of preoccupation that was very intriguing.

" He always does it," untruthfully exclaimed a deserted and slightly piqued hostess. " It is to convey the suggestion that he has an appointment with a Russian princess."

In later life both the impressive manner and fastidious speech became intensified : what he said was always interesting, but he took so long to say it that one felt a growing conviction that he was not for a moment, but for all time. With him it was a moral obligation to find the *mot juste*, and if it had got mislaid or was far to seek, the world had to stand still until it turned up.

Sometimes when it arrived it was delightfully unexpected. I remember in later years walking with him round my little Surrey garden and manœuvring him to a spot where a rather wonderful view suddenly revealed itself.

" My dear boy," exclaimed Henry James, grasping my arm. " How—er—how——" I waited breathless : the *mot juste* was on its way ; at least I should hear the perfect and final summing up of my countryside's loveliness. " How—er—how——" still said Mr. James, until at long last the golden sentence sprang complete from his lips. " My dear boy, how awfully jolly ! "

I also recall his telling of a tale about an American business man who had bought a large picture.

" And when he got it home," continued Mr. James, " he did not know what—er—what——"

" What to do with it," prompted some impatient and irreverent person.

Henry James silently rejected the suggestion. " He did not know what—er—what—well, in point of fact, the *hell* to do with it."

When, quite towards the end of his life, his new face

was evolved, it was a very wonderful one and well worth waiting for. Sargent's painting of it is fine, but lacks a certain something.

" It is the sort of portrait one would paint of Henry James if one had sat opposite to him twice in a bus," said a disappointed admirer, and the statement, though untrue, had some grains of truth in it.

Yet this should not have been so. Sargent and Henry James were real friends, they understood each other perfectly and their points of view were in many ways identical.

Renegade Americans both, each did his best to love his country and failed far more signally than does the average Englishman : they were *plus Anglais que les Anglais* with an added fastidiousness, a mental remoteness that was not English.

Both were fond of society, though neither seemed altogether at one with it : Henry James, an artist in words, liked to talk and in order to talk there must be someone to talk to, but Sargent talked little and with an effort ; why he ' went everywhere ' night after night often puzzled me.

I saw a good deal of Henry James at about this time, then we lost sight of each other for many years. When I next met him, almost unrecognisable in his new face, he seemed much aged and broken. His ever troublesome nerves had now made him more dependent upon companionship ; some of the mystery and remoteness had disappeared.

His final nationalisation as an Englishman came as a surprise to many. His liaison with Britannia was then such an old story, both had completely lived down any scandal, and that he should wish at the eleventh hour to make an honest woman of her seemed almost unnecessary.

His portrait by Sargent, one of the few men who really knew him, should have supplied a clue to the true Henry James that no one else could have found : perhaps the artist intentionally withheld it.

Another friend who volunteered to ' come and sit with me while I was being painted ' (how painters of portraits have learned to dread that offer) was Sarah Bernhardt.

She wished to see what Sargent was ' making of me ' and proposed her chaperonage at an early stage of the portrait's evolution.

I had misgivings ; I could not see Madame Sarah sitting quietly in a corner while I basked in the limelight.

" But it will bore you," I ventured.

" No," said Madame Sarah. " I want to see the picture and I'm coming. You must call for me and take me with you."

" But the sitting is early : you will never get up in time and you'll never be ready."

" I shall get up and I shall be ready. I am coming," said Sarah with finality ; so of course she came.

If the sun had risen in the west that morning it would have surprised me less than the sight of Madame Sarah ready and waiting when I called for her at an early hour, waiting in a neat, business-like walking-dress with a small black hat. She might have been going to shop at White-ley's with a string bag.

Sargent, who disliked the flamboyant type of actress, was completely won over and surveyed the little dark figure with approbation.

" I never saw that she was beautiful before," he whispered to me. " Look at her now."

Sarah was leaning forward, getting a view of the picture in a little hanging mirror : she was poised, the tips of the fingers against the wall, the head thrown back, the delicate profile in relief against a black screen.

I believe that Sargent only narrowly escaped asking to paint her then and there, but that he did escape was perhaps fortunate. They were not sympathetic ; Sargent as a painter of Facts was unrivalled, but Sarah Bernhardt was embodied Fantasy and was only well and truly seen through the golden mist of dreams. Dreams were not in Sargent's line.

241

The Ellen Terry portrait, imaginative and dramatic, was a splendid exception to this rule ; here, I think, the magnificent pomp of colour had fired the artist's fancy, but in the head of Henry Irving, painted in the same year, he had again shown his limitations.

He had painted the great actor with the flame of his genius blown out and had shown that the marvellous face, had it belonged to someone else, might not have been marvellous at all.

Here was a face that might look drearily at us out of a ticket office or haughtily take our order for fancy trouserings ; it might bend over a ledger with a pen behind its ear or stare in listless apathy at small children in a Board School, but never could it blaze like a beacon or lower like a thundercloud, never could it have held crowds spellbound and swayed them with a glance. It was not Henry Irving, but the dreadful thing about it was that it *might* have been, and the sitter, probably recognising this, actively hated it.

He hid it away for some time, but one morning when it shyly peeped from the boot cupboard or crept from under the bed, he took a breakfast knife and—— There is now no portrait of Irving by Sargent.

The admirable little study by Bastian Lepage, far and away the best portrait ever painted of Irving, very nearly shared the fate of the Sargent head and would certainly have been wiped out of existence had not Ellen Terry, recognising its great value, managed to carry it off ; presenting it in after-years to the National Portrait Gallery.

It was possible to understand the actor's objection to it, for, though it is a splendid piece of work and an almost photographic likeness, it represents Irving 'in-time,' Irving as Nature made him, with little hint of the superstructure of dignity and beauty to the raising of which he had devoted his life. It showed a side which he had never given to the public and he saw no reason why it should be thus perpetuated by Bastien Lepage.

His destruction of the Sargent portrait was of course regarded as a great crime, and it was perhaps as well that Sarah Bernhardt was not exposed to a like temptation.

I wonder whether, having us both before him in his studio, Sargent noticed that, all unlikely as it sounds, there was then a vague resemblance between Madame Sarah and myself.

She had apparently realised it before I did. I had paid a sudden visit to Paris without advising her of my advent and had, as usual, gone on my first evening to see her play. When I went round to her dressing-room after the fall of the curtain I found her expecting me.

" But I never told you that I was coming."

" No," said she, " but when I was on the stage one of the actors (he's new and does not know my friends) whispered to me, ' Your son is in the audience, Madame Sarah ' ; and when I said, ' But you have never seen Maurice,' he told me that he recognised him from his likeness to me. Now Maurice is not in the least like me, so I felt sure that it must be you."

" But I am not like you," I said, all incredulous.

" Look," said Sarah, and leading me to the mirror she put her face beside mine.

It could not be denied that there was a certain sort of something, as Sargent would have said, a blurred travesty of her clear-cut face ; but, had I been Madame Sarah, I should not have mentioned it. That she should contrive to resemble the Monna Lisa of Leonardo and the Primavera of Botticelli and also to be rather like me was perhaps one of her most amazing feats.

My face acquired for me a spurious interest for some time after—which reminds me that while I was sitting to Sargent I made a joke.

I know it was a joke because several people laughed at it and it gained me quite a little reputation, but it must have been very subtle as I have never been able to grasp the point myself.

Sargent had asked me why I had not painted myself

and I replied, " Because I am not my style." That was the joke.

Sargent didn't see it until three days afterwards, when he suddenly burst out laughing at a dinner at Sir George Lewis's. That was the birth of the joke *as* a joke. It had a great success ; it went the round of the studios, it was translated into French by Mr. George Moore and the translation revised and re-edited by Walter Sickert. When the latter repeated it to me in its final form I almost saw it, but the illumination was only momentary.

I can't see that joke yet ; in fact, I don't believe that it is a joke.

Sometimes Sargent would give studio parties at which the originals of the various portraits would prowl suspiciously round each other, perforce paying tribute to rival charms, yet each comfortably confident that he (or perhaps in this case mostly she) was sole possessor of the elusive quality—the ' certain sort of a something '—that drew out the greatest powers of the painter.

Once we were summoned to meet and admire Carmencita, the dancer, whose portrait had been one of the first of Sargent's sensational successes. This was to be an unusually large gathering and the artist was rather puzzled by questions of space : the dancer and her guitar players required about half the studio for their evolutions ; there was not much room for an audience. Sargent was the kindliest of men ; unless really roused, it was very difficult for him to say No : the invitation list presented a troublesome problem.

" I suppose I must ask So-and-So," said Sargent dismally.

" Why should you ? " I demanded.

" Oh, well, you know—I suppose—I ought to."

" But do you want to ? "

" No," said Sargent with unusual firmness.

" Then don't."

" All right," said Sargent bravely, as he scratched out the name. " I won't. I'm—I'm damned if I do."

Nevertheless, when I arrived at the party, the first person I met was So-and-So.

The scene in the dimly lit studio was a Sargent picture or an etching by Goya, the dancer, short-skirted and tinsel-decked, against a huge black screen, the *guitaristi*, black against black, their white shirts gleaming. And then Carmencita danced. She postured and paced, she ogled, she flashed her eyes and her teeth, she was industriously Spanish in the Parisian and American manner, she looked beautiful and tawdry, but she was not a great dancer—it was all a little disappointing. Then she retired, to reappear in a dress of dead white falling to her feet, with a long, heavy train ; she wore no jewels, only one dark red rose behind the ear. And she sang the wild, crooning ' Paloma,' and as she sang she circled with splendid arm movements, the feet hardly stirring, the white train sweeping and swinging round her. This was better—this was different. This was not Carmencita of the Halls, but the real dancer of Old Spain.

Then Sargent came to her whispering a request. She looked angry, then sullen, shaking her head violently. He persisted, and opening a great cupboard in the wall, held out to her a beautiful white shawl with long fringes.

She still hesitated, pouting, then snatched the shawl, threw it over her shoulders, flicking him in the face with the fringe with the impudent gesture of a gamin, and slowly crouched down upon a low stool, her face now grave, her hands in her lap. From the *guitaristi* behind her came a low thrumming, a mere murmur, and softly, under her breath, Carmencita began to sing.

Old folk songs she sang, mournful, haunting, with long cadences and strange intervals, and as she sang she clapped her hands, softly swaying to the rhythm. And her beauty changed, the tawdriness fell away, she became ageless and eternal like the still figures of Egyptian sculpture.

She was one with the ' spinsters and the knitters in the sun ' who crooned and swayed thus while the Moors were building the Alhambra, nay, perhaps when Nimrod was building Nineveh.

Sargent told me afterwards that she had held out long against the performance. It was low, she declared ; the common people sang these songs at street corners—they were not for Carmencita of Broadway and the Boulevards ; what would his fine ladies and gentlemen think of her if she thus forgot herself ?

But those whispered lilts laid a spell upon her audience, and the name of Carmencita now brings me no vision of a pirouetting dancer, but memory of a quiet, shrouded figure with darkly dreaming eyes and hands rhythmically clapping.

I wonder that Sargent had not chosen to paint her thus rather than in her short-skirted finery ; I suppose it was because he had already used the white satin and long train *motif* in one of his best early pictures, ' El Jaleo.'

In the summer of 1892 my mother and I took jointly with George Alexander and his wife a little house on the North Coast for a few weeks. It was an old, very dilapidated house, full of quaint surprises and furnished on a plan which was at first distracting to tenants, but which, when approached in the proper spirit, became quite interesting. Nothing could be found when wanted, but in course of time turned up masquerading as something else. The dustbin completely eluded us until I, tripping over a hole in the carpet, fell against a be-muslined dressing-table of odd design which emitted a dull roar like a dinner-gong, thus betraying its true character.

Alexander was completely absorbed in a new play by Pinero which he was going to produce. By all who had read it it was thought to be a very daring, nay, dangerous experiment, and I remember that Mrs. Kendal, when awaiting news of the first night, said, " By this time he will have made the success of his life or will have been torn in pieces."

Nowadays, I suppose, it would be regarded as a bright little entertainment for children in the holidays, but then it was surprising, as it dealt in candid fashion with the situation of a respectable middle-aged man married to a lady whose former profession was, in those unenlightened days, still regarded as a formidable barrier to social success.

Alexander was afraid of the play, yet determined to produce it. He thought at first of putting it up at experimental matinées, but soon abandoned the idea : it must go bravely into the evening bill and he would stand or fall by it.

But who on earth was to play Paula Tanqueray? The choice seemed to lie between Miss Elizabeth Robins and Miss Olga Nethersole. Miss Robins would bring power and intelligence to the part, but could she suggest the less presentable characteristics of Paula, for which there were then still in use a few good, full-mouthed Elizabethan adjectives, but which are now, I think, called ' temperamental ' ? Miss Nethersole was a rough, melodramatic actress who would make Paula into the ordinary stage adventuress. A new actress was wanted, but where was she ?

On our return to town, Florence Alexander and I were deputed to make a round of the theatres in search of her, but she remained hidden. Miss Robins seemed inevitable.

One evening we set dutifully out for the Adelphi to inspect Miss Evelyn Millard, then playing the heroine in the usual Adelphi piece, at that moment called ' The Black Domino.'

Miss Millard was very beautiful, very gentle, very sweet, about as like Paula Tanqueray as a white mouse is like a wild cat ; another evening was evidently to be spent in vain—when the scene changed and the wicked woman of the play came on.

She did not look wicked—a startling innovation. She was almost painfully thin, with great eyes and slow haunting utterance ; she was not exactly beautiful, but intensely interesting and arresting. She played weakly, walking listlessly through the part, but in one scene she had to leave the stage laughing : the laugh was wonderful, low and sweet, yet utterly mocking and heartless.

Florence Alexander and I both realised that there before our eyes was the ideal Paula Tanqueray. If she would only move, speak, look, above all, laugh like that the part would play itself. Neither of us knew the lady, who, the programme stated, was a Mrs. Patrick Campbell.

It is old stage history how Alexander tried to engage her, how the Messrs. Gatti would not break her contract to them, how ' The Black Domino ' failed and Mrs. Campbell was free to accept the part of Paula.

Then came the first rehearsals. Mrs. Campbell had but just recovered from a long illness, she had little strength to bring to her trying task. She, I suppose, rehearsed badly, for during the first week or two Mrs. Alexander and I often wished we had never paid that visit to the Adelphi Theatre.

We were told that we had made a great mistake; that—as Alexander incisively put it—we had seen a second-rate actress in a third-rate production and had thought her good merely because she was not bad. We tried to look confident and superior, but we felt uncomfortably guilty. Then things began to mend. Mrs. Campbell gained strength and confidence. Mrs. Pinero came to a rehearsal and startled the downcast author and manager by saying—" Well, I don't know what you're talking about. I think she's very good." The tide had turned and now began to come in with a rush, and on the night of production Mrs. Campbell scored one of the greatest personal successes ever known upon the stage. Her performance was perfect; beautiful, human and tragic.

Alexander introduced me to her after the fall of the curtain, but I am sure that she did not see me or anybody else. She gazed at the people thronging round her as if they were figures in some strange fever dream from which she wished to wake.

She escaped from the crowd almost at once and I did not meet her again till more than a year had passed.

We next came across each other in Burne-Jones's studio, where I found her established as a family friend. She had become very intimate with his son and daughter, and he himself admired her greatly, her pale face and great eyes making her much akin to the mysterious maidens of his dreamland. In fact, his personal influence and her admiration for his pictures had a very strong effect upon her own work; in parts like the Melisande of Maurice Maeterlinck she might have stepped from one of his canvases.

After the long run of ' Mrs. Tanqueray ' the position of Mrs. Campbell had entirely changed. She had come almost unknown to the St. James's, now she was the most talked-of actress of the day—everything seemed to be within her reach. Alexander had many ambitious schemes for the future, but, with the sudden blossoming of her fame, the lady had grown a little difficult. She greatly disliked her part in the play following ' Mrs. Tanqueray,' the rather crudely sensational ' Masqueraders ' by Henry Arthur Jones. She played it under protest and, truth to tell, played it very badly, leaving the theatre at the close of the season and enlisting under the banner of Beerbohm Tree at the Haymarket.

To the St. James's she came no more until many years later, when she returned to take the name-part in ' Bella Donna,' an effective but not very convincing play founded upon a popular novel. It was only memorable for Alexander's clever performance as the Jewish doctor and for one of Mrs. Campbell's great moments, which occurred within two minutes of the fall of the curtain. The Beautiful Lady (a sordid adventuress), her schemes thwarted, her beauty a wreck, her career at an end, walked up the stage and out through a gate at the back. That was all. What the actress did to get her effect I have no notion and I doubt if she had. Her face was hidden, she never paused or looked round, but the audience sat frozen—they had seen a living soul pass into hell.

At the Haymarket Mrs. Campbell fared less well : under Tree's management she was duly exploited as the coming Sarah Bernhardt and was presented in the very trying rôle of ' Fédora.'

The sensational Sardou plays have had much contempt heaped upon them, but without them should we have known the full range of Sarah's genius ? She well knew what Sardou owed to her, that in her his plays began, continued and ended, but, ever generous in gratitude, she also knew what she owed to Sardou. That she should have given so much of her powers and time to the portrayal of his flamboyant heroines made the judicious grieve, but it must be remembered that the judicious are few. The plays were by no means great plays, but they were magnificent material for an emotional and romantic actress, and Sarah, with what she brought to them of poetry, beauty and melody, raised them to tragic height.

In other hands they are apt to resolve themselves into mere scales and five-finger exercises : Mrs. Campbell in ' Fedora ' only succeeded in showing that she was not Sarah—as indeed was only to have been expected.

Later on she joined Sir John Hare and was again at her best in Pinero's ' Mrs. Ebbsmith ' ; after which she soared into Shakespeare with Johnston Forbes-Robertson.

Oddly enough, Mrs. Campbell could do nothing with Shakespeare ; his great lines seemed to paralyse her, her strange fascination was not felt, her effects appeared modern and trivial. Her ' Juliet ' was pretty and girlish, so, for the matter of that, was her ' Lady Macbeth ' ; but more could not be said. She realised her failure and, I think, worked hard to retrieve it, but in vain.

I remember a conversation with her one evening, after the curtain had fallen on ' Macbeth.'

I was profoundly depressed. Mrs. Campbell, in the night-wear of the Sleep-walker, was sitting in a gloomy little heap.

" Well ? " she asked.

What I said I don't know, but I evidently failed to conceal my feelings.

" Damn," said Mrs. Campbell simply. A melancholy pause. Then—" But look here—that speech in my first scene—the Spirits of Evil—didn't that go ? I worked and *worked* at that."

I was beyond help ; the speech had not made its effect.

" Oh damn," wailed Mrs. Campbell. " I can't do it. I feel all the time that the woman would not speak like that—she couldn't say such things—*I* shouldn't say such things."

" But Lady Macbeth isn't speaking," I ventured. " She's thinking, and her thoughts are put into words by the poet."

" But you can't say such words *naturally*. Ellen Terry

251

tried and what did she do ? She chopped the lines into little bits and pumped them out in staccato jerks."

There was truth in this, although the staccato jerks had ' got there ' and I could hear Ellen Terry's voice working up the rhythmic beat to the final—

> " That my keen knife see not the wound it makes,
> Nor hope peer through the blanket of the dark
> To cry Hold—Hold ! "

the last ' Hold ' turning into a cry of triumph as Macbeth entered and she rushed into his arms.

No, such words cannot be spoken ' naturally,' and were never intended to be so spoken. The Modern School must deign to learn declamation from the old before it can give the lines of Shakespeare with any effect. As well might a *prima donna* in Grand Opera refuse to sing on the ground that it was unnatural.

What exactly was the barrier between Mrs. Campbell and Shakespeare it is difficult to say ; she spoke the periods with due feeling for rhythm and melody, yet, as she gave them, they lacked grandeur and import. Yet she could, on occasion, speak lyric verse most exquisitely : little isolated poems like ' Butterflies ' in ' For the Crown ' or ' The King's Three Blind Daughters ' in ' Pelleas and Melisande ' came with musical perfection from her lips. She was a lyric artist, the epic evaded her ever.

Her ' Melisande ' in the last-mentioned play, Maeterlinck's Fairy Princess seen through the eyes of Burne-Jones, was a pure delight, especially when she played her in the English translation by Professor J. W. Mackail. The play, of course, lost a little, one missed the cadence of the original phrases, but it was beautifully acted ; Forbes-Robertson was a superb Golaud, and Martin Harvey the perfect Pelleas.

Later on Mrs. Campbell played it in the original French with Sarah Bernhardt and her company, and I was supposed to ' help in the production,' though I knew enough of both ladies to limit my ' help ' to agreeing with both of them on all points. I designed Sarah's ' Pelleas ' costume and, to my delight, she was much pleased with it, especially approving of her light surcoat of chain-mail which lent manliness to the figure. Mrs. Campbell wore the dress designed by Burne-Jones for the first production —a costume usually alluded to as ' the gold umbrella case.'

Sarah was in the midst of a strenuous season, playing ' La Sorcière ' every night and frequently twice a day, rehearsing ' Pelleas ' in the mornings and giving a round of matinées at outlying theatres on spare afternoons.

I remember hinting to her son, Maurice, that such ceaseless work must be too much for her—were these constant flying matinées really necessary ?

" Well," said Maurice, who thoroughly understood his parent, " what *is* mother to do in the afternoons ? "

And I think he was right. Sarah Bernhardt, as years went on, had gradually dropped most of her former hobbies and outside interests ; she concentrated upon the theatre, and—as he said—if she did not act, what was she to do ? Fatigue never seemed to touch her ; never have I seen her more placid and unruffled than at these rehearsals. Stage carpenters blundered, lights went wrong, but her calm was perfect. Once, when she leaned from a window into the deep mystery of the night and I observed a brilliant noonday effect upon the back cloth, I held my breath, but no explosion followed. She merely glanced back over her shoulder and murmured—" Rather a *fine* night, isn't it ? "

I think she regarded the performance as a little holiday ; she liked Mrs. Campbell, who interested and amused her, and a peace that really passed all understanding remained unbroken.

And the poetry of her ' Pelleas,' the youth, the innocence !—and all so simple that one could not realise the marvel of it.

The immense care for detail in this greatest of all artists always seemed to puzzle Mrs. Campbell a little.

One evening I was sitting with Madame Sarah in her dressing-room at the theatre, watching her make up. This always fascinated me—it was absorbing to note the subtle touches with which she changed her own delicate features into the sensual, heavy-lipped face of Theodora, the olive-tinted mask of Lorenzaccio, or the fragile semblance of Napoleon's ill-fated son. This evening Sarah was gradually resolving into Cleopatra, and, as final details were being added, Mrs. Campbell entered.

Sarah was absorbed for the moment and could spare little attention : she was painting her hands, staining the finger-tips and palms with the dusky red of henna. Mrs. Campbell watched with some impatience ; she had business to discuss and was in a hurry.

" Why do you take so much trouble ? " she said at last. " What you are doing will never show from the front. Nobody will see it."

" I shall see it," replied Sarah slowly. " I am doing it for myself. If I catch sight of my hand it will be the hand of Cleopatra. That will help me."

She never spared trouble—in fact, I do not think she realised the meaning of the word. Nothing connected with her art was a trouble ; she would always give her best.

I may be wrong, but it often struck me that Mrs. Campbell took her art and her own great gifts too lightly. She would lose interest in a part and play with it instead of playing it, she played with her public (a most dangerous amusement), she exasperated managers, who found that they dared not rely upon her. The very qualities which had brought her triumphantly to the front, the super-sensitiveness, the fastidiousness, the habit of seeing both sides of most things and the ridiculous side of everything (and everybody), actually hampered her later on in her career.

Only once do I remember her deliberately setting herself to tackle and re-study a part in which she had failed to make good. When she played ' Magda ' with Forbes-

SARAH BERNHARDT AS "ADRIENNE
LECOUVREUR"

From a portrait by THE AUTHOR

Robertson she was still at the height of her popularity. Perhaps she had grown careless, perhaps she was not well : be that as it may, her performance was colourless, limp, completely ineffective.

A few years later, under her own management, she revived the play—a daring thing to do after so marked a failure. But now all was different ; she had apparently completely reconsidered the character, or perhaps had taken real interest in it for the first time. Now she gave of her best, and in a part then being played by Sarah Bernhardt and Eleanora Duse, gallantly held her own with both and, in my humble opinion, surpassed them.

Sarah was too great—too much the super-woman for Magda. You felt that she could not have sprung from the dull, respectable, middle-class surroundings into which she was trying to re-fit herself. She acted brilliantly, but it was acting—she was not Magda. Duse, as was her custom, quite simply substituted her favourite character, the noble, oppressed, misunderstood Martyr, for the character in the play. She also played magnificently, but she made no attempt to be Magda. Her greatest effect was made when she re-met the man with whom she had first stepped from the path of virtue : her confusion was painful, her shame terrible. But what was it all about ? Magda was a brilliantly successful artist, the primrose path had led her to the summit of her ambitions, and, when she happened to remember him, she was grateful to this gentleman for pointing it out to her. He had had many successors and would have many more. The blushing, conscious-stricken victim was very fine, but she had nothing to do with Magda. Mrs. Campbell *was* Magda. She played the part beautifully, showing the woman uplifted and transfigured by her art, but recognisably a development of the good-natured, hasty-tempered scamp of a girl who had run away from that respectable house many years before. It was a beautiful performance, full of the highest artistry and well meriting its great success.

For me Mrs. Campbell reached her high-water mark in ' Beyond Human Power ' by Bjornstjerne Bjornson (why could not the man call himself Johnson and get it over ?). It was one of those cheery little pieces from Northern lands which at that time were considered the right thing to talk about, if not to see. The fact therefore that the heroine spent the first Act in bed, paralysed from the waist downwards, was not a surprise, but that in the second and final Act she did not appear at all until just before the curtain fell was a little disconcerting.

I went to the opening performance not altogether blithely, and beside me were seated two pressmen—pressmen of the wrong type. They were profoundly bored by their job—couldn't stand that kind of thing—supposed they must see a bit of it, but would slip out as soon as possible.

The curtain rose upon a log-built room plain to bareness, a dreary glimpse of white mountains through a small window, a narrow bed, and on the white pillow a white face among masses of black hair, dark, haunted, sleepless eyes—the spell began to work. The whole house became as still as the still figure in the bed. Never throughout the Act did the almost painful strain relax until the dark eyes closed in a healing, miraculous sleep and the curtain fell in complete silence.

One of the pressmen said, " My God ! " The other obviously could say nothing.

The second Act was almost entirely taken up by an endless discussion between pastors of various denominations on the nature and possibility of miracles, but so overwhelming was the effect, so tense the atmosphere created by Mrs. Campbell in the first Act, that the disputing clerics were neither seen nor heard ; all attention was fixed upon the unseen woman in the next room. She was waited for breathlessly, and when at last she stood for a moment upon the threshold, radiant, ecstatic, transfigured, then tottered forward to fall dead at the feet of the miracle-workers, we had all had about as much emotion as was good for us.

This was great acting, great among the greatest. This was Mrs. Campbell as she might have been—as she should have been—as, sad to say, she very seldom was.

Her strange beauty and mysterious eyes full of brooding sadness were of great help to her in weird parts of this sort—though I remember her taking credit for the latter entirely to herself.

" My eyes are really nothing in particular," she once observed to me. " God gave me boot buttons, but I invented the dreamy eyelid, and that makes all the difference."

Her sense of the ludicrous was very keen and she could never repress it, even though it told against herself. One evening I was behind the scenes at His Majesty's, waiting to speak to Sir Herbert Tree, who was on the stage officiating as High Priest in some ancient Egyptian ceremonial.

In the dusk of the wings a wonderful figure moved towards me—it was Mrs. Campbell clad in curious mummy-like swathings of black and yellow which clung closely to the shape. She looked magnificent and I ventured to tell her so.

" Nonsense," said the lady, who was often a little ruffled at His Majesty's, " I look like an elderly wasp in an interesting condition."

I never saw that play from the front and it was perhaps as well : I should have been quite unable to forget the interesting wasp.

Painters of course seized upon Mrs. Campbell as a most inspiring subject ; even Burne-Jones, who hated drawing from other than professional models, did several studies of her. She very kindly sat to me for two portraits, as well as for many slighter sketches, and I also costumed for her two entire plays, ' Princesse Maleine ' by Maeterlinck and ' Undine ' by W. L. Courtenay, though only the latter saw the light. Sometimes I would be called in to advise upon or design separate dresses for her in plays the costuming of which was in other hands. This is always a difficult and thankless job, as one is naturally afraid of spoiling and upsetting another man's ideas and colour schemes.

I remember perforce intruding thus into Lewis Waller's revival of 'Ruy Blas' (a version by John Davidson, the poet), in which Mrs. Campbell was playing the Queen of Spain.

Naturally I talked over the matter with the artist who was responsible for the other costumes, and found him plunged in melancholy.

"It's so difficult to get the women to wear the stiff Velasquez dresses," he complained. "They manage to give them a modern look directly they try them on. You'll *never* get Mrs. Campbell into those hoops."

I too had misgivings, but I braced myself for the fray, and Her Majesty of Spain duly 'tried on' at Mrs. Nettleship's.

When she had looked at herself she told me what she thought of the costume : I preserved silence. She next passed on to what she thought of *me*. Here I found it easier to agree with her and still remained calm. She then cast herself upon the floor, like Constance, and uplifted her voice in woe.

"But—but I look such an absolute *fool* ! *Don't* I ? "

"You do," I agreed—it always paid to be quite candid with Mrs. Campbell—"but I don't suppose you mean to play the Queen of Spain on 'all fours.' Won't you get up and look again ? "

After a dangerous moment she rose from where she and sorrow sat, examined herself afresh, and the fact that she looked quite lovely gradually appeased her.

In the end she swept on to the stage like a magnificent frigate with all sail set ; and the other ladies, who had at the last moment reduced hoops and abated stiffenings, reaped their reward in looking limp and characterless.

One always looked for little differences of opinion on the matter of costume, but during our consultations over the designs for 'Undine,' the lady and I had a really serious dispute upon a most unusual point.

I was showing and trying to explain a sketch for the 'Under Waves' scene with mermaids seated in ocean caves.

"Those two mermaids," I continued, "will have to 'stay put' just where they are. They cannot move because of their tails."

"Their tails," repeated Mrs. Campbell dreamily—then her direct gaze was flashed upon me. "And what about *my* tail?"

"You are not going to have a tail."

"*No tail?*"

"No. Certainly not."

All the woman in Mrs. Campbell was roused. Here were these mermaids sitting about complete with tails, and she without one to her back.

"I'll have a tail," she said, and what she said she meant.

"You will *not* have a tail! *Never* will I design a tail for you!"

"Then I shall design a tail for myself. Anyone can design tails."

Really it was almost an estrangement ; we were now both in deadly earnest ; we glared at each other across a table littered with drawings.

Mastering myself by a mighty effort, like the hero of fiction, I rose, pale and determined.

"Then I will have nothing more to do with that scene."

"I'll have a tail," said Mrs. Campbell.

I can recall no more, my emotions must have overpowered me, and, as I never saw the play—it was produced in the provinces—I cannot be certain exactly of what happened ; but, as the newspapers gave no account of 'Undine' entering for a sack race in Act One, I fancy she must have changed her mind.

I had intended this chapter to deal with the St. James's

Theatre under the rule of George Alexander, but Mrs. Patrick Campbell seems, like Aaron's rod, to have swallowed up the theatre and everything connected with it. I can only apologise and say that it is just like her and no fault whatever of mine.

DURING these years my friendship with George Alexander and his wife pursued an unruffled course. I saw much of him both at the theatre and in his home, and we often spent some months of the summer together.

We had further adventures on the East Coast, usually in the neighbourhood of Cromer, and the houses which he took for the season were nearly always marked with strange individuality. In one of them the door of the guest chamber opened sideways on to the stairs and, unless you emerged crab-like, you stepped to your doom. It was a blithe beginning to a day for the old hand, who had been through the mill, to rise early and witness the innocent new-comer prance buoyantly forth, pour himself like a cataract downstairs and roll out into the garden.

Another house was haunted by gigantic insects of terrifying aspect ; the bedrooms were known respectively as The Spider Room, The Black Beetle Room, The Earwig Room, etc. I graduated in the room of honour, The Spider Room, with complete comfort as I do not mind spiders, but, when banished to The Earwig Room to make way for a guest of more importance, I fared less well.

At this time George Alexander always discussed his plays with me, I often heard him his parts and held consultations with him as to colours and effects, but beyond a few sketches and suggestions I did no actual work for him at the St. James's until in 1897 he embarked upon his first big production, 'As You Like It,' and put the costuming of the play into my hands. It was his first managerial attempt at Shakespeare and a very fine one it was. He gave the play almost complete, instead of the usual chopped and hashed version, and, though very long, it never flagged.

I was most conscientious over the dresses, and the forest scenes looked really rustic ; nothing but russets, browns and greens—what a tailor would call 'gent's heather-mixture.'

But I badly wanted some colour to end up with and fastened upon Hymen.

" Can't we make a little splash with Hymen ? " I suggested to Alexander. " A sort of Masque. The stage direction doesn't say ' Enter Hymen ' but ' Enter one representing Hymen.' We need not take him very seriously. Can't we have a Masque ? "

Alexander agreed, old Mr. Espinosa, the ballet master, came in to advise, Edward German wrote a beautiful lilting measure, and between us the Masque of Hymen grew. Flower-decked children danced, demure, white maidens swung their garlands, it was a picture of Spring in the faint pure tints of primrose and anemone.

Then came a burst of colour. A covey of little crimson-robed Cupids fluttered in on peacock wings shooting golden arrows, tipped with red roses, and finally the beautiful golden figure of Hymen emerged from the misty blue deeps of the wood. I had certainly attained my riot of colour, the gentle hues of the opening wiped out by the rush of crimson, the crimson effaced in its turn by the only colour that will efface crimson—orange—and orange against its complementary blue, which doubled its effect.

But at the last Alexander, still young in management, was seized with panic.

" They'll say I've been monkeying with Shakespeare," he said. " They'll say it's not in the play. We ought not to risk it."

I had an attack of inspiration.

" Nobody reads Shakespeare, Alec," I assured him. " They talk about him but they never read him. Put a paragraph in the papers saying that you are reviving the Masque of Hymen, usually omitted in representation."

The idea appealed to Alexander's Scotch sense of humour and the paragraphs duly appeared, with complete success. Not a complaint was made ; the Masque was received with respect, nay with reverence.

Many years afterwards I saw in announcements of an approaching performance of the play that " The Masque of Hymen, as revived at the St. James's Theatre, will be restored." I had created a Tradition.

That production of ' As You Like It ' is a cherished memory of mine ; there was something fresh, vernal, youthful about it. Nearly everyone in it was young and the spirit of happy youth pervaded it. And such a quartette of lovely women cannot often have been seen—Julia Neilson, Fay Davis, Dorothea Baird, and Julie Opp.

I had known the beautiful Julia and her equally beautiful mother for many years, ever since the daughter first gave up the career of a concert singer for the stage. She had sat to me for the first portrait that I painted ' on my own ' after leaving Albert Moore's studio, a careful study in Moore's manner of a white-robed figure against a mass of pale azaleas, that achieved a certain likeness but failed to do justice to the lovely model, as a gay young bachelor of my acquaintance took care to point out to me. He seemed to take an interest in the picture and his name was Fred Terry.

And now she was at the height of her wonderful beauty, the ideal Fairy Princess of romance as she entered as ' Rosalind,' passing along the grey stone terrace in trailing robes of soft blue while a white hound with a jewelled collar paced by her side.

I was rather proud of my costumes and I remember thoroughly enjoying dressing Aubrey Smith as the Wicked Duke, though he was such a huge man that ' to dress ' him was an inadequate term—he required upholstering. I heaped all my magnificence upon him, and he finally stalked on to the stage wearing clothes enough for six ordinary men and looking quite at ease in them.

I should like to put upon record that my ' As You Like It ' was Alexander's most beautiful production, but truth compels me to hand the palm to ' Paola and Francesca,' the poem-play by Stephen Philips, the costumes for which were, I think, designed by Percy Anderson. In his putting on of this play Alexander gave the finest production on Irving's lines ever seen outside the Lyceum : there was a beautiful restraint about it, the picture was always well inside the frame, the lighting was imaginative and perfect. The only blemish, to my mind, was Alexander's own make up as the stern husband. For some reason he suddenly saw himself as Irving, and Irving in an elderly part, and he grew older and older every night to his own deep satisfaction. I did my best.

"Don't you think, Alec," I said, very gently, "that as you and Paolo are brothers and he is eighteen and you to-night are not a day under sixty-five, the Dowager Lady Malatesta must have been a very remarkable woman?"

But it was useless ; Malatesta was a senile seventy before the end of the run—and brother Paolo was Henry Ainley, then a slip of a boy and beautiful as a knight of Giorgione.

The next big production in which I bore a part at the St. James's was 'Much Ado About Nothing,' but on this occasion I had not leisure to undertake the task of dressing the entire play as Alexander wished me to do. I was very busy with pictures which I was painting in the country, and the job was finally shared between me, my friend Arthur Melville, the painter, and Mr. Karl of ' Nathan's,' a past-master in costuming and a charming fellow-worker.

Alexander was anxious that the scene-painters should work with us so that the result might be a complete picture, and nearly all of them were most kind and helpful, though the idea was then regarded as a startling innovation.

Only that fine artist, Mr. Telbin, held out. I think he had been given the idea that we wished to teach him his business, which goodness knows we did not ; anyhow, he would not show us his scene—the Church set—nor even tell us the colour scheme of what was to form the background for our figures.

"It doesn't really matter," said Arthur Melville to me. "The general effect is sure to be brown." So we allowed for brown, and brown it was.

But Telbin had been right in thinking that too many were at work on the production. The result was heavy.

It was magnificent, but ' Much Ado About Nothing ' ought not to be magnificent, but merely bright, sunny, gay. A glimpse of blue sky and a lick of distemper would have better suggested the atmosphere.

In one scene, I remember, we had arranged for a gaily dressed crowd to pass in front of a plain white wall ; the figures *en silhouette* against the whiteness would have produced a dazzling effect of Sicilian sunshine and heat. But never could we get that plain white wall ; it was always carefully ' broken down ' and cut up with representations of crumbling masonry and clinging vines—' to give the effect of age,' we were told.

" But it wasn't old then," I pleaded, " and even if it had been, surely Leonato would have run to a pail of whitewash when he was entertaining Distinguished Company."

But the wall remained a mass of Pre-Raphaelite detail, and the picture was spoiled.

And not many years afterwards Reinhardt brought his wordless play, ' Sumerun,' to England, and all London flocked to see a train of figures pass in front of a plain white wall. The stage is certainly the most conservative of institutions : perhaps that is why it still remains so interesting.

I never felt that this revival, in spite of its splendours, was a real success. The parts of Benedick and Beatrice were unsuited both to Alexander and his Leading Lady, a fact which at rehearsals he did not perceive but which was clearly apparent to Miss Neilson, whom I once found sitting in a heap upon the stairs leading up to the dressing-rooms and crying quietly but hopelessly.

" What is the matter ? " I exclaimed, thinking that she had hurt herself.

" Oh," sniffed the beautiful Julia, " oh—I am making such a f-fool of myself ! "

This was far from being the case, but in truth the radiant beacon-light of Ellen Terry in the part was still too dazzling to allow of any other Beatrice being perceptible.

The successes were Fred Terry's splendid ' Don Pedro,' and the ' Don John ' of Harry Irving, whose sinister, faintly smiling villains were then enjoying quite a vogue. They were all exactly alike, but very effective.

Harry Irving was a very valuable member of the St. James's Company : he played many parts there and played them all well, doing far better and more original work than when, later on, he appeared elsewhere in revivals of his great father's old successes with himself in the leading rôles. In these parts he followed his father as closely as possible and, aided by a strong personal resemblance, produced a very exact copy up to a certain point. But all the wonder, the terror, the fascination of the original lay beyond that certain point. Though a little stiff and pedantic, he possessed the family charm ; he was a likeable man and a pleasant companion.

With Laurence, his brother, all was different. He could not have been called likeable, he was a man to be violently disliked or loved. The perverse devil that had lurked in Henry Irving rollicked fantastically in Laurence, yet without spoiling his kindliness and innate goodness. He came on the stage with everything against him ; he was awkward, ugly, stagy in the worst sense, his too-obvious cleverness seemed no help to him and his painful efforts to give expression to what were evidently fine ideas were distressing to watch. For years he struggled on, not apparently advancing a step, when suddenly—something happened. It was like the birth of a dragon-fly from a caddis, the grotesque shell that had hidden him split asunder and the actor emerged in full panoply.

Ellen Terry and I went together to see him in Ibsen's ' Pretenders.' We could not recognise Laurence. Henry Irving was before us—Henry Irving with his mesmeric personality, his strange pale beauty, his atmosphere of romance and mystery.

The illusion was so compelling that we could not speak of it. Silently we made our way on to the stage when the play ended and stood tongue-tied before Laurence, until at last Ellen Terry burst into tears and embraced him, which seemed to express our sentiments very well.

He had arrived. The long uphill struggle was over—he had conquered. And in a few months more he was dead.

Work was very pleasant at the St. James's. Alexander and I, as old friends, were able to discuss matters comfortably, Florence Alexander, his wife, was always of immense help, and she and I used to make secret and illicit raids upon the sacred ' Wardrobe,' where we often found just what we wanted ready to our hand.

It is curiously difficult to persuade a manager to use up old stuff. I remember Henry Irving once putting the production of a poetical play, ' The Amber Heart,' entirely into the hands of Ellen Terry. He had bought the play for her and gave her *carte blanche* to get what she wished in the way of scenery and dresses. When she presented the bill, which amounted, if I remember right, to a little over fifteen pounds, he was quite annoyed.

" But," as Miss Terry said, " there it all was. Some of the ' Hamlet ' scenery, turned round and differently lit, was just right ; all the dresses required were in the theatre except mine—and that was made of book muslin, damped and wrung, and cost about twopence."

My long memory used to come in usefully here as I was able to call up a picture of dresses in plays past and done with which, with a little management, would supply our present wants.

The same ' long memory ' was also effective when, in the ' pleached alley ' scene in ' Much Ado About Nothing,' I wanted the actors to come up on to the terrace as from a lower garden.

" They cannot come up there," said Alexander. " There isn't a trap there."

" There is."

" There isn't," said the stage manager, also the carpenter.

" But there *is*," I persisted. " It was cut for the White Parlour in ' Guy Domville.' "

And lo, there was a trap. I went up several places with the carpenter, at any rate.

'Guy Domville.' That recalls another beautiful production at the St. James's. I had nothing to do with it, I am sorry to say—I should like to have been responsible for the White Parlour—but I was present on the first night, and that is not a happy memory.

The play was by Henry James. He had tempted fortune on the stage on one or two former occasions but with small success ; now, with the Company and resources of the St. James's Theatre at his back, all would surely be well.

His old friend, John Sargent, and I had dined together quietly and we set out for the first night with high hopes.

The opening act delighted the audience ; all the delicate charm of the dialogue was brought out by careful acting and stage management.

Marion Terry at her enchanting best was an ideal ' Mrs. Peveril ' and Alexander played ' Guy Domville ' with quiet grace, though Sargent, always on the look-out for ' bad drawing,' kept whispering to me, " Why does he open his mouth on one side like that ? It makes his face all crooked."

The curtain fell to general applause and the play seemed safe.

But with the next act came a change. The author had done a dangerous thing in dropping most of the first-act characters and introducing a new set in whom little interest was taken. The excellence of the opening was now a drawback, the audience wanted more of it ; they longed to follow the fortunes of Marion Terry and sulkily refused to be interested in the doings of Miss Millard. An elderly actress entered in a costume which struck them as grotesque.

As a fact, the dress was a particularly fine one, but it wanted wearing ; the huge hoop and great black hat perched upon a little frilled under-cap should have been carried by one filled with the pride of them and the consciousness of their beauty.

But at the unexpected laughter the actress took fright, she became timid, apologetic, she tried to efface herself. Now the spectacle of a stately dame whose balloon-like skirts half filled the stage and whose plumes smote the heavens trying to efface herself was genuinely ludicrous and the laugh became a roar. After this the audience got out of hand ; they grew silly and cruel and ready to jeer at everything.

The last act, with its lovely White Parlour and the longed-for return of Marion Terry, almost pulled things together again, but by this time the hero's continual vacillations between his lady-loves had struck the demoralised house as comic, and when he changed his mind for the last time the irreverent let themselves go. The play ended in a storm of laughter and hisses, during which Alexander led on the unhappy Henry James and held him there in the middle of the stage confronting the jeering and booing house. Why he did this I cannot imagine. Possibly he thought that the appearance of a man of letters, an artist of great and acknowledged reputation, would silence the mockers, but alas, the bewildered and terrified face of poor Mr. James only gave them new delight. It seemed to me that the two stood there for hours—to Henry James it must have been a lifetime—and my discomfort was not allayed by the violent eruption at my side of John Sargent, who had one of his rare attacks of fury and seemed about to hurl his hat at Alexander and leap upon the stage to rescue his friend.

It was a miserable evening, but I think the most acute impression left upon me as I staggered homewards was amazement and admiration at Sargent's eloquent summing up. To think that I had denied to this Lord of Language the gift of self-expression in picturesque and impassioned speech ! He expressed himself for upwards of half an hour without repeating a phrase or an epithet. It was colossal —I never heard anything like it.

But such experiences as that fatal night were luckily rare. Well manned and well steered, the good ship Sant' Iago put forth year after year on fair and prosperous voyages and returned laden to port. Alexander was very wise in his management; he did not rely upon his own great popularity, but always surrounded himself with a good company and, during his reign, made several notable discoveries.

He presented us with Mrs. Patrick Campbell and also with Fay Davis, a comedienne of most compelling charm whose career was brilliant as it was brief. Also, he let us see the delightful art of Marion Terry in many parts, all of which she made memorable by her unerring skill and accomplishment.

The great successes of her later life in rather flamboyant rôles, such as ' Mrs. Erlyn ' in ' Lady Windermere's Fan,' may have slightly effaced the memory of her earlier work, but to me she remained the most perfect portrayer of wistful girlhood; her art in such parts was so finished, so exquisitely subtle as to be imperceptible : few people, I believe, realised how great an artist the stage possessed in her.

Like most of the Terry family she was so much at home on the stage as to be able to do what she pleased. I remember, while I was watching her one evening from the prompt corner in a difficult and rather poignant scene, she gathered up a few flowers from a bouquet in a vase, arranged them carefully, walked calmly across to me and presented me with the bunch, saying in what seemed to me the same voice which she was using in the play, " There's a buttonhole for you." What she was doing and saying was as apparent to me as all the rest of her scene, yet I am positive that no one else in the theatre either saw or heard.

The reign of Marion Terry at the St. James's immediately preceded that of Mrs. Patrick Campbell, and for a brief space they shared the throne, but there cannot be two queens in one hive.

Alexander, with reckless daring, once went on tour with both of them, reaping, I believe, a golden harvest but returning with his brown locks becomingly but perceptibly silvered.

Certainly, in my varied career in the theatre, I got my best chances and did my best work at the St. James's, possibly—though this may seem a self-opinionated point of view—because I was there allowed so much of my own way.

Designing for the stage is not quite such a plain-sailing business as it would appear, and much of the difficulty comes after one's designs have been made. It is one thing to invent a dress, another to make someone wear it, and I have usually found the men more difficult to deal with than the women.

I remember one actor in particular who seemed invariably to dislike the clothes intended for him, and to hanker after those of his fellow-players. In one piece it was absolutely necessary for the balance of my picture that in a certain scene he should wear a certain costume.

I felt sure that he would object to it, so I had it made carefully to his measure and allotted it to a minor character, who at once became an obtrusively conspicuous figure. Soon—as I had foreseen—the leading man drew me aside.

" This costume of mine, you know," he began. " It's fine. It's just the thing of course. But that dress there—right in the corner—oughtn't it to be nearer the centre ? "

I agreed ; it certainly should be.

" I suppose," he went on, " that it wouldn't do for me to wear that dress instead of this ? "

I admitted that it would look very well, but suggested (may I be forgiven !) that the costume might not fit him. He vanished, and soon returned, attired as I had hoped to see him.

" It's a most extraordinary thing," he exclaimed. " It fits me exactly. It might have been made for me. I really think I shall wear it. You don't mind, do you ? "

And I didn't.

George Alexander, at the St. James's, was not a pioneer ; as a producer he broke no new ground but followed quietly in the footsteps of his former chief, his own good taste preserving him from the pitfalls into which blundered others who in going further fared worse.

In my time I have seen no advance upon the stage pictures shown by Henry Irving at the Lyceum : later productions, said to be upon his lines, went far astray despite their elaborate costliness.

At the Lyceum there was no needless extravagance, no pomp and circumstance for their own sakes. All was suggestion, preparing the mind, through the eye, to receive the great actor's interpretation.

I do not, for instance, suppose that the chimes which clashed out from St. Sebald's Church in ' Faust,' to the discomfort of the cowering demon, were really so deep and sonorous. I have heard Madame Yvette Guilbert, when singing ' Les Cloches de Nantes,' produce exactly the same impression of crashing, booming sound by pulling an imaginary rope and saying " Ding, dong," or whatever is its French equivalent. Everything at the Lyceum was *Maya*—illusion ; the master spirit that had contrived all impressed its will upon us and made us see and hear what it pleased.

In the productions at His Majesty's Theatre during the reign of Tree we were given reality ; real magnificence, real brocades and cloths of gold, real streams dashing over oilcloth rocks into still pools of mackintosh, real ferns and grasses, real flowers.

I wish I could forget a scene in which terrace upon terrace of real (stage) grass piled themselves to the skyline while centre stood a lady in a real red dress.

One longed to post letters in her. The grass was greener than any grass could be, the lady was redder than any lady, out of the Apocalypse, had any right to be. Everything was too gorgeous, the soul was lacking ; here were no dreams to sell, no great will at work, illusion fled before the pitiless and all-revealing electric glare.

The beautiful lighting effects of Irving, under which the stage picture looked like a mellow ' Old Master,' were all attained by gas. Augustin Daly, when he rented the Lyceum for a season, installed electric light, but Irving, noting its effect on his return, banished it at once and restored the gas.

Critics of to-day, many of whom cannot have seen these productions, tell us that his way of giving Shakespeare was not the right way. I can only affirm that a better way has not been found since. The ' freak ' performances—the ' No Scenery ' performances—the ' No Clothes '—sorry—I mean the ' Modern Dress ' performances, are mere ' publicity stunts ' and not even new at that. Did not one of Charles Dickens's showmen anticipate ' Shakespeare performed entirely by wooden legs ' ?

I have seen only one production on other lines which held its own against Irving's : ' Twelfth Night,' put on by Harley Granville Barker at the Savoy Theatre in 1914— indeed, it did more than hold its own, it distinctly outshone Irving's presentment of the same play. ' Twelfth Night ' had been one of the few Lyceum failures ; it was wrong in key, it was ponderous, dull : Ellen Terry's lovely ' Viola ' seemed to have wandered into it by mistake, her cry of " What should I do in Illyria ? " held a plaintive note of sincerity. Barker's rendering was poetic, comic, a delight to the eye yet very simple. It was the work of a true artist.

THE 'nineties were passing. It was the end of a period, and with the ebbing of the century many great landmarks were swept away.

The great Victorians were falling fast, leaving the lustre of their names, but taking with them the keen, stimulating atmosphere created by their vivid personalities.

Robert Browning died in '91 and London mourned him as a friend. He had none of the aloofness, the unapproachable pose of the Great Poet, though of reserve he had plenty, for, though nearly everyone knew him, I doubt if anyone knew much about him.

He liked to mix and converse with his fellow-creatures, and it must be admitted that he did most of the conversing, but as an audience almost any fellow-creature seemed to do—he was not particular.

This was borne in upon me when I found that he would, on occasion, even converse with me.

Everyone seemed more or less to interest him or at any rate to engage his attention, and I recall a curious instance of this.

In my scrubbed and most undistinguished youth I was on one late afternoon plodding past Hyde Park Corner in a steady downpour. Cabs and omnibuses had vanished from the face of the earth ; I was rapidly becoming what Mr. Mantilini would have called a ' demned moist unpleasant body.'

Suddenly an umbrella was held over me and a rather loud voice behind me said, " You'll be soaked. Come under this." I was captured and sheltered, and found my unworthy self walking arm in arm through the rain with Robert Browning.

" You're going home ? " he enquired. " Well, that's my way too—in fact, I shall pass your door. We'll go together."

I fell into step, grateful and elated.

" But how do you know where I live ? " I enquired.

" Why you told me yourself," replied the poet. " One evening at the Lehmanns'. Don't you remember ? "

Of course I remembered, but why on earth had Browning remembered ? He must have had a marvellously accurate memory in which all information, however trivial, was carefully placed and docketed.

My kind and much-loved Master, Albert Moore, passed in '92, and his end was at one with his brave but lonely life. He had undergone an operation which had been partly successful, and gave him some years of health, but when the trouble reappeared he knew that nothing further could be done. He had just started a large canvas, ' The Loves of the Winds and the Seasons,' and was determined to finish it.

He shut himself up, refusing himself to friends and seeing hardly anyone save a former pupil, a kind and charming woman, who now came to him, ostensibly for some final lessons, but I think really that she might bring him some help and sympathy.

And he worked ceaselessly at his picture. As it grew he faded. It was killing him, but as his life passed into the fair young limbs of the Winds and the Seasons he was happy.

Like the fabled nightingale, he sang his last song with his breast against the thorn, and when the song ceased he was dead.

It was a beautiful and brave ending and well befitting this most perfect knight of the Lady Beauty, to whose service all his life had been dedicated and to whom in death he was still faithful.

My fellow-pupil, Alfred Lys Baldry, and I helped to arrange a Memorial Exhibition of his pictures at the Grafton Gallery, and Whistler—the real Whistler, not the fantastic cynic known to the public—deeply mourned the loss of his friend. Whistler liked many men—perhaps a little capriciously and fitfully—but Albert Moore was one of the few men whom he respected.

Another link with what are still for me the Great Days was severed by the death of William Morris in '96.

Though meeting him often, I had never known him really well, but many of his intimate friends were mine also and his strong personality was a dominating influence.

It was difficult to connect his exuberant vitality with illness and loss of strength, and I remember calling with a friend upon Mrs. Morris not long before his death without a thought of approaching sadness.

We had been with her in the long upper room overlooking the river and I had, as usual, become lost in watching her strange, mysterious beauty as she half sat, half lay, upon the great couch by the fireside. Morris was 'not well' in the room below, and as she came downstairs with us we asked her for news of him. She made no reply, but turning to the wall, fell against it, her bowed head hidden in her hands, and, in spite of the sudden realisation of tragedy, my mind involuntarily registered the thought—" If Rossetti could have seen that grand, wild gesture, what a picture it would have drawn from him ! "

And now Rossetti's kingship was passing, his Round Table was dissolved, and, with the death of Edward Burne-Jones in '98, the last of his great knights set out upon the last Quest.

The shadow of loss lay long upon Burne-Jones's friends, and the list of them must have included almost everyone to whom he had ever spoken. To me it came as the end of an epoch.

Though he was my elder by so many years, for me he stood for Youth ; his mind was eternally fresh and youthful, a flowery country full of quaint nooks and unexplored alley ways ; no one else could 'make believe' so deliciously, his imagination had the vivid quality, the clear vision that is usually lost with childhood. I never felt so young again after his death.

To his active brain and with his habits of ceaseless industry a long illness would have been unbearably irksome : happily this was spared him and the last day of his life found him at work in his studio as usual.

But during the last two years I had noticed a little change in his daily round. He was hurrying—not by relaxing effort or scamping work, but by forcing himself to concentrate upon and finish certain pictures instead of laying them aside while he fixed some new idea upon canvas.

Thus the huge 'Arthur in Avalon,' which had half filled the Garden Studio for so many years, claimed the lion's share of his time and finally got itself practically completed. It was a grand, solemn picture, though the actual design had never been one of my favourites. It was a little diffuse—scattered—the central figure of the sleeping Arthur to which all eyes were directed seemed to lack dignity and import. I had looked for a great man, in a tiny island tomb ; here was a little man in a vast land of rolling hills and vales.

I felt that the picture was great, but I had, as it were, grown up with it, and familiarity had perhaps dimmed its impressiveness.

When I saw it in the painter's Memorial Exhibition, framed and hung amongst his other works, I was again able to appreciate its beauties, but I have always regretted the removal of two outer panels, part of the original design, which formed the picture into a great triptych. These panels represented the Hill Faeries, the Echoes lurking in clefts of the rocks and waiting to prolong and repeat the trumpet blare that would proclaim the waking of Arthur to the world. These little watching figures, their eyes fixed upon the still form of the sleeping king, conveyed the idea that all Nature waited breathless for a sign, for the long silence to be rent by a mighty sound.

I always mourned the Hill Faeries, rejected at an early stage of the picture's development, and tried to 'keep up' with them after their banishment to an upper chamber at the Grange, and afterwards, when they passed into the possession of the Artist's granddaughter.

Might they not one day be reunited to the picture and take their place in the great design?

Another magnificent canvas of colossal size, ' The Car of Love,' never reached completion, but was luckily left at a moment when the whole design had been painted in and modelled in monochrome, the colour as yet hardly suggested. In this state, though unfinished, the picture can be seen as a whole and reveals itself as one of the painter's very grandest conceptions.

It now recalls to me fantastically a morning spent with him in the Garden Studio and one of our many conversations in which the Puck-spirit, always lurking in him, would bob up unexpectedly—often with surprising effects.

I was sitting harmlessly and innocently watching him as he worked; there was complete silence between us, he seemed absorbed in his task.

Above us towered the great picture, reaching almost from floor to roof.

High aloft, fast bound to his own triumphal car, stood the figure of blind Love, himself at once the god and the sacrifice; behind him swirled splendid masses of wind-blown drapery, leaving the white body naked.

The car, mounted on huge wheels, swept down a narrow street leaving no space on either side and before it, drawing it along by cords, ran a crowd of naked men and women, some laughing and shouting as they sped along, others looking back with a growing terror as they realised that the great car was now moving by its own impetus and that they must run on and on or be crushed beneath its weight.

Suddenly the painter paused.

" I often wonder," he said, apparently in one of his grave, father confessor-like moods, "just what *you* were about when this car passed by."

" There isn't much of me," I suggested. " I expect I slipped in between the wheel and the wall."

" No room," he said solemnly, fixing me with his

mysterious eyes. " The car fits exactly—no one in the street can escape."

" Then probably I had just run in to see the time at the pub," I ventured, at a loss for loftier imagery.

He put down his brush and turned to me ; the father confessor had vanished, Puck undisguised and unashamed regarded me with elfin malice.

" I know of nothing—*nothing*," he observed, " that would give me more pure and exquisite pleasure than to see you get yourself into the most ridiculous mess over some woman."

I gaped at him—here was a nice child's guide !

" Now, taking this into consideration," he went on, " don't you think you might make an effort ? I don't mean a silly little mess that could be swept up in a minute, but a regular howler. You can't imagine how much it would amuse me. Don't you *want* to amuse me ? "

I did, of course ; it was one of my fondest aspirations, but still——

Really this was no way to behave. I was no longer a boy, but a grave and reverend senior stepping sedately into my thirties—my grey hairs should have protected me. But I fancy the ' Car of Love ' was to blame.; it was a great subject, greatly treated, and over-much solemnity always had a dangerous effect upon Burne-Jones—after a prolonged dose of it disturbances might usually be expected. With me, at least, he could never be very serious for long together.

Once and once only during our long friendship did he try to write me a Business Letter—a grown-up letter about Things that Matter.

He got on pretty well for a page and a half—then occurred abruptly the portrait of an unprepossessing person in a tall hat covered with fly-papers and the Man of Business broke off to observe—

" A man has just passed the window in a hat like this. I don't quite like it, yet a Lincoln and Bennett leaves much to be desired."

Though every moment of his day seemed to be occupied, yet he always found time to write nonsense; long letters used to come to me full of fatherly advice as to dealing with imaginary (and usually unseemly) situations in which I had not found myself, patient and saintly forgiveness for injuries which I had not inflicted, dignified rebukes for opinions which I had not expressed.

At one time many of these effusions were for the attempted bewilderment of a beautiful and much-prized model who sat frequently to both of us, who had a delightful sense of humour and who was affectionately known to her large circle of friends as Bessie. The following is a fair example.

Bessie had called at his studio to ask when he would require her to sit and was met by a solemn assurance that, thanks to information received from me, he now knew ' all,' and that—as she must see—this made it quite impossible for him to employ her again.

As she always received any statement from either of us with caution, she was not unduly cast down, but she was entrusted with a letter to deliver to me and gravely and sorrowfully bowed out.

The letter, which the lady insisted upon seeing, and had, of course, been prepared for her inspection, ran as follows :

My dear Graham,

I have had this morning rather a painful scene with Miss Elizabeth Keene. I felt bound in conscience to tell her why I had abstained so long from communicating with her, and when pressed to give my authority for the distressing things with which I charged her, I grieve to say that in the hurry of the minute I gave *you* as my authority, and the scene which followed was painful in the extreme.

I feel on all such occasions that a man is at a great disadvantage in a dispute with a lady. His anxious words are met with such undisciplined eloquence, his severe logic, if I might so term it, with such emotional rhetoric that his position is often pitiable.

I did not come off quite so well this morning as the justice of my cause seemed fitly to promise, nor do I anticipate any victorious issue for you of your next interview with her. I am sorry to confess that I was compelled to sacrifice you entirely and seemingly to acquiesce in the many and withering comments she made upon your character. They are weak creatures and we must have patience.

Yours aff.,

E. B.-J.

Here is another letter, also brought solemnly to me by Bessie, when I in my turn had let some time pass without asking her for sittings.

Thursday, January the Somethingth, 1897.

Miss Elizabeth Keene and Sir Edward Burne-Jones present their respects to Mr. Graham Robertson and would esteem it a favour if he would kindly inform them what he—Mr. G. R.—is up to.

Miss Keene in especial feels that the long silence on his—Mr. G. R.'s—part cannot be other than intentional, and as it has been and continues to be a subject of surprise to her friends she would be glad of a speedy termination of the annoyance she is subjected to.

Sir E. Burne-Jones would like respectfully to suggest that this season—the commencement of a New Year—is particularly fitted for remorseful contemplation and repentance.

Bessie, I remember, 'got back' quite successfully on Sir Edward by giving him a most circumstantial account of my secret engagement to a young lady at Surbiton ; the marriage being indefinitely postponed as the lady was the daughter of a clergyman in reduced circumstances and much occupied with parish work. He was quite worried by the news until Bessie, pressed to name the lady, announced her as a Miss Gertrude Barlow, which title, too evidently culled from ' Sandford and Merton,' gave the story away.

Bessie's mother had been a favourite model of Rossetti's and had appeared in many of Burne-Jones's best-known pictures, ' The Days of Creation,' ' Vivien and Merlin,' and others, but she herself had come to his studio as a very young girl, hardly more than a child. He had always delighted in her keen sense of the ludicrous, for the while she sat to him, her lovely face charged with that rapt expression of combined sanctity and imbecility generally supposed to be peculiar to angels, she would oblige with

281

a flow of thrilling domestic anecdote, as for instance the tale of a timid aspirant to her sister's hand who, on his way to propose, had primed himself for the ordeal and evidently rather overdone the priming. Bessie came upon him at a late hour seated moodily and to all appearance permanently in the middle of the garden path.

"I love Laura," he observed. Bessie felt the delicacy of the situation and gently hinted that he might now rise and go home. "I love Laura," repeated the gentleman, still immovable. "I *honour* Laura. 'F anybody—" suddenly fixing Bessie with a truculent eye—"'f anybody says a word against Laura—knock him down!"

Bessie fled, and finally, I believe, the adored one herself had to appear and assure him that she was Another's —which at the time she wasn't.

Burne-Jones used Bessie's face much in his later work —she succeeded her mother as chief 'angel' and 'nymph' —and he produced one beautiful portrait of her; actually a portrait, though he called the picture 'Vespertina Quies.' It showed her in a gown of deep blue against a background of grey hills under a quiet evening sky.

His pictures had always appealed to me strongly, but more especially his early work, so colourful, so steeped in romantic suggestion, and I had been lucky in securing most beautiful examples in the eight panels setting forth the life of Saint Frideswede, painted very early in the artist's career as designs for a great window in Christ Church Chapel, Oxford. Those lovely panels, perhaps the most spontaneous and fascinating of all his works and far finer than the window for which they were designed, were made into a screen by the artist and were for long in his own house in Kensington Square, until his friend, Birkett Foster, persuaded him to part with them and bore them off to 'The Hill,' Witley, which already boasted stained glass by the same hand and a series of decorative paintings from the history of Saint George.

Birkett Foster was then *the* water-colour painter of the day, and there are still traditions at Witley of heavily laden trains disgorging swarms of dealers at the station who would race each other up to 'The Hill' and sit patiently on its doorsteps to waylay the popular artist and extract from him the promise of a 'little gem.' When in course of time I came to make my home at Witley I did not notice any racing dealers, but found the kindly Lord of the Hill still painting and tramping about the countryside which he so loved and fought hard to protect against the 'improving' and destructive jerry-builder. Alas, what would he think of it now? The great Frideswede screen stood in a seldom-used studio, and I finally induced Birkett Foster to pass it on to me ; when I detached the panels, framing each separately in a narrow band of black, under Burne-Jones's direction.

Then came a difficulty which nearly always occurs when an artist comes across his own early work after losing sight of it for many years. He at once wished to restore and repaint.

Now this puts the owner of a picture into a most awkward position. It would seem ungracious, nay unfair, to deny to the creator of a picture the right to work his will upon it, yet to deliver it into his hands is to court disaster.

If a picture actually wants retouching in order, for instance, to hide an accidental injury, the artist who produced it many years ago is the last man who should be allowed to touch it, because, quite erroneously, he imagines himself still to be the man who painted it and therefore falls upon it without mercy or respect. No artist should ever be allowed to see a picture painted by himself more than twenty years ago.

Charles Hallé once told me of a miserable day spent at the Grosvenor Gallery during the hanging of the Millais Exhibition, while Millais completely repainted one of his early pictures to its utter and hopeless undoing. To watch the earnest young work disappearing under layers of slick commonplace was unforgettably sad.

I fought for my panels.

"There's hardly anything to be done," I pleaded. "Only those little joins to paint over. Let *me* do it. Let us get a man in from Whiteley's to do it. Don't let us do it at all—but *please* don't do it yourself!"

Burne-Jones was kind but quite firm. I was respectful (I hope) but quite firm too. I left town for a few days, and Burne-Jones raided the house in my absence, carrying off four panels. I, on my return, raided the Grange and got all the panels back again. Finally, under stress of other work, the painter forgot about the matter and six of the eight panels remain in their original condition.

These lovely works, with the two tiny water colours, 'Sidonia and Clara von Bork,' are among my most cherished treasures, but dearer still is the memory of their creator and the great gift of his friendship.

The three strong personalities who set their seal upon my artistic life were Rossetti, Burne-Jones and—later on—Arthur Melville, and amongst my small collection of pictures I have the good luck to number a really representative work by each of them—Rossetti's magnificent 'Proserpina,' the beautiful 'Frideswede' panels of Burne-Jones, and Melville's wonderful 'Venetian Night,' the great Piazza after 'lights out,' Saint Mark's and the Doge's Palace dimly lit by a reflected glare from the Piazzetta, and the Campanile towering up to lose itself in blue infinity.

But besides these there was another influence, dating from a day in my sixteenth or seventeenth year, when I came across Gilchrist's *Life of William Blake* in a Southampton bookshop. The poet-painter's all-daring imagination and marvellous powers of design fascinated me from the first, and gradually I became aware that it was still possible to pick up specimens of his (then) little appreciated work. My first 'find' was the famous 'Ghost of a Flea' which I purchased, despite severe qualms of conscience at the vast outlay, for twelve pounds. Since then the collection has grown and now my gallery of Blake is felt to represent one of my few excuses for existence.

284

" THE GHOST OF A FLEA "
by WILLIAM BLAKE
From the author's private collection

Meanwhile during the 'nineties I continued to see much of Sarah Bernhardt, on and off the stage both in London and in Paris.

I painted two portraits of her, one (a large canvas) as ' Adrienne Lecouvreur,' the other (a small panel) as ' Lorenzaccio.' The ' Adrienne ' picture was in the Oriental costume of the second act, when the actress is attired for the stage as ' Roxane.' This dress she was perpetually altering and renewing, but in the costumes for the other acts she took no interest. The period, she considered, was ' all wrong ' for her ; she had to wear powder which she hated, corsets which were torment to her. The powdering of her red-gold hair she always put off to the last minute, then, dashing on a white shower, she would fling down the puff exclaiming, " There ! Now I'm spoiled."

She was then at the height of her powers. Her performance of ' La Tosca ' was a nightly miracle if only from the point of view of vitality and endurance. She ran through the entire gamut of horror and despair and with it gave a first act of the lightest Comedy in which, for delicacy of touch, she rivalled her great fellow-artist, Réjane, for whom she held the most unbounded admiration.

" She is in Comedy what I try to be in Tragedy," she would say to me. " You must see her in everything she does."

The terrific force of that Tragedy I realised one day when I accompanied her to a photographer's where she was to be pictured in various scenes from ' La Tosca.' Several times she fell into the pose of horror and triumph after the murder of ' Scarpia,' but always seemed dissatisfied : there was something lacking—she had not got a corpse. At last she turned to me.

" Come here, Graham," she cried. " Come here and let me kill you."

Now I had on more than one occasion figured as the corpse in ' Fédora ' and found the sensation of being wailed over by the distraught heroine very pleasantly thrilling, so I advanced cheerfully and with confidence. But when the awful eyes of Floria Tosca—full of terror and deadly purpose—blazed into mine at such close quarters I became uneasy, and finally, as she seized me with her left hand and caught up the knife with her right, I disgraced myself.

"Madame Sarah," I yelped. "*Do* remember that you've got a *real* knife and not that one that shuts up into the handle!"

Ellen Terry at this period was also doing some of her best work. I have spoken of her 'Fair Rosamund' in 'Becket' which Irving took to America in '93 after a long run in London. It was perhaps her most perfect part, the tenderness, the dignity, the spirituality of it were unforgettable.

I remember going on to the Lyceum stage one evening, shortly before the departure of the Company to New York, and finding Irving about to start a rehearsal.

"But the play went all right, didn't it?" I asked. "Why must you rehearse?"

"We are to give a command performance of 'Becket' at Windsor," said Irving—"on a stage this size—look." He pointed to a space chalked upon the boards about the size of a bathing machine. "We must rehearse the whole play over again on that scale and I must have every stick of scenery repainted."

"But this will cost a great deal, won't it?"

"Any amount."

"Then—is it worth while?"

"Well worth while," said Irving. "I'm taking 'Becket' to America. For one American who will go to see a play by a great poet, twenty will go to see a play that has been given at Windsor Castle before the Queen. Oh yes, it's worth while."

Which showed that he had not been unobservant during his visits to the Land of Democracy.

Early in '94 Ellen Terry wrote to me from America in an unusual mood of depression.

We hope to get back about the 1st of April. Then 'Faust.' For my part pity me. Henry takes it as a deadly insult to him whenever I beg to be let off such and such a *young* part or to rest for awhile, and so I suppose, as I can't abide to offend or hurt him, I shall go on 'all work and no play' until I'm entirely worn out.

I begged for Marion to play 'Margaret'—just that one part. No—not at all. He was deadly silent for a week and then, when I said I'd do it, peaceful harmony was restored. Oh, I'm tired and sleepy. Good night. What a scrawl—the pen is fast asleep already.

Your affectionate friend,
E. T.

Strange that this realisation of time's passage should have come upon her then, for two years later, in '96, she was to achieve one of her greatest triumphs in a 'young' part. Her 'Imogen' in 'Cymbeline' was such a radiant embodiment of youth that when she first appeared the audience gasped—there was a silence, then thunders of applause.

In the 'Milford Haven' scene her outburst of almost delirious happiness dazzled and amazed : she seemed a creature of fire and air, she hovered over the stage without appearing to touch it. And as a companion picture was Irving's 'Iachimo,' no scowling sinister villain, but a fascinating Italian gentleman, entirely without morals but with exquisite manners and a compelling charm which explained his successes as a liar and scoundrel.

The 'nineties were to me a wonderful period ; the century was dying bravely in no dreary winter of old age but in what seemed a burst of late summer, sunny and fair, though flowers were beginning to fall. But with the end of the decade came war, unrest, in the air was a vague note of change, faint yet perceptible.

The old world was passing and I found myself looking out a little anxiously for the New Jerusalem descending from above.

I never saw it, and what's more I haven't seen it yet.

O<small>N</small> Christmas Day, 1887, my mother and I were returning from a more than usually virulent Family Dinner. Our family resembled most other families in that, while individually we were charming, collectively we were unbearable, and, realising this, we took care to collect as seldom as possible ; but as the great December feast of peace and goodwill came round we responded meekly to the call of tradition and the result was, as a rule, deplorable.

"That was one of our worst," observed my mother. "I knew it would be when Fred began on the teapot before we had even got to turkey."

This dark saying, which seemed to suggest that my uncle Fred had suddenly ' gone dry ' in the midst of our annual Bacchanalia, merely meant that he had shattered the light table talk by hurling into it the great family bone of contention—the burning question of my grand-father's silver teapot. Never should I have suspected my uncle, late dashing soldier and ' beauty man ' of the Bays, of a morbid interest in teapots, still less that the loss of one (shamelessly annexed by a quick-witted and light-fingered sister) should have embittered his whole later life, yet thus it appeared to be—especially at Christmas-time.

I do not suppose that, during the rest of the year, he brooded in his tent over his wrongs, but Christmas evoked old memories, the light of other days shone out, and down the long beam stole his lost teapot, and he told us all exactly how he felt about it.

"This must never happen again," said my mother firmly. "Next Christmas we will go abroad."

"Abroad ? " I echoed dismally, for I had been there and didn't like it.

"Then," said my mother desperately, "we must take a cottage somewhere. We can then say we are spending Christmas at ' our little place in the country ' and we shall escape these dreadful dinners."

So forthwith we began the search for our cottage and, in the autumn of '88, heard of a possible one through an old friend, Madame Bodichon. Now Madame Bodichon, known among a small but perfervid set as Our Glorious Barbara, was in her day a Personage. As a young woman Barbara Leigh Smith had lived much among artists and literary folk, for the most part members of the circle immediately round Rossetti, and had won recognition by her quick wit and artistic gifts ; but perhaps her most striking claim to originality amongst that happy-go-lucky band lay in her possession of a settled income, by no means a colossal one, yet allowing her throughout life to help a perfect procession of lame dogs over stiles, to their considerable surprise and her own good-natured satisfaction.

Rossetti himself had been quite attracted by the high-spirited young woman, whom he described—if I remember right—as having " plenty of fair hair, fat, and tin, and readiness to climb a mountain in breeches or to ford a river without them."

I should hardly have credited the portly and dignified, though incorrigibly untidy dame of my acquaintance with any of these accomplishments, but doubtless time had tamed her.

In my day she was devoted heart and soul to the Higher Education of Woman—with a capital W—and to her is mainly due the founding and rise of Girton College and its attendant consequences.

Whether the intellectual state of Woman is higher to-day, when she knows nearly everything that man knows, than in older times, when she knew so many more things than man ever knew, is to me still an open question, but one that has no place here, especially when I am trying to tell of Madame Bodichon and our ' little cottage in the country.'

" Just the place for us " was reported by our friend to belong to the Allingham's ; William Allingham, poet, editor and *littérateur*, and his wife, the well-known painter of cottages and country lanes. It was situated on the borders of Surrey looking over the Sussex Weald, and its owners were reluctantly leaving it to settle in London.

Supported by the authority of Our Glorious Barbara, but lacking an order to view, we presented ourselves one morning to be promptly refused admission.

" Try Bodichon," murmured my mother, who was subject to attacks of irreverence when naming the Great Ones of her sex.

I unfurled the Bodichon banner and lo—the charm worked. The door flew wide and we were hurriedly shown into a semi-darkness full of perambulators while—as I gathered afterwards—William Allingham was forcibly got up and dressed (it being his habit to lie in bed for most of the day and sit up all night) and Mrs. Allingham rounded up from the remote places of the garden.

" This won't do," said my mother gloomily, whether in reference to the darkness or the perambulators I did not like to enquire ; but soon all was well : our host and hostess came to our rescue and took us into a delightful parlour full of sunshine and looking over the great wooded valley. The garden, bright with old-world flowers, sloped down to an orchard and beyond lay meadows and woods—woods and meadows reaching away to where the distant Downs, softly blue, lay stretched along the horizon between the Weald and the sea.

It really *was* just the place for us, and luckily we recognised the fact. Mr. Allingham took me for a walk, and as he displayed the enchanting countryside, I lured him into speaking of old days and of Rossetti, with whom his friendship had been long and intimate. I knew that in later life they became estranged, probably because Allingham, after his marriage, felt that Rossetti's household was perhaps a little exotic ; but on this he never touched, but always spoke with delight and affection of the man who had been his hero and will always be mine.

I cannot recall much of that talk, but remember a quaint description of Rossetti's carefully explaining to him the points of his favourite model, Fanny Cornforth, in that lady's presence and with almost embarrassing minuteness.

" Her lips, you see "—following their curve with an indicating finger—" are just the red a woman's lips always should be—not really red at all, but with the bluish pink bloom that you find in a rose petal."—Miss Cornforth the while spreading her ample charms upon a couch and throwing in an occasional giggle or, " Oh, go along, Rissetty ! "

Though William Allingham was now white haired and elderly his features were still handsome and he had a charm of manner and speech which quite explained why so many of the great ones in Art and Literature had sought him for a friend and companion. But doubtless, in those early days, his nerves had been under better control, for, as I gradually learned, he had developed whims and eccentricities even beyond the limits of poetical licence. He sat up all night, as I have before noted, and the house had to be wrapt in complete quiet lest his studies should be disturbed. This was simple enough, but as he slept during the greater part of the day and everything had to be kept equally quiet lest his repose should be broken, life must have presented some difficulties to his family. On one occasion the said family, complete with perambulators, were waiting, packed and ready, to set out for the Shelleys' house at Boscombe, where they were to spend the holidays ; but, as the fly came to the door, Allingham remembered that at Bournemouth there were cliffs—down these cliffs the perambulators and their contents must infallibly fall—and so the fly was sent away, the boxes unpacked and the holiday lost.

Burne-Jones also told me of a visit he had paid to a country house where William Allingham was expected. On the day before his arrival came a letter to the hostess enquiring whether the door-handles in her house were of brass—if so, might they all be carefully covered up as brass was most insanitary to the touch.

The lady, slightly annoyed, suggested in reply that

291

it would be an easier plan for Mr. Allingham to wear gloves.

As a poet, I suppose, he has few readers now, a fate which he shares with most other poets—poetry and the sister arts are rapidly dying in the hurry and clamour of this fevered age—but some of his pieces have caught the general ear and find their way into many anthologies. The poem called ' The Fairies ' is perhaps the best known, the weird lilt of ' The Maids of Elfinmere ' has great charm, and the little haunting fragment ' Three Ducks on a Pond ' refuses to be forgotten by anyone who reads it.

> " Three ducks on a pond,
> The blue sky beyond,
> White clouds on the wing.
> What a little thing
> To remember for years,
> To remember with tears."

" A sonnet is a moment's monument," wrote Rossetti, but here is a moment's monument in only six lines.

What would have happened to William Allingham had he not married Helen Paterson it is impossible to imagine. She understood him thoroughly, cared for him deeply and made life smooth and happy for him ; and to do all this for a poet would have provided most women with a fairly arduous career. But she also had her work as an artist and she painted day in and day out ; in fact she hardly ever seemed otherwise occupied.

Her lovely little transcripts of the Surrey lanes and woodlands, of the school of Birkett Foster—but, to me, fresher, more fragrant and close to Nature than the work of the elder painter—are delights to the eye and lasting memorials of the fast-vanishing beauty of our country-side. In a few more years they will seem visions of a lost Fairyland, a dream world fabulous and remote as Lyonesse or Atlantis, but they are no false mirages but beautiful truth ; few painters have ever penetrated so close to the soul of the English country.

William Allingham was an invalid at the time of the

move and only survived the flitting of the family to London for a few months, but Helen, his wife, had many more years of happy and incessant work and bestowed upon me her lifelong friendship, a gift which its possessors held very dear. Her quiet strength and serenity, her unfailing kindness, her quaint humorous outlook and shrewd judgments on men and matters, made her a delightful companion—whenever she found time to be companionable, which was not often. My memories of her wit and wisdom are chiefly in the shape of detached sentences, jerked over her shoulder as she sat at the bottom of a damp ditch, knee-deep in nettles, or poised precariously on a pigsty wall, using her open umbrella as an easel. Though her lot was cast in London, she could not keep away from her old haunts and used to appear at least twice a year in the village, painting away as usual. She did not, I felt, resent our occupation of her beloved Surrey home, and indeed to me it has always seemed as much hers as mine, so subtly does her atmosphere still pervade it.

The house was old-fashioned when we came to it on that autumn morning more than forty years ago ; now it is prehistoric, and to-day I take a foolish pride in its including no electric light, no telephone, no garage (and no motor to put in it), no central heating and no bathroom, but in spite of these drawbacks—or perhaps because of them—it holds a strange peace, a quiet that is not of to-day, but of the long-past age when people had time to be happy. I notice the most unpromising and rampant moderns sensing and enjoying this, the while they abuse the inconveniences roundly.

Witley and its neighbourhood had been quite a centre for artists and literary lights, though of the band several were now missing. Tennyson still reigned at Aldworth, Birkett Foster at ' The Hill ' and the Allinghams at ' Sandhills,' but George Eliot was a memory at ' The Heights,' Fred Walker at ' Tobitt's Farm,' and Charles Keene at ' Tigbourne.'

I remember Burne-Jones telling me of a day spent at

'The Heights' with George Eliot, and of his departure thence on a pitch-black autumn evening. The lady, who, in spite of her genius, was hopelessly vague in mundane affairs, bade him farewell at the door, and saying—" If you turn to the right you will get to the station "—shut him out into the darkness. He stumbled blindly down the drive and into the lane where, hearing the distant approach of the train, he turned to the right as directed (incidentally scrambling over a fence), and—sure enough —got to the station, but upside-down, much torn by brambles and considerably bruised, after having fallen and rolled down a fairly perpendicular bank about thirty feet high. This rather inconvenient vagueness of the great lady was probably fostered by the exaggerated care taken of her by G. H. Lewes, of which another of Burne-Jones's stories gives instance.

He came across her standing monumentally alone at Waterloo Station, and, as he talked with her, they walked for a short distance along the platform. Suddenly Lewes rushed up to them, panic pale and breathlessly exclaiming—" My God! You are HERE! " George Eliot gravely admitted it. " But," stammered Lewes, " I left you THERE! " That his precious charge should have walked by herself, without proper escort and chaperonage, for over ten yards was a portent almost beyond possibility.

Yet, in spite of the incense and high ritual that surrounded her, George Eliot seems to have remained a very simple and kindly woman. Once, during an illness of Mrs. Allingham in London, she arrived to take the children for a drive, and their nurse, in telling me of it, said—" When I got into the carriage I thought she was the ugliest woman I had ever seen, but when she had been talking for awhile, I couldn't see that she was ugly at all."

The said nurse, Elizabeth Haddon, would have followed the fortunes of the Allinghams when they left Witley, but having recently married one Harry Cave, woodman, of this parish, she consented to remain as my cook-housekeeper, her husband becoming gardener and bailiff.

She had lived with the Allinghams since her girlhood and had met at their house nearly all the eminent Victorians of the pen and brush. She had tended Carlyle in his last illness (for which attention he bequeathed to her his feather bed), had entertained Tennyson to nursery tea, and had become thoroughly conversant with the odd world of art and letters which she regarded with a wise and kindly tolerance ; even admitting to me that she was glad I was an artist, as she was now accustomed to them and didn't think she *could* keep house for a gentleman. As she has successfully kept house for me for over forty years, this remark gives food for thought, but anyhow, I hope I have ' given satisfaction ' and made some small return for the care and affection bestowed upon me by her and her husband. Ellen Terry, I remember, on her first visit to me at Sandhills, ran straight to Mrs. Cave, crying, " You knew little Willie Allingham, didn't you ? " and they disappeared together into the back premises ; and to this day, whenever my guests rather pointedly desert me in the parlour, I know they are having a really interesting time in the kitchen.

Sandhills, when first we came to it, was a most unsophisticated little village and might have been many hundred miles from town.

Our house was nameless and, in my new pride of possession, I wished it to bear a title of its own.

" Call it ' Bella Vista ' or ' Mon Plaisir,' " suggested my mother, whose enthusiasm was ebbing. " It's very like a little Putney villa."

" These farm lands and copses," I explained patiently, " all have their fine old local names if only we can recover them. It will be very interesting to find out our real and ancient address."

After some research I found it, but it never adorned our note-paper. It was

Hell Bottom, Lice Lane, Wormley.

The Great Event of the day at Sandhills was the arrival of the postman who walked into our midst and blew a small horn, at which signal we all rushed out of our houses and claimed our letters.

The district was really rustic and unspoilt, ancient legends and beliefs still lingered and the older villagers were still the heirs of the ages and wise with the wisdom of the years. Still, in the remote 'Fold' country, whose villages, with names all ending in 'fold,' were once clearings in the huge pre-Saxon forest of Andreadsweald, could be found old people who had seen the 'Pharisees' (the folk of Faerie) and had watched their moonlight dancing.

I once called to condole with an old neighbour who had lost his son, and found him sitting in his smock frock —he was one of the last to wear this beautiful garment —beside his cottage door.

" I knew he was going," he said to me very quietly. " You see, he trod upon the Blue Flower." I suppose I looked enquiry, for he went on—" Ah, you don't know ? No, likely not. There do grow a little blue flower in the harvest fields and the man who treads on it dies within the year. So I've just been sitting and waiting."

Almost for the first time in my life I found myself living in the real English country.

As a child I had had two favourite day-dreams. In the one I was alone on a bare upland covered with short grass over which I ran and ran and ran. The dream went no further, the running was sufficient. I did not want to get anywhere—in fact, the whole point lay in there being nowhere to get to. In the other dream I plunged deep into a great wood and became lost in its shadows.

And all through my childhood, when, on our short summer exodus, we bumped along in trains, I caught maddening glimpses of fields and woods where these dreams might become reality ; but we always bumped past them and got out somewhere to find flagstones and lamp-posts just like those we had left behind. But now here was the real country. The bare uplands of my dream were close at hand and, from the end of the garden, I could plunge at once into woods stretching to the horizon, woods carpeted in spring with primroses, violets, anemones and bluebells. The woods in particular went to my head and London began to lose its hold upon me.

Many of my friends shared my love of Sandhills, but especially, I think, it appealed to Ellen Terry. She wrote to me from America in 1900.

" Some of my very peacefullest and happiest hours have been at your cottage. Being a long way off makes one see things so clearly, and some of my memories are rainbow-hued."

Although she had not actually stayed there, she had known of Sandhills before I came to it, as the Allinghams were among her oldest friends. She and Mrs. Allingham had met as girls at Lavender Sweep, the house of Tom Taylor, and a discussion had arisen as to which was the taller.

" Helen and Ellen, stand up and be measured," commanded Tom Taylor, and Helen and Ellen stood up together and remained fast friends throughout their long lives.

The poetry of William Allingham was always a delight to Ellen Terry, and the lines which she left as a last message—

" No funeral gloom, my dears, when I am gone——"

were taken from his writings.

Always she seemed to find rest among the woods and fields of Sandhills. In the long-lost days of quiet, when the country lanes belonged to the country folk and had not become speed tracks for Cockney motorists, she loved to jog along the narrow ways in an old donkey-cart ; and, as the donkey had her own ideas as to direction and pace, we often found ourselves becalmed far from home as dusk began to fall.

She loved all the stories and legends of the country-

297

side, and once, on one of these starlight strayings, we actually met the ghost in the Haunted Lane, between Bowler's Green and the Moors.

I was walking ahead, Ellen Terry and the donkey following slowly and of course on the wrong side of the road, when I heard behind us the distant trit-trot of a horse.

" Pull over to your left," I shouted, and while she did so we both listened to the horse coming nearer down the many windings of the lane. At length it rounded the last corner and passed us, but we saw nothing ; horse and rider were invisible.

It was, of course, the murdered highwayman who rides home in the dusk to Lower House where he met his fate at the hand of a treacherous friend.

Moderns tell me that the illusion is an echo from the Portsmouth Road—which I shall believe when I meet a phantom motor-car in the Haunted Lane.

Year after year, the country tightened its grip upon me, longer and longer grew my stays at Sandhills. London friends said—" Very pleasant in the summer perhaps, but how about the winter ? " Now in the country there is no winter as Londoners understand it, no dreary, lifeless time of fog and darkness. Autumn often lingers until she can hear Spring's footfall and in my garden last year's roses meet the first snowdrop. And to a painter, the exchange of smoky gloom for clear light is a priceless boon.

When in 1896 I came across a painter who shared my views and my love for Sandhills, I began to make Witley my headquarters.

One evening, at the house of J. J. Shannon, the portrait painter, I met Arthur Melville, the Scottish artist whose strong, colourful work had been the inspiration, nay, the very origin of what was known as the Glasgow School of Painting.

I know that this paternity has been attributed by many people to numerous other people, but the evidence of the eye is convincing, and the compelling influence of Melville's wholly original and highly characteristic genius is everywhere apparent.

He probably took water colour to the highest point it has ever reached. His pictures of the East, with their dazzling sunshine, their dim interiors full of coloured shadow and stealthy movement, their motley crowds moving through white-walled cities and mysterious bazaars, found many imitators, but no one could fully capture their secret. So much was suggestion ; the slightest hint of a figure seemed alive and real ; but Melville was a perfect draughtsman and that slight hint was not—as it appeared to be—a hasty and wayward slap of a brush, but was a piece of masterly and deeply considered drawing.

He and I became friends almost at once, no doubt owing to our many points of dissimilarity. He was a tremendously vital and athletic man, breezy, strong and adventurous ; I was—well, none of these things and, beginning with a good deal of difference, we advanced almost unconsciously into friendship.

He had a boyish love of fun and almost imperturbable good humour, which, considering his formidable physique, was rather lucky for those who happened to come up against him.

As an instance of this good humour, I recall a story told of his old Edinburgh days. He had been absent for many months, and had returned bringing with him marvellous sun-steeped water colours which seemed to hold all the glamour, the beauty and the savagery of the East ; and with them many exciting stories of perils and escapes.

Notable among these was the tale of his riding alone from Baghdad to the Black Sea, of his encounter with a band of robbers who stripped him of all he had and left him for dead in the desert, of how he dragged himself to an Arab village where he was kindly received and tended, of his riding with a punitive expedition while hardly yet able to stand, of the tracking and dispersal of the marauding band and the recovery of his effects (a bullet-hole in a large Scotch plaid, now in my pos-

session, grimly hinting at the fate of the robber who
annexed it), of his placid resumption of his lonely ride
and of what further befel him by the way, made a stirring
tale of romance and high adventure. In fact, the tales
proved too tall for his friends, who decided that, during
his Arabian Nights, he must have met the Sultana Scheherazade and caught some of her sublime gifts of imagination. They therefore, in a highly jocular spirit, invited
him to relate his experiences at the Edinburgh Artists'
Club before a large gathering.

Melville at once realised that they did not believe a
word of his story, but told it again in his best manner and
with even more romantic colour ; ruffled not a whit by
the loud laughter and ironical applause, but calmly enjoying the joke of which he alone saw the point. Some time
afterwards, one of the scoffers met a friend from Baghdad
who confirmed the story in every detail. He therefore
presented himself conscience-stricken at Melville's studio
and confessed that he had taken for ' travellers' tales '
what he now knew undoubtedly to be fact.

" My dear fellow," exclaimed Melville, " for goodness'
sake don't tell anybody. You'll ruin my reputation in
Edinburgh ! "

Soon after our meeting I asked him down to Sandhills,
and he came, saw and was conquered, returning again
and again, discovering subjects for pictures in the surrounding country and finally settling down to serious
painting. As some of his canvases were large, the farmer
who was our nearest neighbour kindly lent us as a studio
his big barn, which we shared with a large black sow who
evidently looked upon herself as our hostess and did the
honours with much affability.

For longer and longer periods we remained there together painting. My mother did not care for a permanent
life in the country ; she missed her friends and the wonted
round of her London days, but she came down to us
often and she and Arthur Melville became great friends,
he at once sensing and appreciating the wisdom and

strange quickness of perception which she tried so hard to conceal. He painted a very remarkable picture of her, unsuccessful as a likeness, but a marvellous piece of work which, after a *succès de scandale* in London, met with an ovation in Paris.

Many of his friends became ours. F. S. Selous, the mighty hunter, an almost legendary figure owing to his frequent appearances in works of romance, would come and sit to us both, in his white open shirt and great sombrero, and Edith Rhodes, sister of Cecil Rhodes, the South African Colossus, struck up a friendship with my mother, though, as a rule, she showed a decided preference for the male sex. She was a strange rugged figure, curiously like her brother, though with a certain grandeur which he lacked, and, on the strength of this appearance, she considered herself extremely virile and cultivated enthusiasms for large powerful men, whom she thought she greatly resembled. At the time I speak of the throne was shared by Arthur Melville and Captain ' Bobby ' Marshall, the playwright ; Melville by right of his biceps and Marshall for his heroic proportions and remarkable good looks.

" I know you like me," she once observed to me, " because you're fond of Melville and I'm exactly like him."

It was the aim of her many friends to conceal from her the fact that she was the most essentially feminine woman of our acquaintance.

Ellen Terry became much interested in Melville's work at Sandhills and used to lend him draperies and ' properties ' for his pictures, and it was during this period that he and I made costume and scene designs for George Alexander's ' Much Ado About Nothing ' at the St. James's.

Mr. Karl (of ' Nathan's ') who collaborated with us (and took the lion's share of the labour) very kindly came down to Sandhills to work with us in our studio. I remember, in after-days, his paying me one of my most cherished compliments. " I wish you would take up costume work for the stage again," he said ; " we could always tell where your designs buttoned."

Melville, though his name had been made as a painter of water colour, was now working almost entirely in oil. He felt that he had fully expressed himself in water colour and reached the extreme limit of the medium as far as he was concerned, and he now wished to devote himself to oils and apply his theories to work on a larger scale. After painting some landscapes, the subjects taken from Sandhills common and its immediate neighbourhood, he started upon an enormous picture representing ' The Return from the Crucifixion ' and four other canvases, smaller yet still of large size, which he called ' The Christmas Carols ' and which showed the Arrival at Bethlehem (' There was no room for them in the inn '), the Nativity, the Vision of the Shepherds, and the Coming of the Kings.

The question of models troubled us for a time. I could oblige as St. Joseph and some of the rabble in the ' Return from the Crucifixion,' but posing for the principal figure in that picture I found distinctly trying and was glad to turn it over to a very charming Italian organ-grinder whom a kindly Fate sent our way and who became model-in-chief to both Arthur and myself for two years, his mother going round with the organ in his absence.

There was then a little Italian colony at Godalming, organ men, ice-cream men, etc. ; Antonio's friends would drop in at the studio from time to time and we became quite popular among them—indeed, I verily believe that we could have had anybody's throat cut in the neighbourhood for a very small consideration.

I sometimes think we rather neglected our opportunities.

One day, before the advent of Antonio, I had been sitting in costume for the crucified figure—though sitting is not the word and costume is equally inaccurate. I was hanging by my hands from two ropes high up in the studio

gallery, and from my exalted position could see all along
the road which lies across the common. Every muscle
was aching and I had distinct premonitions of cramp, but
my plaintive hints at a rest were completely ignored by
Arthur, who was deep in his work. At length I perceived
the Great Event of the day dawning upon us over the
hill.

"Here's the post," I cried, snatching at a chance of
respite. "Shall I get the letters?"

"Yes, do. Run," grunted Arthur, still absorbed.

Joyfully I made a Descent from the Cross and ran as
directed—and only as I was opening the garden gate to
the postman did I recall the completeness of my *décolletage*.

Those years of work with Arthur Melville were a
wonderful time for me ; I practically went back to school
and took up my studies where I had dropped them after
leaving Albert Moore.

And, as during my apprenticeship to Moore, I gradually
became able to make myself useful. I could make studies
for Melville and finally could start pictures for him, en-
larging his preliminary sketch and laying it in on the
larger canvas, sometimes carrying it well over the first
stages. Of course, when he took up work upon it, my
work was entirely obliterated ; still, it saved him some trouble
and a certain amount of mechanical labour which anyone could do for him—if they happened to know how.
In after years I destroyed the few canvases, started by
me, on which he had not worked, but I remember being
obliged to forbid the appearance of one at his Memorial
Exhibition.

"It's quite unfinished," I urged. "It ought not to
be shown."

"Ah," said the promoters, "but look at the mastery,
the etc. etc."

"Yes," I had to admit, "I don't think it's bad ; I
rather like it myself, but—I painted it."

After that, oddly enough, the mastery seemed to grow
less conspicuous—in fact, we heard no more about it.

The great picture of 'The Return from the Crucifixion' was a huge canvas covering one entire wall of the studio. The rabble rout surges down the hillside, half exultant, half terrified by the gathering darkness, the Centurion and other soldiers riding amongst the crowd, their long lances rising out of the shadow into the lurid sunshine which still glares upon the summit of Calvary and the three naked forms, hung all aflame against a background of brooding storm. It is a splendid conception, and, had it won to a finish, might have been one of the great pictures of the world.

On this, and on its four smaller companions, Arthur Melville expended all the work and thought of his last years, but, alas, not one of them reached completion, although the first of the ' Christmas Carols,' ' There was no room for them in the inn,' was carried sufficiently near a finish to allow its wonderful qualities of imaginative beauty to convey almost their full message.

It is an unforgettable picture, simple in the extreme, but full of tense feeling. It represents realistically an actual happening to actual human beings, yet is so charged with mystery, with tenderness, with reverence, that, without aureoles, watching angels, or any of the paraphernalia of the ' sacred picture,' its deep import is unmistakable. The canvas is soaked in moonlight. It falls upon the white wall of the inn, throwing upon it flickering leaf patterns from an unseen vine pergola, and deep shadows of the waiting travellers, who gaze through a small open shutter into the warmth and glow within. Joseph, the yellowish-white of his long *burnous* turned to pearl by the moonbeams, stands leaning forward on his staff, evidently pleading for admission, while the weary ass and its weary burden wait with a patience that is half the sleep of exhaustion. Mary's head falls back, her hand mechanically holds together the folds of her purple cloak, yet her very stillness speaks of trust and resignation. The spirit of quiet is over all ; the travellers are the only beings astir in the moonlit street

To me that canvas still seems a part of the summer nights on which it was painted. The whole of the picture, as it now stands, was painted by moonlight. Arthur Melville watched and studied the effect he wanted night after night ; then mixed his tones by daylight from memory and started work on the actual canvas when the moon sailed clear of the surrounding woods. I stood as Joseph in the white *burnous* beside the old grey donkey, and work went on in a silver silence only broken by the sleepy beast shifting her feet and the distant churring of the nightjar.

The other three ' Carol ' pictures were not taken nearly so far. The Nativity was but a rub in, though the watching figure of Joseph, dark against the lantern light, was very fine ; in the Shepherds the effect is almost secured ; the Three Watchers, brilliantly lit, stare wildly out into the supernatural radiance, while behind them is the blue mystery of the night, with a few puzzled faces of sheep dimly emerging from the darkness ; but the Coming of the Kings is still a mere sketch, the figures barely indicated.

That these four pictures, with the great Crucifixion, would have been the crown of Arthur Melville's career I have no doubt. That they were left incomplete is a grave loss to the world of Art.

THE years passed quickly at Sandhills, happy, busy years. We painted nearly all day, then, in the summer evenings, rode, walked or drove in the pony cart, an interesting antique to which had happened about everything that can happen to a pony cart. The back had come off, the bottom had fallen out, each wheel had an adventurous history, and once, when going up Hindhead, the whole thing came in half, the pony placidly plodding uphill with the two front wheels, while the remainder drifted downhill and subsided in a ditch. This lent great variety to our drives, and when we were finally obliged to abandon the wreck and set up a more road-worthy vehicle which only I could upset, carriage exercise became comparatively monotonous.

I had meanwhile possessed myself of the neighbouring farm and fields, and when, in 1900, Arthur Melville married, he rented the farmhouse from me, and together we turned it into a really enchanting little habitation. The old house we touched as lightly as possible, but the grounds—that is, the potato patch, the horse pond (a very smelly one) and the pigsties—we transformed into a small terraced garden, its primness contrasting quaintly with the wild wood which lay round and beyond it.

Melville had a genius for work of this sort; he took advantage of every accident, destroying nothing that was beautiful or characteristic, but gently coaxing what was rough into order and harmony. When finished, it was one of his best pictures; any alteration made since by others has always seemed to me unskilful restoration.

Antonio, the organ-grinder, had risen to affluence and gone back to Italy to fulfil his life's dream, the purchase of an estate (it always sounded like an estate when he spoke of it) near Naples, where he was to settle down and found a family. Some of the family seemed to be founded already, but perhaps he meant to make a fresh start.

Organ grinding was very lucrative in those days.

"I shall go back when I have saved two hundred pounds more," he used to state, and when asked how long that would take, replied, "Oh, about two years." And so it did.

Into the void thus created stepped my old friend 'Bessie,' the popular model, who came to stay at Sandhills for weeks at a time and helped us round many corners. It was her proud boast that she could sit for anything, and she certainly sat for some very odd and unlikely things to us, though this was no new experience for her.

One of her stories told of a prolonged sitting to an artist for the Flight into Egypt. Bessie was a devout Catholic, and took her frequent posings for the Holy Mother very seriously. On this occasion she had, as she thought, excelled herself, and could not help feeling that her rapt and spiritual expression, held fast regardless of fatigue, was actually inspiring the painter, so intently, so passionately was he working. At length he was called away and Bessie, returning to earth, stepped down to inspect the picture. On only a small space of canvas was the paint wet—the artist had been working entirely upon the eye of the donkey. Poor Bessie was only comforted by the reflection that it is not every model who can sit for a donkey's eye.

She soon collected a large and strangely various circle of friends in the neighbourhood. She was, I consider, the only genuine Socialist that I have ever met ; she did not despise social distinctions because she never recognised their existence. She did not dislike the Duke because she was interested in the Dustman, but gave each his chance and was equally charming to both. It was an experience to see her walking quietly round the garden with the local great lady, our nearest neighbour and kind friend, a stately and rather awe-inspiring dame to those who did not know her, and clad in the stiff rustling silks of the day and an imposing bonnet. Bessie wore a much-bedaubed painting smock of mine—and nothing else—as the day was hot and we had been tackling the strenuous job of stretching and priming a large canvas. Yet both were equally at ease, each a *grande dame* who understood the other perfectly.

Work on the great Crucifixion went on continually, leaving Arthur Melville little time for other painting. He was constantly altering the composition, sometimes the whole shape of the picture, and drastic alterations on so large a canvas entailed much work, not a little of it destructive. Never could he be persuaded to try experiments with studies, to make small sketches. I even painted several small copies and begged him to try his new ideas upon them, but he would always attack the great picture itself and reduce it to wild confusion.

" Accidents," he would insist, " are the makings of a picture."

I was able to illustrate from my own works that this is not always the case, but without effect.

I am haunted by the remembrance of a day when the great conception dawned in full completeness out of the chaos of paint. I begged him to consider it final.

" There's your picture," I pleaded. " I've watched it from the start and I know that you have now got what you set out to get—and it's magnificent. If you alter it again I shall know that it will never be finished."

But the artist was tired—not well—he had worked upon his picture until he was not really seeing it. When next he showed it to me it was again half painted out and—never was it finished.

In 1902 Arthur Melville's baby daughter was born. She showed an early preference for the country life, in that she refused to be born in London, where preparations had been made for her arrival, but put in an abrupt appearance when least expected at Redlands (as the little farmhouse was called) and held her first receptions in a clothes basket and one of her father's flannel shirts. She was soon installed as my model-in-chief, sitting to me for two portraits before she was six months old, and I began to write little plays for her—plays that grew out of her daily life. Thus, on the evening of her first Epiphany, the Three Magi came out of the mysterious night to where she sat by the fire in the old oak-panelled kitchen, bringing to her the Gold Casket of Happiness, the Blue Casket of Dreams, and the Green Casket of Memory ; and again, on her first birthday, a little Water Nymph rose from the lily-pool calling the Spirits of the Winds and Flowers to give her greeting.

These were happy, fanciful days when we, as loyal subjects of her small majesty, lived for awhile in her dream kingdom of Faerie, but dark clouds were gathering ahead.

In the summer of 1903, Arthur Melville and his wife went for a holiday to Spain, where they both contracted typhoid and returned with the deadly malady upon them, she to recover after a long illness, he to pass away, leaving, it is true, a splendid record of achievement, but with what might have proved his greatest work yet unfinished.

This sudden ending of a partnership so intimately connected with my Art life seemed at first to take away all incentive. For a period I could paint no more, but fell back upon writing and making picture books for children—or rather, for one child—which led finally to my doing a good deal of book decoration, both in black and white and colour. Most of this work was produced for John Lane, the publisher, and from time to time he used to send me MSS. to read for him, usually with a view to illustration.

Once, when I was particularly busy, arrived a bulky parcel containing a novel by G. K. Chesterton, which I regarded dubiously, wondering how I should find time to read it. But as I glanced at it, my eye fell upon the first phrase—" The Human Race, to which so many of my readers belong——" and at once dispatched to Lane an enthusiastic recommendation. A book which began like that must be all right ; no one could afford to throw away such a gem in the opening sentence who had not plenty more to follow.

I was enlisted to illustrate the work which turned out to be a witty and fantastic picture of a future England, reigned over by an elected King who appeared to be none other than Max Beerbohm, or at least a recognisable caricature of him. But Max, himself a caricaturist, was fair game ; besides, he was in the secret and made no objections, and John Lane used to ask him and me to meet Mr. Chesterton, so that the collaboration between novelist, model and illustrator might become the more harmonious.

Poor Max and I, in the freshness and innocence of our budding middle age, gambolled dutifully round the big man, all unconscious that—as he afterwards set down —he bracketed us together as interesting survivals of a bygone and evil period.

He found us, it seems, ' most charming people '— always an ominous opening—and then went on to describe the type which, to him, we represented. It wasn't a very nice type. It had—' an artificial reticence of speech which waited till it could plant the perfect epigram.' Now that couldn't have been I or I should have gone through life dumb. It was—' a cold, sarcastic dandy ' —(a dandy ! I, whose clothes always look like somebody else's misfits after I have worn them twice !)—' who went about with his one epigram, patient and poisonous, like a bee with its one sting.' Now I'll take my oath that this wasn't Max : of all the witty men I have met he has the kindliest and most strictly disciplined tongue. Sometimes a hint of sly malice creeps into his caricatures, but there it is surely in its right place.

I consider Max Beerbohm the perfect companion, because I always part from him with the impression that I, myself, have been brilliantly amusing. He is the most generous of wits ; he not only casts his pearls before swine, but actually gives the swine the credit for their production.

I regret that Mr. Chesterton did not appreciate us all the more because we both thoroughly appreciated him.

Meanwhile, Sandhills, coupled with the fascinations of

little Miss Melville, now nicknamed Binkie, still held me captive.

Ellen Terry, who was Binkie's godmother, came often to stay and became very fond of her godchild. On one of her visits she was busily studying 'Hermione' in 'A Winter's Tale,' which was shortly to be produced at His Majesty's Theatre. The play had an additional interest for her in that her first Shakespearean part had been the child, Mamillius. I left her one morning under the great pear-tree, dutifully occupied with Hermione and 'minding' her god-daughter who played round her on the grass.

On my return, Hermione seemed to have gone to the wall and Binkie was getting a thorough grounding in 'Mamillius.'

As she taught the child, her old part seemed to come back to Ellen Terry and I could see just how she had played it. Over and over again Binkie was pulled up on the line—"Nay, that's a mock," Ellen patiently explaining, "No—he's really angry. He knows he's being laughed at. He could almost cry with rage if he were not such a big boy. Now—try again." And Binkie, purple in the face with concentration, again boomed out —"Nay, that's a *mock*!" At last she appeared to give satisfaction, and got praise for her 'dreadful, growly voice' in her rendering of—"There was a man dwelt by a churchyard."

If only those lessons could have been continued. Binkie had her father's Celtic imagination and a quick ear for rhythmic cadence—as quite a baby she spoke verse with appreciation of its music. If these gifts could have been developed by her Fairy Godmother she might have found herself—and her father.

Living daily with a child and trying, in order to become a satisfactory companion, to see the world from her point of view, I began to be filled with ideas for a Fairy Play for children. What laid the foundation for it was an actual happening in her baby life.

A little way within the wild wood which circled her

domain was a barrier of wire netting to keep the rabbits out of the garden, and in the barriers was a small wooden gate which, for Binkie, led to the Unknown and was terribly attractive. To prevent her from straying, I invented the legend that the Rabbit Gate, as it was called, led to Fairyland and could only be passed by persons over four years old. This stratagem worked wonderfully and kept the child within due bounds till she was four —when I was faced with a problem.

Either she must still be denied passage through the Rabbit Gate—which would be false to tradition—or she must go through the gate and find Fairyland. And Binkie at four was growing sceptical and had more than a suspicion that the whole tale was a fable, and only framed to keep her from the joys of a delightfully muddy brook which ran through the lower woods.

So I was in desperate case, but, setting to work, I made certain preparations, and on her fourth birthday, when the shadows began to fall, when bushes and trees took on aspects unfamiliar and faintly disquieting and the woods became caverns of mystery, Binkie was led with much ceremony down to the Rabbit Gate, wholly incredulous and inclined to scoff. But no one can keep up that attitude for long in a twilight wood, and she arrived at the gate duly chastened. Then we knocked and spoke strange words of conjuration—

> " Under the Moon and under the Sun
> Will the Gate unclose for a Woman of one ? "

and Binkie gasped and clutched me when a tiny voice from beyond replied—

> " Woman of one, it may not be done."

We spoke the next words of the spell—

> " Under the Green and under the Blue
> Will the Gate unclose for a Woman of two ? "

And again the tiny voice answered—

> " Woman of two, 'tis not for you."

" BINKIE "

From a portrait by THE AUTHOR, 1908

And so on up to four, when the Gate swung mysteriously open and Binkie, now much wrought up, passed timidly through.

Within stood the Guardian of the Gate, a small figure in robes of silver, flower-crowned and holding a sceptre of purple iris ; while it spoke rhymed words of welcome, there was a sound of distant singing which drew nearer, until out from the wood crept the Fairies with their pale faces and shadowy hair and glittering green robes ; and they gathered round the child and sang to her and drew her away down a wonderful alley where strange golden fruit hung and impossible flowers bloomed, and then the last of the daylight faded and Binkie came out into a clearing and—there were no more Fairies, no more singing, only the grey woods and silence.

The Adventure of the Fourth Birthday was over. Strangely enough, she never expected the wonderful experience to repeat itself, but she knew that she had walked with the Elf Folk through the green twilight, and the wood was the Fairy Wood always.

It was rather a dangerous experiment, and, had I then known what I know now about that wood, I should not have risked it ; but luckily, for the moment, there were no unpleasant consequences.

In later life—that is to say, in a few months' time— a little boy cousin called Tommy (chiefly because that was not his name) came to live with Binkie, and doubtless they found their own Fairies in the wood—but of course they did not mention them to me.

Not long afterwards, perhaps as a result of meddling with things and beings better left alone, luck seemed to desert me and grey days in plenty set in. I had a long illness from which recovery was slow, and I was sent for convalescence to Sidmouth.

There Mrs. T. P. O'Connor, who was wintering at a neighbouring hotel, told me of a musician friend, Frederic Norton, who was in search of a ' book '—preferably of the Fairy Tale order—to which he could write music ;

and gradually the idea of ' Pinkie and the Fairies ' began to come to me.

I took it up in the most desultory way, making notes from time to time, writing down scraps as they suggested themselves ; but later on, after the loss of my mother, which occurred in 1907, I turned wholly to the dream play and tried to lose myself in it—dreams seeming all that was left of a world which, for the time, had lost meaning for me.

' Pinkie,' if it had any aim, which I doubt, was an attempt to put upon the stage the passing of a day and a night in the life of an imaginative child, to show the ' workaday world of everyday ' from a child's point of view.

Whether this idea was ever logically carried out or made clearly apparent I do not know, but I experienced a genuine thrill when Mr. H. G. Wells once said to me —" I like your ' Pinkie ' better than any of the other plays for children because it represents life as seen through the eyes of a child."

I hope I am blushing becomingly while I set this down, but I am going to set it down all the same.

The elves who dwell in the haunted wood of Pinkie's vision were, of course, Fairies as they exist in a child's imagination ; figures evolved partly from picture books, partly from dreams of personified flowers, birds or insects. They were, I hope, removed from the acrobatic sprites and ballet ladies of pantomime, but were no more, though no less, real than the rest of the children's dream world.

Stage Fairies are seldom convincing, though once, when Harley Granville Barker put on ' A Midsummer Night's Dream,' I registered a distinct shock. The production was interesting, though less perfect than his ' Twelfth Night ' which it followed ; a faint suspicion of the ' stunt ' hung over it, its *art nouveau* wood lacked mystery and its Elizabethan folk dances held no hint of elfin revels. But at the entrance of his ' First Fairy ' I stiffened in my chair. Its swift, flitting motion without apparent use of the feet, its suggestion of progress without movement, like the dart of a dragon-fly or a humming-bird moth, was so strangely true that, for the minute, it frightened me. I really felt that one of those beings, whoever they may be, who still allow themselves to be glimpsed, rarely and by few, in the woodlands of our rapidly disappearing countryside, had been brought before us on the stage.

If the resemblance was purely accidental, Barker must have formed the habit of ' dreaming true ' like ' Peter Ibbetson.' I asked him if he had ever seen one of Them, and he said nothing—which looks suspicious.

And yet it is unlikely that Granville Barker has had any such experience. He is brilliant, his vision has a crystalline sharpness, a frosty clarity, while the man who can catch even a momentary glimpse of the Other Side of Things must, I think, be a bit of a fool. Is not the country word for a fool a ' natural ' ? And the ' natural,' often being very closely in touch with Nature, may some-times see—a little more than most people.

Meanwhile ' Pinkie ' had got herself finished. Frederic Norton had composed his music, though never could he be induced to write it down, and all was ready for production if an enterprising manager would come forward.

I am bound to admit that there was no rush. The play, like the efforts of most beginners, went through the familiar course of wandering from theatre to theatre and being rejected. Barker and Vedrenne seemed to dislike it rather less than many, but finally refused it. Lena Ashwell actually accepted it in '97, and Norman McKinnel, who was then producing for her, was quite enthusiastic and full of excellent ideas ; but it was too late to get it ready by Christmas, and a Christmas production appeared to be essential. George Alexander, out of pure good-fellowship, for he had not read it, offered to put it up for matinées at the St. James's, but I was ambitious and stood out for the evening bill. Finally, in October 1908, when the play and its wandering were almost forgotten, a sudden summons arrived from Herbert Beerbohm Tree to come to His Majesty's and discuss it with him.

I did not even know that he had it under consideration, but presented myself obediently and read the whole play through to him in his ' palatial suite of apartments ' (I can find no better description than this well-worn phrase of the House Agent) situated in the dome of the theatre.

I had heard from many sources that to read a play to Tree was a formidable ordeal, that it was almost impossible to catch and hold his attention, but this must have been one of his ' off ' days—I certainly never had a more sympathetic audience. He accepted the play, talked over the cast, and promised to start rehearsals at once.

Frederic Norton, the composer, was in America and I swore that he would return immediately, bringing the score with him, though I had an uncomfortable conviction that not a note of the said score had been committed to paper. Such was indeed the case, but Norton duly arrived with the score complete, how and when set down I cannot imagine.

I had written telling Ellen Terry of these happenings : she had lately married and was then living much in the country with her husband, James Carew, good actor and good fellow, whose friendship I have always valued. She replied at once from Small Hythe.

" Nov. 9th. Blow the trumpets, beat the drums ! I am delighted, my dear. Did you read it to Tree ? I do like Tree, he *does* things. But take care. You must have your say in all of it or—— I'd so much like to see your alterations (cuts, I suppose) in the last Act. Keep well and let me help you in bits of your work if I can."

Then came the question of the cast. Charming Iris Hawkins was the obvious ' Pinkie,' Marie Löhr, at the height of her girlish beauty, was ' Cinderella,' Viola Tree, with her stately presence and beautiful voice, was ' The Sleeping Beauty,' Stella Campbell lent her lovely gravity to ' Molly.' Then came another astounding letter from Ellen Terry.

" Nov. 12th. Do you know I believe I really would like to play ' Aunt Imogen,' for I think I might be very funny in that very funny part. I wonder would Tree think it worth while. I feel I should love to do something of yours. Do you think I'd be of use as ' Imogen '? If you don't, don't speak to Tree."

When I showed the letter to Tree he refused to believe in it and complimented me on my skill as a forger ; but when convinced, he telegraphed to clinch the bargain on the spot.

Then work started and things began gradually to take shape, but I well remember my bewilderment during the first few days of rehearsal. I had been accustomed to the all-compelling personalities of Henry Irving and Sarah Bernhardt, to the iron rule of Augustin Daly, to the quiet, business-like atmosphere of the St. James's, under George Alexander. Here all seemed confusion, everything drifted haphazard and apparently without a guiding spirit. Tree was, I suppose, producer ; then there was an Acting Manager who had much authority, another Manager (what he managed I never found out), two very efficient Stage Managers, without whom nothing could have gone forward, the Composer, the Author, and, in addition to these, any passing author, actor, newspaper man or critic, all of whom appeared to be at liberty to drop in and give advice. To me it seemed like a return to back drawing-room theatricals or to the charade parties of my youth.

My principal anxiety was to prevent this dream play, for and about children, from becoming a musical comedy. It would have taken so little to push it over the edge ; a few sentimental songs, a ' red-nosed comedian,' and a ' strengthening of the love interest' (strongly recommended) would have done it in no time. Oh, that love interest ! It was always being strengthened, and the whole construction of the play—written from a child's point of view—demanded that the love interest should be entirely uninteresting. One morning a beautiful young man, complete with tenor solo, was all but engaged for a character which I had carefully kept off the stage, though, like Queen Elizabeth, you expected him to come on every minute. Intimating that anyhow his entrance would be effective, as it would be made over my dead body, I contrived to decoy Tree into a box by himself, where I begged him to watch the Act quietly through and then tell me if he still missed the beautiful young man ; and when he finally said, " Not a bit," the danger passed.

Sometimes, at rehearsals, the fantastic element, always rife in Fairyland, led to strange happenings.

One day something—I forget what—had to be done upon the stage which seemed to belong to no one's part. It was not quite the job for a Fairy or a Frog, the Court Officials were occupied.

" Cinderella's Footman ! " I exclaimed. " He's not doing anything."

" Of course," said the Stage Manager. " Now, Mr. ——, you come down and——" He explained the movement in full.

But Cinderella's large Footman hung back ; he was very shy, but managed to convey in an inaudible voice that he either couldn't or wouldn't.

" Come, Mr. ——," said the Stage Manager, firmly, " get on with it." More reluctance, more faint disclaimers. " Now don't *make* difficulties," roared the Stage Manager. " How much longer are we to hang about here for you ? Why can't you do it ? "

It was too much—the worm turned. Cinderella's sorely tried Footman suddenly found his voice and exclaimed in tones of thunder, " *Why* can't I ? Becos— I keep on tellin' yer—I'm a *mause* now ! "

And it was quite true. His hefty appearance had misled us. Twelve o'clock had struck and he was now a mouse. We apologised.

His liege lady, the Princess Cinderella, in the person of pretty Marie Löhr, was a very busy lady just then.

She was playing 'Margaret' in 'Faust' every evening and rehearsing 'Hannele,' the tragic little waif of the German fantasy, as well as preparing for 'Pinkie,' and her rather incongruous rôles got oddly mixed when the Stage Manager once sped us from the theatre with the anxious request—shouted after us down the street—" Mr. Robertson, will you *see* that Miss Löhr tries on her trick dress and gets measured for her coffin, please ? "

I remember coming into a rehearsal of 'Hannele' and finding her sitting up in the aforementioned coffin and trying to combine the luxuries of a 'good cry' and the absorption of a bun and a glass of milk. It was the oddest and most pathetic little picture.

Sir Herbert Tree—he became Sir Herbert in 1909— must often have been described as a 'born actor.' I have known several born actors, but, as a rule, they are not very good actors.

Their habit of perpetually acting, in and out of season, on and off the stage, weakens their grip on the realities of life ; they are so much absorbed in registering their reactions to each emotion that the emotion itself is barely realised, the shadow outweighs the substance. They use speech not to express their thoughts, but to arrest attention, to 'get across' well, and the result is usually a lack of sincerity and simplicity—two qualities of the utmost importance to an actor.

Tree frequently did himself injustice by not allowing his warm-hearted, generous self to be seen, but exhibiting instead a perfect gallery of assumed characters, none of them very convincing and none of them with half the attraction of the genuine Herbert Tree. When the real man put in an appearance—as if by accident—it gave one a pleasurable start, like the sudden sight of a friend's face among a crowd of strangers. In life's comedy he cast himself for a man of mystery, dignified, yet full of fantastic eccentricities. The carefully thought-out eccentricities frequently came off all right, owing to his strong sense of humour, but the mystery he could not manage.

There was nothing mysterious about Tree; he would have been horrified to discover how perfectly he was understood in the theatre, and perhaps a little surprised to find how much he was liked. He had the lovable quality of liking to be liked, he hated enmity and rancour.

Once, after a ' scene ' at rehearsal (in which he was entirely in the right) and the abrupt departure of the offender, he came to me quite distressed.

" Do you think I should apologise ? " he amazingly enquired, and when I pointed out the difficulty of apologising to people for their own rudeness, he only said regretfully, " Yes—yes, of course. I suppose so. But it seems a pity." His own anger had completely evaporated, he only wanted to put things straight.

He was an extraordinarily clever man and a kind friend; he gave me my big chance and I am very grateful to him.

Of the actual First Night of the play I recall little. On the day before it came out, I had learned that Mrs. Arthur Melville was giving up the little house in the wood and leaving the neighbourhood of Witley, so, with the birth of ' Pinkie,' came to me the loss of Binkie, her prototype, and the latter took all joy out of the former. In fact, with this in my mind, I was thinking hardly at all of the play or its fate and gained quite a reputation for coolness and self-command among the Company and staff, all rather wrought up after a hectic dress rehearsal lasting well into the small hours.

My chief memory is of the terrific outburst of applause that greeted Ellen Terry. She had not been seen for some time, and when she stepped upon the stage a storm seemed to break. It crashed out suddenly, like a thunderclap directly overhead, pealed on for a few moments, then settled into a steady roar which rolled on and on with a rhythmic throb like the beating of great drums and seemed as though it would never cease.

It is always difficult to foretell to what section (if any) of the public a play will appeal. ' Pinkie,' intended to interest the Nursery, captured—the Military. Night after night the stalls at His Majesty's looked like a parade at Aldershot. I was much puzzled by this phenomenon, and finally asked a little soldier of my acquaintance to enquire into it.

"Do ask them why they come so often—what it is that attracts them."

He returned to me with a most unexpected explanation—"They say it makes them cry."

And I who thought I had written something mildly humorous !

Apparently, what they found most devastating was the close of the second Act, when the children's dream ends and the vision of Fairyland slowly fades, the lights twinkling out, the music dying away, until all is darkness and silence save for the murmur of the stream among the shadows. And in the darkness Aldershot sat weeping for its lost Fairyland, and the lights went up upon rows of bedewed shirt-fronts.

The play achieved a considerable success and was revived at the same theatre in the following Christmas-tide.

One of the offshoots of ' Pinkie ' was a playlet given in the back drawing-room of 88 Portland Place, a tiny stage with a great tradition.

Sir George and Lady Lewis, old and kind friends of mine, were in the habit of getting together there one of the most remarkable and unique gatherings of the year on the occasion of a great annual dinner and reception on New Year's Eve, and it would be easier to make a list of absent Notabilities than of those present. A short play was always given—though no entertainment was really needed beyond the mere presence of most of the guests—and, for the festival of 1909–10, the production of the ' book ' was entrusted to me and the music to Paul Rubens, that strange genius who masqueraded as a good-looking boy wandering listlessly through his days in the vague hope of amusing himself, and who got through more good work in his short life than many a composer of fifty has to his credit.

We built up the play at top speed during a hasty lunch together and it took the form of a burlesque of the Play for Children, then enjoying a vogue. It treated of the reception of a Fairy Visitant by a family of modern children, all complete sceptics and much annoyed at the interruption.

The poor Fairy can do nothing with them ; the visions she evokes fail to appear, or appear all wrong, distorted and vulgarised by the chilly atmosphere of unbelief. She is retiring in tears, when in trip the Parents, full of the Christmas Spirit and babbling of Cinderella and Bo-Peep. They are delighted with the Fairy, and the poor thing, realising that they are her only supporters, concentrates all her charms upon them. " Come, oh true believers ! " she cries, and they come joyfully, crowned with paper flowers and played upon by coloured lights and, as the trio flit away through the nursery wall to the Rosy Realms of Radiant Rapture, the relieved children return to their normal avocations and the baby settles down in his cradle to a quiet cigar and the evening paper.

Nigel Playfair ' produced ' for us and also made the histrionic hit of the evening in the part of a six-months-old baby. A few cavillers hinted that he was too old for the part and looked at least one and a half, but they were silenced by the roar that broke out when he sat up in his beribboned basinette and uttered his first withering cynicism. He himself has recorded that this was his Great Moment on the stage, and it was certainly my great moment as an author. The sight of that audience, comprising most of the finest intellects in London, helplessly rocking with laughter is an abiding memory.

Few imagined that this was to be the last of those wonderful gatherings. I vaguely remember being dragged up the room by Tree and Arthur Bouchier to ' take my call '—Paul Rubens was ill, as he too often was, and could not share it with me—and feeling, as I looked round upon that assembly of the talents, a certain chill sense of finality. It was the end of a period ; the end of the world, as we then understood it, was near at hand, and that absurd ' transformation scene ' was almost the last glimpse of Fairyland for a good many of us.

WE are drawing to the close of my period which ended abruptly in 1914, and it would be unbecoming in me to attempt any record of a new age to which I do not belong and which I do not understand.

I and a few of my friends have accidentally slopped over into it (the verb is inelegant but expressive), and perhaps the best thing we can do is to hold our tongues and efface ourselves.

But though this volume purports to contain an account of my Notable Acquaintances, I have hitherto left unmentioned the most Distinguished of all.

Those who have never been privileged to enjoy the affection and intimate acquaintance of an Old English Bob Tail Sheep Dog will not understand this chapter. How should they? Nearly all dogs are charming and lovable, but the Bob Tail as a companion is unique : his store of true friendship is so inexhaustible, his sympathetic understanding so profound, his love, if you are lucky enough to gain it, so limitless that he seems to belong to a race apart. He possesses all the canine virtues, but adds to them others which I hesitate to call human because they are seldom to be met with in humanity.

I have known four Bob Tail Sheep Dogs intimately and, if only for that reason, I have not lived in vain. The dynasty began with

B O B

BOB came to me, a gift from my mother, when he was two years old. He had belonged to a butcher and had been ' thoroughly well trained ' ; that is to say he had been systematically ill treated, beaten and abused, was as hard as nails and quite without illusions. He feared no one, for fear was not in him, but he mistrusted everyone—with good cause—and neither gave nor expected affection. It was sad to meet the hard, undoglike glance of his yellow eyes, to see the involuntary flinch before he stiffened himself to bear the punishment which he felt sure must be coming.

It took about a year to thaw his icebound but un-broken spirit, and indeed all through his life the memory of evil days remained with him ; he was stern and grave, unable to play or to take a joke, chary of his friendship and difficult to approach. But all the stunted and un-wanted love hidden in his deep heart he gradually bestowed upon me ; at first grudgingly and tentatively, but at last with a fierce concentration almost tragic in its intensity. It was by no means the worship usually attributed to dogs by their chroniclers ; if anyone had suggested to him that I was his god, Bob would have told him not to be a b—— fool (he had been brought up in a rough school and his expressions were probably crude), but it was a grim, unswerving devotion lavished upon me despite my many faults and shortcomings which he forgave but could not deny. How well I knew the look of pained displeasure on his face when I said or did the wrong thing or, in his opinion, made a fool of myself. He deplored my lightness of mind and lack of dignity, he thought poorly of my intellect and general information, he expected little con-sideration from me ; all that he asked, nay demanded, was that he should be always with me. Where I went he must go, where I lodged he must lodge, though my people were by no means always his people, but frequently quite the contrary.

Where I went he did not care so long as he might go too ; London or the country were the same to him ; he would thread dense crowds at my heels like my shadow, he would wait patiently outside galleries or the residences of those strange people who ' like dogs in their proper place ' ; nothing came amiss to him save only separation from me.

Anything might happen if he were not there to look after me. He was sternly upright, a stickler for law and order ; in fact, the only being capable of turning him from the path of rectitude was a railway porter. These officials had decided that he was too large a dog to travel in a carriage with me ; he himself thought otherwise and would take infinite trouble to set their authority at naught.

It was an understood thing between us that at a station we did not belong to each other. I chose my carriage and took my seat innocently dogless. Bob apparently had ' found the receipt of fern seed and walked invisible,' for, though he never got into that carriage, he always got out of it at the end of the journey. When and how he entered, where he disposed his large body I never knew, but when I alighted, so did he.

Once, on a very tumultuous Boxing Day, I was wedged into a much overcrowded carriage into which, as the train was moving off, shot a little pink man, finding a temporary resting-place on my lap. As there was nowhere else for him to sit, he stayed there amicably conversing, and as we neared Witley I said to him, " Now watch—you'll see something in a minute." Sure enough, as the train slowed down, the apparition of a large grey sheep dog materialised in our midst and was received with an incredulous gasp, then with shouts of wonder. On the following Easter Monday, I, in my turn, nearly missed my train, and hurling myself into a crammed carriage, found myself on the lap of—the little pink man. But this time he was preoccupied, evidently filled with but one idea, and, after we passed Milford, he whispered in tones of awe, " Is it going to happen again ? " I nodded, and soon the usual sensation announced the mystic burgeoning of Bob.

" Well," cried the little man, bouncing me on his knee in his excitement, " I'm glad I've seen that again ! I didn't believe it last time, but I suppose seeing it *twice*——" He said it with such fervour that it suggested a ' Nunc Dimittis.' We have never met since.

As a father, Bob belonged to the old school. His sons (who I am sure addressed him as ' sir ') were permitted to take no liberties, were allowed few privileges. I had to be very careful to observe his rules in dealing with them or they were apt to suffer for my misdeeds. One morning, when Bob was unwell, I ventured to take his son, Portly, for a walk into Godalming. In the afternoon I had again to go out without my bodyguard, and a lady, staying with us, volunteered to ' take the dogs for a turn.'

As they walked up the common, Portly, always tactless, evidently observed to Bob, " I went into Godalming with the Old Man this morning."

" Did you, damn you," replied Bob. " Then take that——" And he flew at his throat.

Portly was hefty and put up a good fight and the battle raged round their unfortunate escort, finally knocking her down and sweeping over her prostrate body.

Suddenly Bob noticed an unfamiliar taste in his mouth. " I say, that *was* your leg, wasn't it ? " he shouted.

" No," puffed Portly, " you've never touched me yet."

" Then—what was it ? " gasped Bob, and the combatants paused, struck by the same uncomfortable idea.

Portly was right ; it had not been his leg. Bob's teeth had nearly met in my guest's arm. The dogs stared at each other—then fled ; Portly to the sanctuary of a chair which had been the refuge of his puppy-hood and under which he could now barely get his large head, Bob to report in the kitchen.

" There has been a—a slight accident on the common," he probably said. " Someone had better go and see about it."

Towards the end of his long life—he lived to be nearly sixteen—Bob became almost blind, and the son of his old age, Benny, tended him like a nurse, waiting for him, going back for him if he were not in sight, pushing him gently round corners just as a professional plough horse will turn a novice at the end of a furrow. Despite his rigorous upbringing—for Bob was still a stern parent—Benny loved his father deeply and had the greatest reverence and respect for him.

Once, when out for a walk, we had scrambled out of a sunk road up a very steep sandy back, almost a cliff, and I had gone a little ahead to help a lady who had chosen a rather less precipitous ascent. Suddenly Benny rushed up breathlessly shouting (and if ever a dog spoke, he did then) —" Come—quick—father—down there—— Drop that woman and come—quick ! " I dropped my guest like a hot potato and ran back. Bob had made a rush which had almost taken him up the bank, but he could not climb over the crest. He was hanging, one leg crooked over a projecting tree-root, and on his face was the grim look which I had hoped never to see again. He knew that he must soon let go, that when he fell he would break his back ; he perhaps hoped faintly for help, but did not count upon it. I had gone that way, he had tried to go too—all was quite as it should be, but this was probably the end.

When I pulled him up, Benny got no thanks, only a sharp reprimand for ' making that damn noise and fuss,' but I think Bob knew what his son had done for him and grew gradually very gentle towards him. His dauntless spirit never flagged. In his old age he had to undergo an operation which, though it was successful and gave him two extra years of happiness and good health, was an alarming experience and, I know, put his nerves to a severe test. Yet, when brought back to the surgeon to have the stitches taken out, he walked resolutely into the torture chamber, got up on to the operating-table and lay down.

In his last year I could hardly leave him. He was well but feeble and seemed to live only in my life. If I were away he would lie by the door waiting ; he did not want food nor companionship and would hardly stir from his post lest he should miss the first sound of my footstep. As I came round the garden gate, I would see the grand old figure at strained attention, the sightless eyes striving to pierce their veil of dimness, then—the sudden shock of joy—the transfiguration, as, with a rush, a young dog—young again for one wild moment—hurled himself towards me across the grass. Then—his body pressed against me,

328

his grey paw in my hand, and there would come a deep quiet. His vigil was over, we were together again, all was very, very well, but—" don't let us make a fuss about it."

That was Bob, the grandest, most gallant creature I have ever known.

PORTLY

Bob married twice. His first choice fell upon a pretty, rustic maiden in a neighbouring village, and of their union was born Portly—Portly, the gay, the stout, the irresponsible, dowered with all the qualities denied by Fate to his father, the light heart, the merry eye, the happy-go-lucky, devil-may-care temperament of the born Jester. Portly loved everybody, and if everybody did not love Portly, the only exceptions were the occasional victims of his craze for practical joking. To him life was a joke, and if people were not entering properly into it, he would try to shake them up until they did.

" Now, Portly," said I one day as we sallied forth, " we're going for a long walk."

" Long walk ! " yelled Portly on the fatal rising note of hysteria. " Lo-ovely—lo-long—walk ! " and he seized a passing boy by the slack of his breeches and waltzed him round and round out of the purest *joie de vivre* until those useful garments were rent in twain like the veil of the Temple.

One of his most deeply thought-out jokes, and one which might have proved most disastrous, was the deft plucking of people off bicycles. I had certainly noticed one or two odd mishaps to riders, but had naturally never connected the same with Portly. But one day, when I was standing at our gate, a young man on a bicycle came slowly by on the up grade. Close behind him trotted Portly with an odd, rapt expression which I knew and feared. Suddenly he rose on his hind-legs, took the tail of the rider's coat softly between his teeth—and gave a sharp tug. Off came the young man backwards,

Portly vanished into the hedge, and there was nothing to account for the catastrophe.

I trust that this joke was not repeated. I had, of course, to take violent measures, but even during the painful scene between us, Portly was evidently still shaking with laughter and gasping, " But it *was* fun, wasn't it ? Did you see how neatly he came off ? "

As a puppy, Portly was irresistible—so fat, so round, so jolly. Kenneth Grahame, that exquisite and only too occasional writer, was then at work upon his delightful ' Wind in the Willows,' and I have a proud suspicion that the fat puppy had his tiny share in the evolution of that great chapter, the poem in prose called ' The Piper at the Gates of Dawn.' For Portly is the little fat baby otter who sleeps at the feet of Pan.

" I hope you don't mind," said Kenneth Grahame in his courteous, deliberate way as he showed me the MSS. " You see, I *must* call him Portly because—well, because it is his name. What else am I to call him ? "

So Portly is among the immortals, for ' The Wind in the Willows ' is already a classic.

Poor Portly : he was the child of misfortune, always in scrapes, always meeting with accidents. Disasters of all kinds were perpetually overtaking him, yet never could they crush his high spirits nor sour his sunny nature.

I will not tell the tale of Portly's short life : it is a sad one and he would not wish it to be told, but would be remembered only as the Joy Dog, the jolly dog, the dog who laughed—he was the only dog I ever met who could throw back his head and roar with laughter—the dog who made the best of everything.

BEN

Bob, in his second marriage, looked higher for a mate. He married a lady of title, the daughter of Lord Linford, a redoubtable grey Bob Tail who held a high position in the sheep-dog world. I never saw the Hon. Mrs. Bob, but, as a mother, I fancy she showed that careless incompetence which should be (and isn't) the sign of the patrician. Be this as it may, she one day took her very young family for a walk in a wood and lost them. The poor babies were found next morning, after a night of terror in the open, and Benny, who was to be my puppy, never wholly got over the experience ; his nerves, as a young dog, were completely shattered.

Gentle, timid, deprecating, he was in nearly all things the opposite to his ' strong, silent ' father. Very lovely to look upon, with long rippled coat of pale silver, he was the shyest, most elusive creature, slipping through life like an apologetic shadow : one had always to remember never to shout at him, never to startle him, never to take him among crowds or into noisy places. In later life he recovered self-command and concealed his nervousness, but I saw that he always had to pull himself together to face any crisis, and counted it to him as the truest bravery.

He never lived down his horror of thunderstorms—I could sympathise with him there—and if one began to rumble in the distance when we were out, he would look at me, ashamed yet beseeching, obviously saying, " Do you mind—would you think it very rude of me—if I went home ? " And when I gave leave, he was off like a streak, rushing home and curling himself up in a certain corner of a little upstairs sitting-room, which was called the Thunder Room and brought him a strange sense of security.

Unlike most nervous dogs, he had the sweetest temper ; even when he was frightened he would never snap or growl. Of other dogs he had no fear, which was lucky, as Bob, his father, was perpetually getting into street brawls in which Benny was of course expected to stand by him ; but cows were a great trial to him, and he would hover miserably round the edge of a field trying to find courage to cross. I argued with him in vain.

" It's all very well for you," he would say plainly. " Cows don't run after you."

331

" Yes, they do," I replied, " because you always get between my legs. But they don't do any harm."

But it was of little use—he never really acquired the cow habit.

Except for this nervousness he was happy and light-hearted, remaining a puppy in his irresponsibility and love of play long after he should have become a serious-minded dog. He had one treasure, a fetish which he adored and was inordinately proud of. Originally a soft toy of some sort, it rapidly lost any figure that it ever possessed and was generally known as Ben's sausage. If new-comers found favour in Ben's sight, which was seldom, he would produce this highly objectionable object and lay it gently before them as if conferring a boon ; and indeed it was his highest mark of approbation. Much of this childishness came from the very tight leading strings in which he was kept by Bob, who was determined that, while he ruled, Benny should remain an infant and not butt in on the affairs of his elders and betters.

But evidently there had been long and serious talks between them as to Benny's future duties, for when in the fullness of time Bob died, Benny immediately took over various little intimate services and attentions which his father had rendered me and in which he had never been allowed to take part. " This and this you must do for the Old Man when I am gone," Bob had evidently said, and even on the day after his death, Benny fell into line.

Towards the end of his life Benny himself became sponsor and tutor to a puppy. Richard, his great-nephew, was suddenly planted upon him and, though we well knew the sweetness of his character, we hardly expected him to be pleased. But jealousy was as far from Benny as all other forms of uncharitableness ; he accepted the little creature at once, tending him with the utmost kindness and by his gentle rule gradually shaping a very hot-headed, rebellious little dog into a well-behaved and reasonable member of society.

Beloved by all, Benny stayed with us till he was

fourteen, and, with his passing, there came to me a strange experience. Tranquilly as he had lived, Benny lay a-dying. Death was coming softly to him as if loath to disquiet his gentle spirit. I sat by him holding his paw. Suddenly, and entirely unprompted by any previous train of thought, my mind became dominated and possessed by the grim, strong personality of Bob. If I had seen and touched him I could not have been more keenly aware of his presence—in fact, I looked hastily round for him, forgetting that he was long dead.

And Benny's quiet breathing ceased—he was gone.

Benny had always waited for his blind father, had gone back for him and guided him gently round corners, and I shall always feel that Bob, the strong-hearted, came back in his turn for the timid Benny to help him across the great barrier.

RICHARD

RICHARD was not born into my family. Richard happened.

I had written and produced a Pageant for the neighbouring village of Chiddingfold, and at the close of its successful run, I became uncomfortably aware that a Presentation to me was on foot. I could see the 'handsome marble timepiece with suitable inscription' or the silver cigarette-case the size of a small portmanteau for which I should have to return thanks, and looked forward to the ceremony with lively apprehension. I should have had more trust in the good taste of my village friends.

When the dreaded day arrived, I received some beautiful old, silver-handled knives and forks, a set of 'rummers' and—what was this entrancing furry object suddenly plumped into my arms? A Bob Tail puppy, the like of which for beauty I have never seen. He was indeed a distant relation of my family, Benny's great-nephew, but he came from far away and his father was the celebrated Champion, Night Raider.

Richard as a puppy was prideful. He could hardly

333

have been otherwise: his extreme beauty and local celebrity made him a centre of interest wherever he went. Effusive admirers seized upon him and exclaimed over him, and if by chance an unobservant or beauty-blind person was about to pass him by, Richard would plant himself solidly in the path, evidently saying—" But—you haven't looked. I am Richard, the Pageant Pup—everybody looks at me."

All this adulation I felt would be bad for his character and, by way of a cure, I took him to London that he might become absorbed into the great universal life and realise his insignificance. Vain hope. In London crowds collected round him whenever he went out, policemen held up the traffic for him, complete strangers buttonholed me, full of enquiries as to his age, birth and parentage : in fact, an old friend, after the ordeal of a walk with Richard down Kensington High Street, observed that he remembered nothing like it since the early days of Mrs. Langtry.

It was far worse than the country, so I gave up and Richard remained prideful. But it was an innocent pride and did him no harm ; he was, like the King's Daughter, ' all glorious within and without,' his disposition was as charming as his appearance.

Yet this pride fostered a certain self-consciousness which his Uncle Ben and I regarded with a growing apprehension.

" If he is not very carefully treated," we thought, " this love of publicity will lead him to learn tricks and one day we shall witness the shameful spectacle of a Pedigree Bob Tail sitting up and balancing biscuits on his nose. Better that he should go on the stage at once and have done with it."

And, with the thought, came to me the conviction that this would be the best way out of the difficulty. What Richard wanted was some means of self-expression. A stage career, though perhaps not quite what his parents would wish for, would not in these days seriously damage a dog's social position. There was none of the ignominy

RICHARD AND THE AUTHOR

of the nose and biscuit business about it ; he would be a serious artist working legitimately in a fine profession. And luckily I was in a position to offer him an engagement.

One result of the Pageant which had given Richard to me had been a sturdy band of Village Amateur Players, for whom I ' produced ' and who were more or less under my guidance. They would rehearse a play during the autumn and then tour with it throughout the winter, giving performances at the neighbouring towns and villages. What more natural than that Richard, the Chiddingfold Pageant Pup, should make his debut in a small part with the Chiddingfold Players ? Of course he must first appear in a small part ; it would be abuse of privilege and gross favouritism to put him, the merest tyro, into Lead.

Yet what was to be done ? Here again we were up against his fatal beauty. Whatever his part and however small, his wonderful appearance and compelling personality would at once force it into undue prominence.

Fate was again too much for us ; we capitulated at last, and finding a play with a strong part for him which, with a little writing up, fitted him like a glove, I installed Richard in the title rôle and gathered round him a gallant little company, all much attached to the ' star ' and ready to support him loyally.

Richard took to the stage at once. He rehearsed with the greatest gravity and concentration, only getting bored by the scenes in which he did not appear, and on his First Night he was perfectly calm, though his Company were in a state bordering on hysteria. I remember the breathless group at the wings as he went on for his ' crack ' scene, one of the actors reporting progress with his eye glued to a hole in the canvas.

The action depended upon Richard, at a certain cue, climbing into a large arm-chair (centre) and from thence solemnly addressing his attention to the low comedian, with whom he had a long ' back chat ' scene across a table. The cue rang out—" Now then, Lot 49, let's have a look at you." The strain in the wings was almost too much.

" Is he up ? " gasped someone, and when the reporter at the peep-hole almost shouted, " Went up like a shot," we knew that all was well. He had a fine ' exit round ' after his big scene and, from that evening, settled down into being a Popular Success.

Without doubt, Richard loved the stage. We were giving other little pieces at the time in which he took no interest, but directly he saw the ' props ' for his own play being put together he became full of excitement and would jump joyfully into the taxi which was to bear him to his next triumph.

Being a great favourite in the neighbourhood, he usually expected and received much applause at his entrance, but on his first appearance at a place where he was personally unknown and where he entered to a chilly silence, I never saw a dog more surprised and hurt.

He stared at the audience, half incredulous. What was the matter ? Why no reception ? Was he really to come on without a hand ? He could not pull himself together, but gave a limp spiritless performance and came off quite uncheered by his ' exit round,' which indeed he had not deserved.

But as a rule he was a most conscientious actor. Once, during the run of his play, I passed him lying apparently asleep in his dressing-room and remarked, without any idea that he would understand, " You'll be on in a minute or two, you know." He at once got up and slowly, for he knew that there was no hurry, walked out of the room and away to his post at the wings, there to await his cue.

On another occasion he had obtained an engagement to appear with his Company at Guildford and a rehearsal was necessary. I was ill and could not attend, but only a run through for words was needed, and I thought all would be well. However, after rehearsal, one of the actors wished to speak to me.

" I think we ought to tell you," said he when he came in, " that Richard has completely altered the end of the Act. We didn't like to do anything because, of course, it's *his* play, but we thought you ought to know about it."

" Well," I said, " is Richard's arrangement better than mine ? "

" Yes, I think it is," admitted his fellow-player with candour. " More effective."

So Richard was allowed to stick to his new reading, which turned out to be a flagrant ' star ' stunt, bringing him dead centre for the fall of the curtain.

Perhaps this public career was too exciting, though I cannot really think that his stage experiences did him any harm. But Richard's life was not a long one. He lies with Bob and Benny in the little green orchard below the garden, and my dear friend, Gordon Bottomley, the poet, who loved Richard as he loves all beautiful things, wrote the epitaph carved on the grey stone that marks his grave.

> " Richard, in this place of peace
> Love returns, love does not cease.
> Wisdom, beauty, faith and mirth
> Sleep with you in this dear earth,
> And with you shall still return
> When the fires of springtime burn
> In our hearts and in the boughs
> Overhead of your green house
> With an eager blossoming—
> Thoughts of you and scents of spring."

With Richard's death the dynasty of the Grey Brethren came to an end.

Gracious and benign had been their reign and I think the whole neighbourhood took a pride in them. My friend, Alfred Sutro, the dramatist, who rented ' Redlands ' for some years after Binkie's departure thence, was also blessed with a Bob Tail, and when the whole muster turned out together it was an impressive sight—so much so that an old lady, meeting us for the first time in a narrow lane, rushed up the bank and tried to scale the hedge screaming, " What are they ? What *are* they ? "

The loss of Binkie made a sad gap and the little house in the wood seemed very desolate and empty without her. But Fate or Nature, or whoever the lady is who abhors a vacuum, did her best, and one day there swept by me in her carriage—or perhaps it would be more correct to say trundled by me in her perambulator—a dangerously charming woman. She was but a few months old and already possessed two most satisfactory parents, but seemed quite ready to welcome another, and she and I have been boon companions ever since. For though this happened many years ago Rachel still trundles often down the hill with her perambulator, though she now pushes it, and a new Rachel with equally dangerous attractions sits enthroned therein.

Meanwhile I was growing older and older. To mix with the Immortals is a wonderful experience, but it has its difficulties. Advancing years, which take no toll from the Ever Young, seem to weigh all the more heavily upon their satellites.

My friendship with Ellen Terry thus passed through several phases. We began, of course, as the Goddess and the Little Boy ; not that Miss Terry ever considered herself a goddess, but I naturally regarded her in that light. Then I became a bigger boy and was admitted to a greater intimacy, though still, very properly, ' kept in my place.' Then I caught her up and for a glamorous few years we were contemporaries ; discussing things together from the same age-point, having ' larks ' together as two young people with high spirits and a sense of humour. Then I began to draw away from her ; my years increased, hers did not. I became almost respected. Finally I settled down into the old Family Solicitor, sent for in moments of difficulty, consulted on family and other matters and confided in generally.

I always had a talent for holding my tongue, the most valuable quality in a confidant, and I have every reason to believe that I discharged my duties at least with discretion.

With the equally immortal Madame Sarah my passage through the years was marked by fewer phases. I remained the Little Boy for a much longer time—in fact, for many years after my locks were growing scanty and my slimness a mere memory.

But at last came a day when, as we sat together in her dressing-room and Madame Sarah, attired as the boy in 'L'Aiglon,' was, in high good humour, addressing me in affectionate diminutives, she suddenly looked keenly at me and paused.

"But, Graham," she said slowly, "you're—why, you're old!"

"Yes, Madame Sarah," said I meekly. "I can't help it—it's not my fault."

"Really old," repeated Sarah, taking me in as if for the first time. "You look—you look like a fat priest."

"I don't," said I indignantly, for there are just a few things that I do not want to look like, and that is one.

"You do," said Sarah firmly. "Why aren't you married? You must marry at once." And she looked round the room, evidently in search of a bride.

Luckily only the dresser was present or I feel sure that my nuptials would have been arranged then and there.

"If you don't marry now," went on Sarah, in visible anxiety, "nobody will ever take you!"

And sure enough nobody ever has.

Great Sarah! Greatest artist of her century, greatest actress of our time and perhaps of all time; those who have never heard or seen her will never, I think, know beauty in its fullness.

There is an old French folk rhyme with a little tune like tears falling, with the refrain—

"Félicité passée qui ne peut revenir,
 Tourment de ma pensée,
 Que n'ai je, en te perdant,
 Perdu le souvenir?"

339

Its 'dying fall' is haunting, yet its sentiment is wholly false.

Past happiness is not past if its memory is still fragrant. I would give all my future—to be sure there is not much of it in store for me—for the lovely and gracious past, though it be but a memory.

" Why do you never go to the pictures ? " my young friends enquire.

I have no need ; the pictures come to me and I have tried to show just a few of them—a very few, and selected, I hope, with discretion.

A really interesting book could be compiled from my omissions and I think I could promise that it would prove a Best Seller.

I know I can promise that it will never be written.

INDEX

INDEX

INDEX